A Very Private Public Citizen

A VERY PRIVATE PUBLIC CITIZEN

The Life of

Grenville Clark

NANCY PETERSON HILL

UNIVERSITY OF MISSOURI PRESS
Columbia

Cataloging-in-Publication data available from
the Library of Congress
ISBN 978-0-8262-2091-2

∞™ This paper meets the requirements of the American
National Standard for Permanence of Paper for Printed
Library Materials, Z39.48, 1984.

Cover design: Susan Ferber
Interior design and composition: Richard Farkas
Typeface: Palatino Linotype

Cover photo courtesy of Library of Congress

For Dr. E. Grey Dimond (1918–2013)

Contents

Foreword

by Samuel R. Spencer Jr.

In this masterfully researched and beautifully written book, Nancy Hill brings to front and center one of the most effective, but least known, Americans of the twentieth century. Although born of wealthy parents and at home in the highest levels of society, finance, and government, Grenville Clark chose throughout his life to live and serve as a private citizen. Consequently, although he had many friends who loved, admired, and worked with him on important matters, his name never became known to the general public. As Hill clearly shows, however, he had enormous appeal to the people around him. He was a tall personable man who loved sports, excited others with his ideas, and led them in adventures that they would remember for the rest of their days.

In 1947, the first of two summers I spent in graduate school at Harvard, I went to Dublin, New Hampshire, to help Grenville Clark with the writing of his memoirs. This he was doing on the advice of his doctors, who had told him that at age sixty-five, with a serious heart condition, he should give up the demanding work that was his standard. On our first day together at his country home next to Dublin Lake, we talked long into the warm afternoon. Clark suddenly said to me, "Would you like to take a swim?" I said, "Yes, but I have no bathing shorts." "You won't need any," he said. "Let's go." I followed the older man's lead as we walked briskly through the woods, shucked off our clothes, and plunged into the cold lake. I thought to myself, "This is no ordinary man." To work with Grenville Clark and get to know him was one of the blessings of my life.

Having been interested in Clark for some time, Nancy Hill was aware that the sheer volume of material available would make chronicling his life a difficult job. Still, she plunged into the literally tons of correspondence, writings, clippings, photographs, and other myriad items that would await her among the Clark Papers at Dartmouth College. She sought out Clark's former associates, surviving friends, family members, and previous Clark researchers. She visited Dublin, Dartmouth, Harvard, and other places that figured prominently in Clark's life. In short she immersed herself in the life, work, and world of Grenville Clark for nearly five years; this scholarly yet accessible and enjoyable book is the result.

Why did Hill want to write about Grenville Clark? In her introduction she states, "He remains one of the most important Americans that most Americans have never heard of." What could be more alluring to a writer than that? Hill's extensive study of her subject led to a level of knowledge and understanding few of his old friends could have matched. Who among them would, for example, have guessed that Clark's concern for others would frequently have led him to "bail out lowly civil rights workers, accused communists, and other disreputables"? Who would have known of the tender and loving letters he wrote to his young daughters? And who wouldn't have laughed to know that their esteemed friend could "barely drive a car, much less change a tire," as a family member later recalled.

Hill brings readers inside Grenville Clark's life, offering a view of his triumphs and tragedies as if through his own eyes. She shows him at eighteen as he leaps from a trolley to rescue a woman from drowning in Boston's Charles River and later as he becomes recognized as one of Wall Street's top lawyers. Then he succeeds in establishing a special officer training camp at Plattsburg in World War I and manages twenty-five years later to have Congress pass the first peacetime draft just before World War II. Hill also depicts Clark as he leads others in strong opposition to the court-packing plan proposed by his old friend President Franklin Roosevelt and as he maintains a fierce twenty-year stand for freedom of speech, press, and assembly for all institutions while serving on the board of the Harvard Corporation.

The author's broad knowledge of Clark's modus operandi also made it possible for her to capture the essence of the man in her own words: "With [a] . . . brawny mind, ferocious powers of concentration, an apparent lack of fear, and a willingness to do literally whatever it took to get the job done, Grenville Clark could be daunting. . . . Grenville Clark would spend his lifetime seeking and formulating rules that could be applied to the real and urgent problems of the day."

Hill asks at the beginning of her introduction, "So who was Grenville Clark?" One of her answers is this: "A fundamentally modest man, Clark accepted the many honors and awards he received graciously but always with a touch of discomfort and an eagerness to get the spotlight off himself." But even more telling is how Hill concludes her introduction: "Clark's lengthy record reveals an important American, one from whom we have much to learn about the possibilities and proper role of a citizen in our democracy, and as he believed even more important, the possibilities and responsibilities of a citizen of the world."

Her book, a real pleasure to read, will enable any reader to understand and appreciate the powerful spirit and important contributions of this exceptional man.

Acknowledgments

Writing this book brought many joys but also challenges. The passage of time since Grenville Clark was alive and active on the world stage, combined with his penchant for avoiding publicity, did not always make research easy. Happily Clark left a substantial paper trail. Many helped me access that trail. Perhaps the most invaluable assistance came from the superb staff of Rauner Special Collections at Dartmouth College, led by Sarah Hartwell, supervisor of the Reading Room. The collection of Grenville Clark's papers at Dartmouth—350 cartons full of correspondence, writings, clippings, photos, and other memorabilia painstakingly catalogued by Clark's long-time secretary, Ruth Wight—is as rewarding as its setting is beautiful.

David Boutros, director, and Tonya Crawford, archival specialist, facilitated access to the Mary Clark Dimond Papers in the Western Missouri Archives of the University of Missouri—Kansas City. That those archives share space with the Edgar Snow Reading Room makes for a lovely and comfortable place to peruse the well-organized materials.

A happy surprise and excellent resource was the Fanny Dwight Clark Botanic Garden in Albertson, Long Island. The Clarks' longtime family home and its twelve acres are now an active and beautiful public garden and horticultural education center run by the town of North Hempstead. The gardens' knowledgeable, helpful, and interested staff, especially Debra Fiorentino, filled many gaps about the Clark family's private life, sharing writings, local history, and photographs, as well as infectious enthusiasm.

A special privilege for me were the many illuminating conversations with some of the increasingly few people who knew "Mr. Clark," especially his early memoir collaborator, Samuel Spencer Jr., and Ava Spencer, his wife and repository of memories. As a young Harvard doctoral student in the 1940s, Samuel Spencer spent two summers with Grenville Clark in Dublin, New Hampshire, immersed in research that would become a 600-page doctoral dissertation on Clark's Selective Service campaign during World War II. Spencer later became the longtime president, then president emeritus, of Davidson College in North Carolina.

J. Garry Clifford, a distinguished professor of political science at the

University of Connecticut, was an enormous help. Clifford wrote the brilliant book *The Citizen Soldiers: The Plattsburg Training Camp Movement, 1913–20.* His book, which won the Frederick Jackson Turner Prize, is the authoritative text on the Plattsburg movement. For the Plattsburg chapter in this book I shamelessly mined *Citizen Soldiers,* especially for Chapters 4 and 5, with Clifford's kind permission, and I explored related books he recommended. He also meticulously reviewed—and improved—the entire manuscript more than once.

Late in the process came the insightful review and good suggestions of the author and historian Joseph P. Baratta. His encyclopedic two-volume history of the world federalist movement, *The Politics of World Federation,* is a gold mine of information about this unfortunately little-known movement. His work greatly informed the chapters involving Clark's tireless efforts for world peace. As goes the classic line: Any errors, misstatements, or omissions are mine alone.

A constant source of information and inspiration has been the Diastole Scholars' Center, founded by Grenville Clark's daughter Mary Clark Dimond and her husband, Dr. E. Grey Dimond. Diastole is home to a special assortment of Clark memorabilia that "Mary D." inherited from her father. Highlights include books from her father's personal library, including cloth-bound treasures from his school days, plus volumes that date to the mid-1800s that once belonged to his father and grandfather. In Diastole's Mary Clark Dimond Photo Gallery is Clark's original Root, Clark partners desk, of the clever design that allowed two partners to work facing each other across an expanse of polished mahogany. The working sketch from a Clark portrait by the artist Alexander James hangs above the desk. Next to it is an original Vietnam-era line drawing of a *Dennis the Menace* cartoon titled "Starry Night." In it Dennis and his pal, Joey, lie beneath a summer sky and wish on a star that people "wouldn't have wars anymore." The artist Hank Ketchum gave the piece to Mary Dimond in honor of her father's tireless work for world peace. Copies of Clark's writings, books, and articles by and about him are here, as is a glass-encased, U.S. postage stamp of Grenville Clark—a final grace note Mary D. added to her father's legacy before she died unexpectedly in 1983. To work daily in such an inspiring space and with its extraordinary cofounder has been a joy; throughout this project it was also a big help.

My boss, mentor, and great friend, Dr. E. Grey Dimond, died one month shy of his ninety-fifth birthday, just as this book was going to press. As a physician, scholar, medical educator, writer, collector, artist, gardener, citizen-diplomat, and more, he embodied the oft-overused label Renaissance man. He inspired the lucky few who came into his orbit to be and do more than they ever imagined, or even necessarily wanted to do. He first introduced me to the largely unknown life and work of Grenville Clark, and was an invaluable source of stories and private information about Clark, Edgar Snow, and Paul Dudley White. Dr. Dimond quite literally made this book possible, and for that and so much more I am eternally in his debt.

I owe a large debt of gratitude to my colleagues, professors, and friends at the University of Missouri—Kansas City. Dr. Max J. Skidmore, along with the late David N. Atkinson and Harris G. Mirkin, formed my master's thesis committee in political science. That thesis was the early basis of this book. As committee chair Atkinson, especially, gave invaluable direction and support, always with good humor and patience even as the project expanded well beyond intended boundaries and timetables. Sadly, he lost his battle with cancer just before this book was published. But he knew it was in motion, and I like to think he is nodding in satisfaction (and relief) somewhere. My deep thanks and admiration also go to the amazing Nancy Hoover for her technical assistance in producing early versions of this manuscript. Nancy is a wizard.

The twists and turns leading to the book's publication were straight out of Mr. Toad's Wild Ride at Disneyland. The details would fill another book, but the process started and ended at the University of Missouri Press, and I am so glad it did. John Brenner, an acquisitions editor, first shared my enthusiasm for Grenville Clark and for this manuscript. His friendly and intelligent help was picked up by Gary Kass, after John made an exciting career move. Sara Davis and the sharp-eyed Polly Kummel saved me from countless blunders after I thought I was finished. Jane Lago guided the whole operation, and I am grateful to the whole group.

Just as Grenville Clark always began at the beginning, I must mention my (excellent) parents. When my indomitable mom, Roberta "Bobbi" Bohen, told three headstrong and independent kids they could do or be anything, we believed it, and benefited—even if at times she may have regretted the encouragement. Grenville Clark would have saluted my mom's crusading spirit and her unflagging sense of social justice, as do I. My dad, Laurel C. "Chuck" Peterson, a retired navy aviator, was and is the epitome of an officer and a gentleman. He demonstrated no small amount of grace, and restraint, with his unflagging tolerance and affection for a free-spirited (his description) young peacenik daughter, while he flew sensitive missions over ballistic missile–equipped submarines in the Atlantic to deter a Soviet first strike at the height of the Cold War. Both have long since remarried and brought two equally fine people into the family. Mom, Dave, Dad, and Melva, I love and admire you all.

Finally, it is no secret that cramming a large, complicated, multiyear project on top of five already busy lives is asking a lot of a family. Mine couldn't have been better sports. My husband, Larry, and our three superb sons, Cody, Duncan, and Spencer, are the warm and happy base that makes the rest of my life possible and worthwhile. They kept me on my toes, gave great advice, and were the perfect antidote when life became overly academic. They also coined the novel use of *Grenny* as a verb, as in, "Are you Grennying again tonight, Mom?" Finally, kids, the answer is no. Thanks for putting up with me.

A Very Private Public Citizen

Introduction

June 26, 1901, was a big day for Grenville Clark. It was commencement day at Harvard with full pomp and ceremony; the excitement in the air was contagious, even though the eighteen-year-old's own graduation was still two years away. But Clark was anticipating something even bigger. He and two classmates had been invited by then–vice president Theodore Roosevelt, a family friend, to his Sagamore Hill estate on Long Island to meet the famous Major Frederick Burnham, an American scout for the British Army and recent hero of the Boer War in South Africa. It was a rare opportunity but logistics would be tight—a postcommencement trolley from Harvard Square to Boston with just enough time to catch the midnight train for New York.

Clark's friends had gone ahead of him. A commotion in the street stopped his trolley; a woman had just jumped off the Harvard Bridge into the Charles River in an apparent suicide attempt. The passengers poured off the trolley to peer over the edge of the bridge and saw the woman struggling in the water below. Whether his primary motivation was humanitarian or pragmatic ("I saw that I was going to miss the train [to New York], which would have been a frightful disaster from my point of view"), the athletic and decisive Grenny Clark ran around to the riverbank, leaped from its high wall into the river, and rescued the distraught woman. Still thinking about his outbound train, Clark, in what he later described as a "rather cold-blooded way," handed the woman over to police custody, jumped back on the trolley, and made it to the station just as the train was beginning to pull out.

Clark's friends were waiting on the steps as he, "running madly . . . barely made the train by seconds." Explanations were clearly in order or, as he put it, "since I was soaking wet they got out of me what had happened."[1] Once aboard, understatement surely gave way to an adrenaline-fueled recounting of the dramatic event to his excited friends. The next day at Roosevelt's home Clark made no mention of the incident. But it was too good a secret to remain one for long, and one of Clark's companions privately told TR all about it. Roosevelt was so impressed he saw to it that the Massachusetts Humane Society awarded his young guest its humanitarian medal for his actions and dashed off a personal letter:

1

My dear Clark: July 3, 1901

I have only just heard of what you did in rescuing that woman from drowning the night before you came to my house. It gave me a thrill of pride as a Harvard man, and as a friend of your father and mother, when I learned of it. Will you please give me just one or two rough details for my own pleasure?

Faithfully yours, Theodore Roosevelt[2]

So who was Grenville Clark—this Harvard sophomore who paid home visits to future presidents, performing seemingly offhanded feats of heroism en route? He would become a powerhouse Wall Street lawyer, the architect and prime mover of vital military preparedness campaigns before both world wars, and a close adviser to presidents and cabinet members on matters ranging from economics to national security to civil rights to world peace. In a series of unpaid, unpublicized public service roles throughout his lifetime, Clark would stand up for civil liberties, academic freedom, constitutional integrity, and other frequently unpopular causes, leaving a string of achievements that improved his and our world. It is not too big a statement to say that Grenville Clark remains one of the most important Americans that most Americans have never heard of.

This book explores the life of Grenville Clark, and it is based on the premise that a thriving democracy requires informed and engaged citizens; Grenville Clark is a prime and still relevant example. True, Clark entered the world with many advantages. Born and raised in a wealthy New York establishment family, he received a top-flight education at private prep schools, Harvard, and Harvard Law. He later served for two decades on his alma mater's elite governing board, the Harvard Corporation. He cofounded the premier Wall Street law firm Root, Clark with his close friend Elihu Root Jr., son of the celebrated U.S. statesman of the same name. Clark's distinguished legal career ultimately netted him the American Bar Association's highest honor, the ABA Medal. Yet as a law partner once said, "In a very real sense his client was the people of the United States."[3]

In 1915 Clark's early instinct for public service led him to start and lead the Plattsburg military training camp program when he was just thirty-two. Against a strong national tide of isolationism, the young lawyer was convinced that the United States would soon be forced into the Great War raging in Europe and that the small loosely organized U.S. military would face disaster in its current condition. Clark worked closely with

U.S. Army General Leonard Wood to design and run a large-scale, highly concentrated, all-volunteer officer training program that became known as the Plattsburg camps. In what has been called a military miracle, the camps produced about 100,000 U.S. officers by the war's end.

Twenty-five years later Clark found himself back in the preparedness business under uncannily similar circumstances as Americans hotly debated U.S. entry into World War II. Convinced that it was imminent, the Plattsburg founder, now middle-aged, actually wrote the 1940 Selective Service Act and gathered a dedicated and influential group to promote and ensure its highly contested passage through Congress. The Plattsburg camps and the Selective Service Act were widely recognized as important factors in winning their respective wars.

Yet Clark was no one-dimensional military hawk. In the interwar years he informally advised his old friend Franklin D. Roosevelt on economic policy as the new president strived to lead the country out of the Great Depression. In 1933 Clark was the primary author of the Economy Act, one of the most important and successful pieces of legislation in FDR's famed Hundred Days. Just four years later Roosevelt announced the Judiciary Reorganization Bill of 1937, his controversial court-packing plan to enlarge the Supreme Court and thereby thwart an obstructionist bloc of justices that was repeatedly striking down his New Deal programs. Citizen Clark agreed the justices were a problem but felt strongly that packing the court would jeopardize crucial judicial independence. Principle trumped friendship, and Clark's Committee for Independent Courts—a group of lawyers and business people opposed to the president's plan—became a little-known but important participant in the defeat of the court-packing plan.

Clark also vigorously defended civil liberties, academic freedom, and civil rights for African Americans. In his final three decades he wrote, spoke, and traveled the world promoting what became his major passion, world peace through international law. As with the Plattsburg and Selective Service campaigns, he made all these efforts as a private citizen and carefully downplayed his own role.

As a result of this strong bent for privacy, Grenville Clark's was not a household name to the general public, even in his own time. Yet he was quite well known within the inner circles of business and government. He was close to many presidents: both Roosevelts called him Grenny, Woodrow Wilson belatedly supported his World War I preparedness efforts, Herbert Hoover offered him a top Justice Department assignment, John F. Kennedy admired his work on disarmament. Throughout World War II Clark's office was next door to that of the secretary of war, Henry L. Stimson (Clark maneuvered Stimson into that position and served as his confidential adviser throughout the war). Clark's friends and associates included Supreme Court Justices Felix Frankfurter, Charles Evans Hughes, Owen Roberts, and John M. Harlan, and in his relentless quest for world peace Clark counseled, lobbied, and often befriended a stream of world leaders and global thinkers, among them, the British prime minister Clement Attlee; India's first prime minister, Jawaharlal Nehru; Albert Einstein; and Pope John XXIII. These people knew Clark as a lawyer, adviser, ally, and occasionally a formidable opponent. As public servants themselves they valued all the more his talent and tenacity, and perhaps most of all his prescience, in seeing what needed to be done and then getting it done, often well before the experts had identified a problem.

One of Clark's secret weapons was that he never sought public office and was masterful at diverting the spotlight. He was called "statesman incognito" because he preferred to work behind the scenes and liked to point out "there is no limit to the good a man can do if he doesn't care who gets credit."[4] This strong preference for anonymity was perhaps his most defining characteristic. It was likely part modesty, part pragmatism, part noblesse oblige but at its core was pure stubborn independence. Samuel Spencer, a friend of Clark's who collaborated on his early memoirs, notes that "above all, Clark cherished his independence, so much so that he could not have accepted the pragmatic consequences necessary to being elected, or the submergence of individual position necessary to a bureaucratic team effort."[5] During the four years Clark spent at the War Department as Henry Stimson's private adviser during World War II, Clark refused the nominal dollar-a-year salary, "throwing legal advisors into a tizzy trying to determine if he could see top secret documents without having taken a formal oath of office."[6] (Of course, he was shown the documents.)

A fully engaged citizen, Clark was unclassifiable politically. He described himself as "by inheritance a Republican" but showed early evidence of his global outlook when he left the party in 1920 because of its sabotaging of the nascent League of Nations.[7] Clark was a self-described political independent from then on, remaining conservative in many matters but with a natural affinity for the so-called liberal causes increasingly identified with the Democratic Party. Reflecting this ambivalence was a note in Clark's files from 1936: "Voted Roosevelt for President—otherwise straight Republican ticket."[8] Whether he was a Republican or Democrat was irrelevant to people who knew Clark—they often compared him to the Founders. Norman Cousins, longtime editor of the influential *Saturday Review of Literature*, said that Clark "made one think he would have been much at home with . . . Madison, Franklin, Jefferson or Adams. He had the breadth of outlook, strong rationalist strain, enlightened purpose, and intellectual versatility that one associated with leaders of the Philadelphia Constitutional Convention. He had the gift of leadership. He knew how to draw people together of widely varying viewpoints."[9]

Clark's strongest feeling about government had less to do with party or politics than with basic citizenship. He was steeped from early childhood in the notion that the strength of a nation rests on the vigor and integrity of individual citizens. He enjoyed quoting Abraham Lincoln (whom Clark's grandfather knew personally): "The people will save their country if the government does its job only indifferently well."[10] These foundational beliefs did not spring from any hostility toward government but rather from the understanding that government, with its built-in balances and slowness of movement, simply could not quickly come through in a time of crisis. At such a time the citizenry itself had to do at least part of the job.

Clark was as impossible to pigeonhole on religion as on politics. In another link with many of the Founders, he sometimes called himself a deist, defined as someone who has a rational belief in God based on reason rather than revelation and involving the view that God has set the universe in motion but does not interfere with how it runs.[11] Not inconsistently, Clark also used the term *meliorist*, which had been made popular by the American philosopher and psychologist William James. Clark explained to an interviewer: "I guess I'm a meliorist. I don't believe that God destines things to go to the dogs or destines them to come out well. I do believe there is a middle region where God gives a man a chance to work out his own destinies."[12] In sharp contrast to his own High Church baptism, Clark chose not to have his children baptized, letting them make their own decisions about religion when the time came. Later in life he became active in his community's small Unitarian church, finding a natural affinity with the Unitarians' inclusiveness and relative lack of dogma. In the end Clark did not have a religion as much as he had an outlook: a stubborn optimism, faith in people, and a forward-looking orientation. Clark's daughter Louisa made that point at a dedication speech for the Fanny Dwight Clark Memorial Gardens on Long Island in 1966, just months before her father died: "A striking quality of both my parents equally has always been, unlike many older people, an absence of nostalgia; they talked with enjoyment of the past, but never with an atmosphere of the 'good old days.' Until she died my mother was always more excited by the present and future than by the past. My father still is. I think that is the spirit of this gift."[13]

Indeed it was the spirit of his life.

This book examines Clark's life with an emphasis on the man behind the resume. It begins, as he always did, by exploring his early influences. In a 1950s memoir attempt he explained:

> I begin with my earliest memories . . . in the late [1880s] and early [1890s]—partly because if I never get any farther, some memories of that so different a period may be of the most interest on their own account; but also because, if one wishes to judge the motives and purposes that impelled me in later years, it essential to know something of the early environment.
> No one, I am convinced, can wholly escape either from his inheritance or the early influences that surround him. In exceptional cases, he may, if they were bad, almost free himself from them; or, contrariwise, if they were good, shake off most of the aid they should have afforded. But, in the usual case, the formative influences, for good and ill, have a lasting effect; and certainly in my case, I remain—69 years afterwards—very conscious of them from day to day.[14]

Behavioral science has amply borne out Clark's hunch about the importance of early childhood influences. He was equally correct that his memories of growing up in "so different a period," not to mention in such rarefied style, are most interesting indeed. We start by tracing his inescapably blue bloodlines to some the earliest inhabitants of New York (and America) and then take up his recollections of growing up in Manhattan during the Gay Nineties—including sleigh rides in Central Park, playing tag at the Met, and letting baby alligators loose in Central Park. We then review his liberal education—academic and otherwise—at private schools in Manhattan, the brand new Pomfret prep school in Connecticut, then Harvard and Harvard Law School.

We explore the details and dynamics of Clark's domestic life, including his long and happy marriage to the former Fanny Dwight of Boston and the raising of their four children (three surviving), for their strong influence on virtually everything he did. Similarly, an early biographer once noted, "Clark's most remarkable quality was a capacity for friendship."[15] Reminiscences by his myriad friends, famous and otherwise, appear throughout these pages, as these people did throughout his life.

We devote a separate chapter to his legal career and the powerhouse Wall Street law firm he cofounded. Being a lawyer and having a profound regard for the law were central to Clark's life. Similarly we examine in detail his extraordinary Plattsburg effort before World War I and his showdown with his old friend Franklin Roosevelt over the court-packing plan two decades later. We also explore Clark's many other extracurricular projects—defending civil liberties and academic freedom, promoting civil rights for African Americans, championing world peace—both for his impact on national and global events and for their effects on him.

Clark, of course, was a particular man of a particular time. His long life (1882–1967) spanned a series of landmark events that profoundly shaped the modern world: World War I, the Great Depression, the New Deal, World War II, the Cold War, the civil rights movement. Clark's generation not only witnessed these major milestones, they participated in them. During the same period came unparalleled advances in science, industry, and medicine. From automobiles to space flight, antibiotics to robotics, in Clark's lifetime the impossible was repeatedly made possible. His outlook and worldview reflected an unshakable optimism and sense of adventure. When told one of his lofty goals was unattainable, he would point out that when he was a boy no one had ever heard of airplane travel. The underlying premise of his life was "Why not?"

Clark's particular life and times also help explain why he seemed compelled to devote so much time and energy to public causes. A writer in Clark's day called him "a sophisticated, modern exemplar of that deep New England tradition which has long urged men to like their friends, to do good for their country, to revere nature, and not to think about themselves—the doctrine of simple living and public service."[16] The lingering Puritan ethic and classical education that shaped Clark and so many of his friends put a high premium on civic obligation, citizenship, and giving back. It may seem quaint now, and certainly was not universal then, but in Clark's day select members of the nation's elite, the best and brightest, were fully expected "out of duty and desire . . . [to heed] the call to public service."[17] Men of wealth and power rotated in and out of top government roles not for self-enrichment, as would be the immediate assumption today, but from a sense of duty. The authors Walter Isaacson and Evan Thomas dubbed them the wise men in their 1986 book of the same name, and even within this notable subset, Clark made an impression.[18] John J. McCloy, one of the six public-private powerhouses profiled by Isaacson and Thomas, revealed in a moving tribute, "I am frank to admit that I have always been somewhat awed by Grenville Clark." He elaborated: "All who had heard of Grenville Clark knew that he was a great patriot and a man of extraordinary perception and energy, but those who really followed [his life] sensed that he was something more. Now and then a figure comes along who possesses these attributes to such a marked degree that, set apart from his fellow men, he becomes a leader and a factor in history."[19]

Clark would have deftly deflected the "factor in history" suggestion, supportable though it is. But there was no denying his gift for quiet leadership, and it followed a specific pattern. In a public-spirited version of the classic old boys network, Clark would identify a problem, round up a group of well-connected friends, create a plan, and then relentlessly work that plan through to completion. As the noted federal judge Henry Friendly once described it: "[Clark] would have a program, and a sensible one, one that something could be done with. A group of people would have met in a downtown or uptown club, each would emerge with a task assigned, and something would happen."[20] This method worked remarkably well with Plattsburg, the Selective Service, and many of Clark's early public service projects, when Washington was smaller, Congress somewhat more collegial, and professional interest groups less entrenched.

After World War II Clark's effectiveness at the national level was more limited. As Washington and the Cold War became bigger and more intractable, and the issues facing the United States grew ever more complex, the influence of Clark and other well-connected amateurs like him gradually diminished. He had also ostensibly retired, and lived primarily in Dublin, New Hampshire, physically removed from the power centers in New York and Washington. And he had reached his middle sixties, a career point at which the days of active battle often are exchanged for more steering, mentoring, and advisory roles.

But there is perhaps an even more important reason Clark achieved fewer demonstrable successes later in life: after World War II he deliberately turned his attention to national and international problems so large, issues so complicated, and solutions so difficult that they allowed no total victories. Clark well understood that working for world peace and equal rights were marathons, not sprints, and that trophies would not be awarded to the winners in his lifetime.

Throughout his life Clark's infectious optimism, dogged determination, and unshakable faith in human progress touched virtually everyone with whom he came in contact. These qualities also made possible an extraordinary roster of achievements, both those completed and those yet unfinished. Clark's lengthy record reveals an important American, one from whom we have much to learn about the possibilities and proper role of a citizen in our democracy, and as he believed even more important, the possibilities and responsibilities of a citizen of the world.

CHAPTER 1

Ninth-Generation Manhattanite

Grenville Clark's heritage was textbook early American; his ancestors trace to the earliest European settlers of New England and New York in the early 1630s. His family tree includes no *Mayflower* originals, but they were not far from it. On his mother's side Grenville was the ninth generation born on Manhattan Island. As he put it: "In that sense, at any rate, I was born a good New Yorker."[1]

His mother's forebears, the Cannon and de Forest families, were largely French Huguenots—Protestants who were "very well-to-do and solid people" in France but fled to escape increasing persecution by Catholics. The de Forests came first to Manhattan Island, arriving from Europe around 1630. The Cannons arrived at New Rochelle, New York, fifty-five years later when conditions had grown even worse for non-Catholics in France under Louis XIV. Clark's great-grandfather Cannon was an early ironmaster with a foundry and plant in Troy, New York, where a street is still named Cannon and many generations of Cannons are buried in family plots.

On his father's side were the Clark and the Crawford families from England and Scotland, respectively. The earliest Clarks came to Dedham, Massachusetts, from England, also around 1630. Near the end of the seventeenth century they migrated to the Connecticut Valley at Northampton, where they "had a farm for something like a hundred and fifty years on the [present] site of Smith College." Grenville's grandfather, Luther Clark, was one of three close brothers who headed west to seek their fortunes around 1830. The brothers prospered, starting a trading post and a number of banks in the St. Louis area.[2]

By the end of the 1830s they had returned and fanned out along the east coast, settling, one each, in Boston, Philadelphia, and New York. Luther Clark cofounded the Wall Street banking firm Clark, Dodge and Company in 1845. (The company now is headquartered on Long Island.) The other two brothers became similarly well established in their respective cities, and the three remained close throughout their lifetimes. In the twentieth century the Clark name "pretty well died out" in the New York branch after nearly half (three of eight) of the male descendants were killed in World War II. (The Philadelphia Clarks, on the other hand, were quite prolific. The most famous was Grenville Clark's younger cousin and close friend, the two-term U.S. senator Joseph Clark.)

The Crawford branch of the family arrived from Scotland around 1730 and settled in Putney, Vermont. They were mainly farmers, successful enough to build a "very good-looking substantial brick house back in the country." Clark's grandmother Crawford probably met his Grandfather Clark in the Connecticut Valley "since Northampton, Mass and Putney, Vermont are not so very far apart." The couple ended up in New York City at 18 Gramercy Park "in a great big brick house on the corner of Irving Place next to The Players House, which still stands there, although [the Clark home] has long been demolished to make way for an apartment house."[3]

All these substantial forebears notwithstanding, Clark's strongest family influence by far was his maternal grandfather, Colonel LeGrand Bouton Cannon (a marvelous homophonic name—it has the roar of cannons when spoken aloud). Grenville Clark remembered Cannon (1815–1906) as "a man of great force and ability who influenced me greatly. . . . a small man in stature, but [he] had a very piercing eye and an air of great authority, and he was a man of immense vigor and natural authority —acquired, I suppose, partly from his inheritance from his Huguenot ancestors and partly from his experience in life as a builder and employer of labor, and also very largely through his experience in the Civil War."[4]

It is easy to see what a powerful impression Colonel Cannon would have made on his grandson, or on anyone. He was a railroad builder and industrialist, an early member of the Republican Party, and a personal friend of Abraham Lincoln's and the New England statesman Daniel Webster's. A staunch Unionist, Cannon served with distinction in the Civil War, which he invariably referred to as "the rebellion." Cannon wrote with characteristic flourish of his battlefield and administrative experiences in his autobiography, *Reminiscences of the Rebellion,* published privately for his family in 1895. The book includes accounts of intimate conversations with President Lincoln on matters ranging from their shared love of Shakespeare to the shattering loss of Lincoln's cherished son Willie. It also details Cannon's role as the first Union officer to allow freed slaves to serve in the Union army.[5]

Cannon's lofty position and influence in the railroad industry meant travel by private railcar for the family. His friends in high places at the New York Central line also allowed Grenville and his brother Louis the considerable rush of a ride in the engine's cab with "our hands on the throttle" of a powerful locomotive steaming through New York City's Grand Central Station tunnel to the next junction and back. In an era when train engineers might be compared with today's jet pilots or even astronauts, it was "a terrific thrill" for the two young boys.[6]

"The Colonel," as Cannon was usually called, lived half the year in New York, where he was senior vice president of the Delaware and Hudson Railroad company, which operated iron and coal mines as well as railroads. The other half of the year he spent in Burlington, Vermont, where he ran a steamship company on Lake Champlain in addition to a large farm where he bred dairy cattle and trotting horses. He also had an interest in "one or two" Burlington banks, among various other business concerns. In Burlington Cannon lived in a great mansion called Overlake that he built in 1850 on sixty acres high on a bluff overlooking the town of Burlington, Lake Champlain, and the Adirondacks to the west, and the Green Mountain range to the east. The home was described as one of Vermont's premier mansions in its day.[7]

The young Clark family joined the Colonel for summers in Burlington, staying in a house on the property built for that purpose. During the summer of 1894 Cannon took eleven-year-old Grenville to find the neglected gravesite of the abolitionist John Brown in North Elba, New York, across the lake from Burlington. Few historical figures are as controversial as John Brown—leader of the doomed Harper's Ferry raid to start an armed insurgence among captured slaves in Virginia. But LeGrand Cannon was an unequivocal supporter, calling Brown "the rugged, heroic man whose name is one of the greatest and brightest in the history of America and the world."[8] They found Brown's grave covered with weeds and virtually abandoned. Cannon worked with the local preservationist Kate Field to purchase and restore the gravesite and its 250 surrounding acres as "an enduring monument [to] perpetuate the memory of the famous martyr to liberty."[9] In 1895 the group donated the property to the State of New York, where it remains an official historical site within the national Adirondack Park.

Cannon's reverence for John Brown was just one manifestation of his strongly held "ideas about slavery and the Negro." These ideas had a serious and formative influence on Clark. So did Cannon's overall philosophy of life: "That you must look after yourself and as to government doing everything that was required, don't trust that at all; and if government didn't do the right thing or wouldn't move, take things in your own hands and try to move them yourself." Testament to the mutual affection and respect between grandfather and grandson was that the twenty-three-year-old Grenville Clark served as executor of Cannon's substantial estate when the august maverick died in 1906 at age ninety-one.[10]

Clark's parents do not factor nearly as prominently in his childhood reminiscences. The son describes his father, Louis Crawford Clark, with ambivalence: "[He] was well educated and read considerably, devoted to sport, especially shooting ducks and upland game, fond of horses, very popular with men, had weaknesses of habit and temperament but was hard working and devoted to my mother."[11] Louis Clark went to Harvard, as had his father. Louis married Marian Cannon in 1880 and spent his career at Clark, Dodge and Company, his father's Wall Street banking firm. By Grenville's account, Louis seems to have coasted on his inherited wealth and social station—by no means a novel or sinister course but one his second son found inadequate.

Clark's mother, Marian de Forest Cannon Clark, was LeGrand Bouton Cannon's youngest daughter and clearly his favorite. A complete picture of Marian is difficult to form. The collected family history, handed down for generations, burned in a fire in the home of the Colonel's only son, Henry LeGrand Cannon (1856–1895). (Henry Cannon became an accomplished and recognized artist during his short life. The *Genealogical and Family History of the State of Vermont* calls him "one of the most brilliant and promising American sculptors of his day.")[12] Throughout Grenville Clark's numerous, fairly detailed family remembrances, his mother's name invariably triggers a memory, story, or some other connection to her colorful father. She seems to have enjoyed a good relationship with her son, however, with much warm maternal correspondence through his early adulthood. Louis and Marian had five children and an apparently happy marriage until Marian's death at fifty-two, in 1912, of "pernicious hardening of the arteries."[13]

Grenville Clark's childhood in late nineteenth-century New York City seems pulled from the pages of a Gilded Age novel. He was born on November 5, 1882, in the stately home of his grandfather Cannon. The infant Clark was, as he later chuckled, "quite carefully baptized, I assure you!" Elaborately baptized might be more accurate, beginning with a spectacular procession along the streets of Manhattan in Grandfather Cannon's ornate horse-drawn carriage, complete with uniformed coachman and footman. The procession began at Cannon's Fifth Avenue mansion and made its stately way to Grace Episcopal Cathedral on Broadway. There a High Church ceremony was performed, after which the christening party returned to the Cannon mansion for a lavish feast. The requisite gifts given to satin-gowned Baby Grenville included, naturally, a silver chalice from his godfather, H. Walter Webb, senior vice president of the New York Central railroad.[14]

The Clark family lived in the Cannon mansion for Grenville's first eleven years, sharing the home when the Colonel was in residence in

Manhattan and serving as its primary occupants during his considerable time elsewhere. The house had plenty of space for multiple generations. The property included a stable out back and "a good pair of horses" to pull the two carriages or the sleigh. A fleet of servants attended the family. As Grenville Clark matter-of-factly explained, "It was the custom for anyone with a good amount of money in those days to live in a good deal of style."

Grenville was the second of Louis and Marian's five children, with an older brother, Louis Jr., two years his senior; a younger sister, Mary; and two younger brothers, Harry and Julian. Louis, along with two nearby cousins who were a year or two older than Grenville, formed his early play group. They spent their childhood roaming Manhattan with a freedom and independence hard to imagine today. Their major playground was Central Park, where Clark and his pals "went continually to walk and play." They had regular football games on the Great Meadow at Sixty-fifth Street on the park's west side and rode the newly popular bicycles all over the park and throughout Manhattan. ("There was at the time a very good bicycle path all the way up Riverside Drive from 72nd Street to Grant's Tomb, which, as I recall it, was then under construction.")[15]

One of Clark's most amusing Central Park memories involved two small alligators his father brought back from the South for Grenville and Louis to play with. It was a questionable parental move but one surely popular with the boys: "We kept [them] up in our room on the third floor. . . . But as they got a little bigger they began to crawl all over the place and my mother rebelled and said we had to get rid of them. So we took them up to the Park and dumped them in the Swan Boat Lake right by the 59th Street entrance." The story approached urban legend status nearly thirty years later when "an item turned up in the newspaper saying that, to the surprise of everybody, two good sized alligators had been found living in the Swan Lake."

Clark's early recreation included every manner of sport—shooting game (mostly ducks), all ball and racquet games, and rowing on Central Park's lakes. Winter play was equally zestful—Clark fondly recalled how frequent snowstorms and few snowplows meant serious sledding down Fifth Avenue, either solo or hitched to the back of a lumbering carriage, taxi, or bus. Conditions permitting, the family also enjoyed Currier and Ives–worthy horse-drawn sleigh rides through Central Park in his grandfather's elegant sleigh.[16]

Weekly attendance at the Met (New York's newly opened and already famed Metropolitan Opera) was mandatory and enjoyed. Clark mostly remembered ingenious games of tag and "hare-and-hounds" played in back of the plush boxes and long corridors of the Met. The world-class performances on the stage, although at the time a mere backdrop for mischievous amusement (including "making up little packages of water to [throw] down from the box onto the people in the orchestra [section] and spatter them a bit, although not doing them much harm"), must have had a lingering subliminal effect on Clark. He acquired a deep lifelong fondness for opera, despite cheerfully admitting to having "no ear at all" and apparently no natural talent for singing. (Clark's children recall their enthusiastic father would burst into full-throated and unfortunately tuneless arias when the mood struck him.)[17]

Dancing lessons at Dodsworth's Dancing School on Fifth Avenue were another requirement. These were less well received than the Met, although creative mischief availed at least a temporary solution: "We had to wear gloves, besides patent leather shoes, and the whole thing was considered very obnoxious and rather sissy. [So] it was a regular practice of some of us bad boys to put pins in our gloves so that when we took hold of a little girl's hand to dance with she'd give a shriek and then we'd be sent downstairs and sent home and we'd get out of any further instruction."[18] By his own account Clark never did become much of a dancer.

Life for a young boy in late nineteenth-century Manhattan was not all culture and tea dances, however. From around 1890 until he left for boarding school in 1894, he engaged in regular bare-knuckle dustups with "the tough boys from Sixth and Seventh Avenues who kept a running feud with us boys who went to Cutler School." Clark recounted one early and humbling episode in which "my brother, Louis (who was two years older than I, although considerably smaller), and my first cousin, Crawford Blagden, were sitting on my Grandfather's front stoop and a group of 'Micks,' as we called them, came along and taunted us and put forward a champion to fight one of us if we had the nerve." Clark's brother and cousin "united in putting me forward," as the young Grenny was large and strong for his age. Clark's personality was anything but street fighter, and he warmed slowly to the challenge: "I hadn't any quarrel with this boy, of course, and it was all in absolute cold blood so that I didn't have, I guess, very much spirit for the fight. . . . [So] this other boy who was a well-practiced fighter very soon hit me a tremendous uppercut and knocked me out cold. The next thing I knew was that I had been carried upstairs to my bed and was being revived."

While not violent, Grenville Clark was competitive. Boxing lessons became part of his weekly regimen "under a very good instructor [from whom] we got excellent teaching and practiced among ourselves with the straight left and the right hook and ducking and dodging and became fairly accomplished for boys of that age." Clark continued to box through prep school and some in college, and he credited the training with giving him "all through life a certain amount of self-confidence about looking after myself." In later altercations with the local rivals, the now-prepared Grenny Clark "didn't always come off so badly," and the boys "got quite a lot of practice in defending ourselves in those years."[19]

In 1893 Clark's parents moved to 21 West Forty-seventh Street, and Grandfather Cannon bought the house next door. As to why the Clarks always lived with or near Colonel Cannon, the record says little other than that Cannon and his daughter Marian were very close. A classic story involves Marian's nearly truncated relationship with Louis. After a proper and undoubtedly closely monitored courtship, Louis had finally ratcheted up the courage to ask the formidable Colonel for his favorite daughter's hand. The Colonel turned him down flat, sending a letter that became famous within the family: "Marie is especially dear to me. She is the only one left & I shall not consent to part with her unless I am fully satisfied that the man is entirely worthy of her. I shall not object to her receiving your attention but it must be with the distinct understanding that it does not involve an engagement."[20]

Louis persisted and the couple were married in 1880, presumably with the Colonel's hard-won blessing. Cannon spent six months a year at Burlington and at the height of his career traveled a lot, giving the young Clark family a good deal of private time. In his later years the aging, long-widowed Colonel undoubtedly found comfort in having his daughter and grandchildren nearby, and they undoubtedly enjoyed living close to him.

The move to West Forty-seventh Street brought Clark into "an entirely new lot of experiences." He changed schools and became close to two distant cousins on his mother's side, the Goelet boys, whose family "had come to Manhattan some generations before . . . and acquired a lot of real estate and become extremely rich."

The Goelets weren't the only ones to become wealthy—decades later Clark described this "peculiar age . . . which . . . was correctly called the Gay Nineties" in New York:

There was in New York, at least, and doubtless in a half a dozen of the other big cities, an extraordinary new wave of wealth created partly, or largely, by the opening of the West, and the exploitation of coal and iron, and largely by the creation of new and profitable industries and in large part, I suppose, merely by the increase of population and the immense rise in the value of real estate—such as enriched the Astors, the Goelets, and other families in New York.

At any rate there was a lot of money around for the sporting proclivities of the younger generation who were the descendants of fathers and grandfathers who had made their way by the hardest kind of work. . . . Somehow or other, the psychology was in many cases that fathers and grandfathers, having worked so hard and struggled so intensely, thought it was quite all right for the grandsons and sons to take it easy and they didn't seem to mind their indulging in polo and steeple chasing [sic] and yachting and having four-in-hands . . . [with] shining harness and a footman and a very elaborately dressed lady sitting on the left of the driver.[21]

In a nod to the abundant social fluff of the day, Clark recalled "the dandies and young swells . . . lolling in the windows [of New York's Knickerbocker Club] and strolling with their canes and top hats." He also enjoyed telling an amusing yet cautionary tale about his mother's cousin George, who had "an extremely aristocratic appearance, with perfect manners and self-confidence. Yet [he] seemed to be the 'Last of the Valois' [the end of the line of opulent Burgundy royalty]. Cousin George had not, I think, ever thought it necessary to take part in business and his tastes were luxurious. This situation led him, I know, to raise an occasional loan from my father who would occasionally comment on George's expensive tastes, but good naturedly, I think; and indeed it was hard to resist Cousin George's urbanity and charm even when one realized his uselessness to society."[22]

Without seeming condescending or overly judgmental of such fondly recalled "dandies and swells" or even the "useless to society," Clark steered his own life on quite a different course. Of course philosophical reflection and thematic life choices develop over time. As a child, like all children, Grenville Clark took his life as he found it—his circumstances and the customs of the day simply were what they were. His summary of his childhood: "Altogether New York was quite a pleasant place to live in, as I remember it, in those days."

Clark's education was first rate, typical of his time and family status. It began with private schools in Manhattan. In the early Fifth Avenue years he attended a facility at Thirty-seventh Street and Lexington Avenue run by a Headmistress Ketchum and her assistant, Miss Cook, that the pupils referred to, with great amusement, as "Ketchum and Cookum's." After the move to Forty-seventh Street he enrolled at Cutler's School on West Fiftieth Street, just off Fifth Avenue opposite St. Patrick's Cathedral. A Cutler classmate who became a lifelong friend was Ulysses S. Grant III, grandson and namesake of the famed Civil War general and eighteenth U.S. president. Clark remembered the younger Grant as a remarkable student and distinguished West Pointer who "graduated on even terms with General MacArthur, one of the highest marks in the history of West

Point. For some reason, however, he never had an especially brilliant military career . . . never quite realized the promise of his youth—possibly perhaps handicapped by the weight of his name."[23]

In 1894, at age eleven, Clark went off to boarding school at Pomfret in the northeastern Connecticut countryside. Pomfret was a brand-new prep school founded by a disgruntled headmaster from St. Mark's (one of the five classic New England "St. Grottlesex" schools—an acronym for Groton, Middlesex, and Saints Paul, Mark, and George—run on the English model of molding leaders of society through classical studies and rigorous physical education). Clark's older brother, Louis, had attended St. Mark's the year before, and when its charismatic leader, William Peck, quarreled with the St. Mark's trustees and decided to form his own school, the Clark boys' father was loyal. Thus Grenville was sent along with Louis to beef up Pomfret's inaugural class, even though at eleven-going-on-twelve he was substantially younger than most of the other boys.

The early days at Pomfret were an adventure in many ways. The first class included "about twenty of the worst behaved boys from St. Mark's who they were happy to let go, and they were on the whole a pretty tough crowd." The facility and site were similarly rugged: "There was just one single building . . . an old barn used as a make-shift gymnasium. It was all quite primitive and yet in many ways quite stimulating." One aspect that either shaped Clark or at least suited him was that "being a new enterprise . . . the boys had to engage in self-help . . . [and] had the opportunity at least to take a great deal of responsibility and certainly a good deal of it was put on me." As was the custom at the elite New England prep schools, physical fitness was on a near par with classroom education. The athletic young Grenny Clark developed a strong enthusiasm for running track and also participated vigorously in rowing, hockey, boxing, football, baseball, and "all that anyone could possibly do in the way of sports."

When he graduated from Pomfret in 1899, Clark received a gold medal for general excellence, which invited "a lot of trouble for some years afterwards [with] good-natured ridicule by other, younger members of the family [who] would keep saying, 'How's General Excellence today?' and that sort of thing, making me very much embarrassed." Clark's explanation for why he received the medal was typically deflective: "I got that medal, not because I was very good at anything in particular, not the best athlete in any sport, not the best student in any subject, but I imagine because in general, considering my interest in the whole field of school activities, studies, sports, discipline, and responsibility and so forth, I had done fairly well in the headmaster's opinion."[24]

Already evident in prep school, achievement and understatement would become lifelong themes for Grenville Clark. After Pomfret the inevitable next step was Harvard.

There is something verging on mystical about Harvard, something people outside Cambridge struggle to fully fathom and people on the inside rarely seem to recover from. Perhaps it is the irresistible status of being first—established in 1636, Harvard is widely considered both the first institution of higher learning and the first corporation in the United States. Uniquely, its bylaws are a permanent part of the original and still functioning Charter of the Commonwealth of Massachusetts.[25] Harvardians would point out that its mystique also has to do with continuing excellence; Harvard is consistently ranked among the world's top handful of universities in national and international listings of such things. Whatever the reasons, the "school in Boston," as careful alumni obliquely refer to it, has held a matchless position of prestige and sway, even among other Ivy League institutions, since its inception.

The Clarks were not immune to the lure of Cambridge, and young Grenville became the third-generation Harvard man in his family. (Keeping the legacy intact, his son would be the fourth, with his daughters attending Radcliffe, Harvard's "sister school" before women were admitted. One daughter went on to Harvard Law.)[26] In 1931 Clark became a member of Harvard's select governing board, "the Corporation." His association with the college in all its various roles was among the most important and enduring of his lifetime.

Grenville Clark began college life at Harvard the same way incoming freshmen most places do—slightly overwhelmed by the whole experience. Entering at the tender age of sixteen because he had started Pomfret so early, Clark was perhaps a bit immature: "I went there too young at sixteen, nearly seventeen, it's true, but I was at least eighteen months on the average younger than my fellow classmates." Still, he did well enough in school: "As to studies, I took quite an interest in them and did moderately well."[27]

It was an exhilarating time to be at Harvard. Charles W. Eliot, its visionary president, had "turned the university over like a flapjack" during his forty-year tenure (1869–1909).[28] He exhorted university-trained men to engage in public service, whether they held public office or not. Clark remembered Eliot's "great vigor of mind and great reliability of character, [he was] very insistent on speaking the truth under all circumstances no matter how hard it was, [and had] great shrewdness in selecting men." Clark's professors at Harvard were luminaries in their fields. He studied philosophy under William James and George Santayana, economics under Frank Taussig, and government under A. Lawrence Lowell, who would follow Charles Eliot as Harvard president in 1909 and stay for more than twenty years. (At the end of Lowell's tenure then–Corporation member Grenville Clark would play a prime role in selecting Lowell's replacement.)[29]

At Harvard Clark maintained a full roster of extracurricular activities. As a freshman he joined the fencing club and in later years the debate club, the latter earning him the nickname "the Wrangler" from his friends "since others of my social crowd, so to speak, took no part in such things and thought it very queer." He was also active in rowing, "which I was a crank about, and got a great deal out of and became President of the Newell Boat Club, [and] came to know very well [Oliver Dwight] Filley who was the famous oarsman and captain of the crew." Apparently Clark rarely engaged in another venerable extracurricular pursuit—dating. Whether it was attributable to his youth or perhaps lingering effects from Dodsworth Dance Academy, "as to girls and dances, I had nothing to do with them all those college years, as I remember it, [I] perhaps went twice in four years in college to any dance."[30]

As a sophomore Clark was initiated into the ultraexclusive Porcellian Club, an assemblage of such rarified air that not even Franklin Roosevelt rated an invitation. (FDR, one year behind Clark at Harvard, reportedly told a friend that being turned down for Porcellian membership was the greatest disappointment of his life.) The Porcellian, founded in 1791, is similar to Yale's Skull and Bones (founded 1832) and Princeton's Ivy Club (founded 1878), in that it represents the most elite of the so-called final clubs—destination points atop the heady and steep social ladders at Ivy League schools. The *National Review* columnist and Dartmouth emeritus professor Jeffery Hart gently lampooned the club's exclusivity, given its limited tangible offerings: "[The Porcellian] is devilishly hard to join. But there is nothing there, hardly a club at all. The quarters consist entirely of a large room over a row of stores in Harvard Square. There is a bar, a billiards table, and a mirror arranged so that members can sit and view Massachusetts Avenue outside without themselves being seen. And that's it. Virtually the sole activity of the Porcellians is screening applicants. Porcellian is the pinnacle of the Boston ideal. Less is more. Zero is a triumph."[31]

Clark took this triumph, along with his many other distinctly nonegalitarian birthrights, more or less in stride. Some inner sense of equality, or perhaps just playful irreverence, led to his being reprimanded by the Porcellians—some years after his graduation—for twice bringing non-members into their hallowed confines, which was strictly verboten. A stern letter began: "Inasmuch as you have persisted in breaking the rules by bringing non-members into the Porcellian Club—" Clark's unauthorized guest whose presence triggered the letter was none other than Henry Stimson, then–secretary of war under President Howard Taft, but even that lofty credential held no water in the absence of official "Porc" membership. Equally amusing is the club's long memory. Clark's first transgression had occurred as an underclassman, more than a decade before he crashed the Porcellians' sacred precincts with Secretary Stimson.[32] The unrepentant rule breaker surely chuckled as he tucked the frosty letter away for future generations. This pattern of moving smoothly among, but not in lockstep with, the inner circles of power and influence continued throughout Grenville Clark's life.

If attending Harvard was a given in the Clark family, law school was not. Grenville could easily have slid into a comfortable position in his father's banking business or any of the railroad, mining, or other concerns of his Grandfather Cannon, let alone the myriad opportunities his own prodigious abilities and connections would have availed. Instead with characteristic independence he chose an unprecedented (in his family) career in law. In retrospect it was a perfect choice and near seamless fit for Clark's thorough logical mind, his bent for fairness, and his methodical personality. He entered Harvard Law School in 1903.

At Harvard Law Clark met fellow student and future Supreme Court Justice Felix Frankfurter. Frankfurter was a brilliant young Jewish immigrant from Austria who had come to Harvard from the coldwater tenements of New York's Lower East Side. He could not have been more different from Clark in upbringing, personality, and modus operandi, yet they shared a reverence for the law and an unshakeable belief in good governance through active citizenship. The two became close friends and sometime conspirators on public service projects throughout their lives. Both went on to enjoy distinguished careers and notable public service accomplishments—Clark as a lawyer, private citizen, and agitator and Frankfurter as a Harvard Law professor, member of FDR's brains trust, and ultimately a long-serving justice on the nation's highest bench.[33]

In their law school days Frankfurter was undoubtedly the more serious scholar. He wryly noted that while he spent his time and energy on the intellectually challenging *Harvard Law Review* board, "Grenny was more interested in rowing."[34] And yet Clark was not frivolous. Another law school anecdote illustrates his thorough, meticulous method of thought and his innate pragmatism. One day, presumably to stimulate abstract thinking and discussion, a well-known law professor presented the class with "a preposterous theory, trying to reconcile the irreconcilable." According to Frankfurter, "the hunt was on" as many eager nimble-minded students (FF included) raced to match wits with and impress their esteemed professor and each other. Finally students and teacher wearied of the game and moved on to another topic. All except Clark, who continued to reflect on the needless complexity of the original question. He abruptly announced: "But Mr. Beale, the rule you've formulated is very difficult to apply!" The teacher condescendingly replied, "This is not a cinch course, Mr. Clark," much to the other students' snickering amusement.[35] Yet Clark was right and the event was prophetic. Grenville Clark would spend his lifetime seeking and formulating rules that could be applied to the real and urgent problems of the day. Intellectual gamesmanship and showing off for a crowd never held appeal.

After law school Clark and Frankfurter both found themselves back at Harvard. Frankfurter became Harvard's first Jewish law professor while Clark joined its top governing body, the Corporation.[36] Their old roles became reversed as Clark found himself frequently defending his brilliant friend, who ruffled feathers with his frequent absences from Cambridge for ongoing government consulting roles in Washington. This criticism was undoubtedly coupled with some degree of anti-Semitism, latent or overt. Most offensive to Harvard's elite conservative governing board was Frankfurter's public support of controversial political causes, especially his outspoken defense of the two Italian anarchists in the infamous Sacco and Vanzetti case.[37] Clark and Frankfurter did have several heated disagreements over the years. In 1937 Frankfurter's deafening public silence during FDR's court-packing attempt would greatly offend his old classmate. Even more so would several of Frankfurter's distinctly illiberal, as Clark perceived them, Supreme Court rulings in civil liberties cases.[38] Ironically the immigrant Frankfurter grew steadily more conservative through the years as his manor-born friend became ever more broad-minded.

Despite these differences the bond of friendship remained. The two men visited each other's homes, kept up a voluminous correspondence, and ran up large phone bills to discuss, debate, and sometimes conspire on important matters of the day. The childless Frankfurter became an honorary uncle to Clark's children, who were routinely greeted with a hearty kiss whether at home or the Supreme Court's marble palace in Washington. When illness forced Frankfurter to retire from the court in the early 1960s, Clark quietly arranged through Justice John Harlan to make certain neither Frankfurter nor his wife, Marion, would have to worry about money for medical bills.[39]

Besides Frankfurter, other notable Harvard Law classmates were Clark's future law partners, Elihu Root Jr. and Francis W. Bird. Both came from distinguished families. Root was the son of Elihu Root Sr., then a senator from New York after long service as secretary of war and secretary of state under presidents William McKinley and Theodore Roosevelt, respectively. Bird was the son of the colorful and prominent Massachusetts paper manufacturer Charles Sumner Bird, who was also the leader of the Progressive Party in Massachusetts. Clark considered the younger Bird the most brilliant and promising man in the class, a "top student with great originality and imagination and a reformer in politics" who left the firm early to join his father's newspaper-publishing business in Boston. Tragically Francis Bird died soon after, in 1913 at thirty-two, cutting short what Clark called "an almost certainly remarkable career."[40] Root and Clark remained fast friends and frequent partners; they died within months of each other in 1967.

Other friends from the impressive Harvard Law class of 1906 included George A. Washington, descendant of the first president's brother, and Delancey K. Jay, direct descendant of the first chief justice of the Supreme Court. Clark considered Jay "the most admirable character in the class." Jay served in the diplomatic service, practiced law, and was an active participant in and organizer of the Plattsburg Officer Training Camps before World War I. He sustained severe injuries as an infantry officer in the war and received the Distinguished Service Cross. According to Clark, Jay "always did the right thing, however difficult; . . . a man of the highest standards in every way." The Clark and Jay families were friends and neighbors, and the two men remained close until Jay "died in 1941 largely as the result of war service."[41]

Clark's sterling education and the contacts and opportunities it afforded mattered. They still matter today. The author William Deresiewicz recently wrote of his own fourteen years of Ivy League conditioning: "From orientation to graduation, the message is implicit in every tone of voice and tilt of the head, every old-school tradition, every article in the student paper, every speech from the dean. The message is: You have arrived. Welcome to the club."[42] In 2013 eight of the nine sitting Supreme Court justices (not to mention three of the last four presidents) had Ivy League diplomas, causing a sociology professor at the City University of New York to quip: "What I think [President Obama] means by 'diversity' is Yale, Harvard, Princeton, and Columbia."[43] From birth Clark was already a member of the club, of course. Still, his time at Harvard and Harvard Law in every way delivered on their promise of a stimulating education and unmatched network of future colleagues and associates. After seven years in Cambridge the next natural stop on Clark's seemingly preordained path was Wall Street.

CHAPTER 2

Life on the Street—Wall Street

After completing Harvard and Harvard Law School, Grenville Clark was admitted to the New York State Bar Association in 1906. He took the customary two-year clerkship at the distinguished Wall Street law office of Carter, Ledyard and Milburn. The firm's founder, then retired, was James C. Carter, described by Clark as "the acknowledged leader, I suppose, of the American legal profession at that time." Underscoring the power of his Harvard connections, Clark recalled that he was likely selected for the prestigious spot "because of my friendship with Devereux Milburn at . . . the Law School and in the Porcellian Club, of which we made him an honorary member."[1] (Despite Clark's irreverence toward and scolding from the Porcellians, membership in the club nonetheless quietly opened doors.)

A fellow law clerk at Carter, Ledyard was Franklin Delano Roosevelt. Besides their overlapping time at Harvard, Clark and Roosevelt shared the rapport of old east coast families that had known each other for generations. But boot camp camaraderie as lowly law clerks forged a closer friendship. Together the young men labored under the famously dictatorial Louis Cass Ledyard, whom Clark described as "a very powerful high tempered and able man." A Clark daughter remembered that her father's favorite reminiscences included "those sometimes hilarious days when he and FDR were among the most junior terrified 'slaves' of Ledyard, the formidable head of the firm. When Mr. Ledyard occasionally summoned [the clerks] into his office to recite on some intricate legal questions, the young FDR sometimes performed worst of all and got in the most trouble because his mind was not fixed on a career as a lawyer but instead was already mapping out his path to the Presidency."[2]

Roosevelt freely shared his future plans with his fellow clerks. Clark always remembered "the engaging frankness with which [FDR] described the road which he intended to follow and did actually follow to the Presidency . . . [telling] us of the successive steps by which he hoped to reach the goal—election to the state Legislature, service as Assistant Secretary of the Navy, the Governorship of New York. I remember him saying: 'Anyone who gets to be Governor of New York has a good chance to be President; and anyhow I'm going to try for it.'" Presidential ambitions didn't stop the young men from enjoying summertime in New York. One afternoon on the way back from a "routine service of papers in New Jersey," Clark and Roosevelt stopped by the Polo Grounds sporting park to take in a baseball game. They also apparently took in a few beers. Back at the office they were intercepted and interrogated by Ledyard, who cut short FDR's elaborate explanation with an abrupt: "Roosevelt, you're drunk!"[3] The future president took his lumps cheerfully and got back to planning his political ascent.

In 1909 Clark left Carter, Ledyard and formed a partnership with friends Elihu Root and Francis Bird. Root, Clark, and Bird hung out its new shingle at 31 Nassau Street in the heart of lower Manhattan's mecca for elite law firms collectively known as Wall Street. Its exclusive location masked the firm's modest beginnings. Clark remembered:

> It was extremely meager. We had a small, bare office . . . [three partners], one stenographer . . . and two office boys. . . . We had a considerable bankruptcy business, however, by favor of friends of ours who were United States Judges, particularly Judge Learned Hand and his cousin, Judge Augustus Hand, both of whom had just gone on to the Federal bench. My very first client, I remember, was The Swastika Lunch Club, a club of stenographers of which my cousin's . . . secretary was Chairman. I am sorry to say the Swastika Lunch Club dissolved very quickly and the fee, if any, did not exceed $15![4]

In 1913 Bird left the firm to run a newspaper in Boston, so Root and Clark brought in Emory Buckner and Silas Howland, who had been a year behind them at Harvard Law. Buckner and Howland were from completely different backgrounds than the founding trio. Buckner was the son of an impoverished Methodist minister in Nebraska, and Howland came from similarly modest circumstances, but the talents and personalities of the four partners meshed well. Grenville Clark said later that between them there was virtually no case at least one could not take on with confidence.[5]

When the United States entered World War I in 1917, the financially secure Root and Clark took time out for military service—Clark at the Adjutant General's Office in Washington, D.C., and Root as a field officer. Buckner and Howland, whose families were dependent on their earnings, stayed to run Root, Clark. At the same time the firm was given an inestimable boost when Root's distinguished father, the former secretary of state, secretary of war, and senator from New York, agreed to become counsel to the fledgling firm. In his words, he wanted to "help hold the business together while the boys were at war." If his original motives were paternal, the senior Root relished getting back into the practice of law. When his son and Grenville Clark returned after the war, the senior Root stayed on, lending invaluable guidance and letterhead weight until his death in 1937. Clark described Senator Root as having "pretty much set us up in business. His prestige was enormous and his kindness and interest in us beyond measure."[6]

That prestige undoubtedly helped attract some impressive early clients, including Andrew Carnegie and Marshall Field, the first of many business and industry titans the firm would represent. Through talent, hard work, and well-placed connections, Root, Clark soon took its place among the so-called lions of the blue-chip bar. These elite firms are immortalized in the legal reporter Paul Hoffman's 1973 insider look at Wall Street, *Lions of the Street.* Hoffman describes the peculiar Wall Street ethos:

Here the law differs from the other learned professions. . . . Their power and influence comes not only from the clients they represent. The system itself nurtures power—through its recruitment, training, and promotion of men able to cut through the thorny issues of business, finance, and government. The [Wall Street] legal establishment is like an octopus with its head in Manhattan and its tentacles stretching into the power centers of American society. The lions sit on the boards of banks and business, foundations and universities. They graduate to posts in the Cabinet and seats on the Supreme Court.[7]

Root, Clark in many ways exemplified the power, entrée, and influence that flows through and from the top Wall Street law firms. (According to Hoffman, by the 1940s "there was no finer array of legal talent in New York than the aggregation known as 'the Root, Clark firm.'") In other ways, however, the firm was quite different. Clark and his partners cultivated an atmosphere of collegiality throughout their organization in sharp contrast to the hierarchical culture prevailing on Wall Street. Just one example: Root-Clark's star litigator, Emory Buckner, reportedly coined the more respectful term *associate* for junior members of a law firm, replacing the more subservient sounding *law clerk*.[8]

Root, Clark was also the first major law firm to pay its associates an annual bonus from the firm's profits. These were distributed, along with profit shares to the partners, at the highly anticipated "Dough Day" dinners each January. The dinners were held at a private club, with gourmet food and good liquor, which was completely legal even during Prohibition since the alcohol was not purchased, sold, or transported. The entertainment program was an uproarious lineup of original ditties lampooning senior partners, sung to the tunes of popular songs. "Club Boy Clark," to the tune of "Oh My Darling, Clementine," was typical:

There are many, who think Grenny,
Is the Club-man's, maximum;
But the highbrows, lift their eyebrows
When he snaps, his chewing gum.

All beholders, love his shoulders
And that long, determined jaw;
All his clients, have reliance
But the boys, look up the law.

All Porcellian's, sainted hellions
Stuffed the ballot, box for Clark;
Now he's lost on, trains to Boston—
Just a Harvard, hierarch.[9]

The last stanza alludes to Clark's recent appointment to the Harvard Corporation. It is accompanied in the printed program by a caricature of a smug and aristocratic Clark, feet propped on the desk, telephone in hand, demanding to be connected with Harvard's President Conant. Clark was an enthusiastic participant in the evening's antics as well as a frequent target. His children recall their normally dignified father rehearsing the silly songs in the weeks leading up to the dinner "in full voice and gesture" until all were collapsed with laughter. Afterward he would dryly remark on the cost of the legal hours put in on the program by the firm's top lawyers but then would chuckle, "It was worth it."[10]

Root, Clark was also the first of the so-called white shoe law firms to hire lawyers who were not Anglo-Saxon Protestant men. In the 1920s, only a few short years after women secured the right to vote and at a time of rampant anti-Semitism, Root, Clark hired both its first woman attorney and its first Jewish attorneys.[11] Clark considered this logical and proper, and the firm's then–fairly radical hiring policies were followed as a matter of course and good business.

These policies and, more important, the attitudes and character behind them, helped Root, Clark become especially well known for the

Root, Clark "Dough Day" dinner program, 1939.

many bright young lawyers it trained and prepared for positions of prominence. The dazzling and gregarious Emory Buckner was the firm's chief trial lawyer. He was also responsible for recruiting and grooming many other top legal talents, including the future Supreme Court justice John Harlan, who joined Root, Clark in 1923 fresh from a Rhodes Scholarship at Oxford. In 1925 Buckner left to serve for two years as U.S. attorney for the Southern District of New York. Harlan went with Buckner, serving as his assistant U.S. attorney.[12] Both men returned to Root, Clark in 1927. When Buckner suffered a serious stroke in 1934 from which he never fully recovered, Harlan took over as the firm's top litigator and performed ably for many years. Eventually President Eisenhower tapped Harlan for the U.S. Court of Appeals for the Second Circuit and later elevated him to the Supreme Court.

Another star who began at Root, Clark was Henry Friendly. Such is Friendly's stature in the legal world that people argue about whether Friendly, Felix Frankfurter, or Louis Brandeis was the highest-ranked student ever at Harvard Law School. While impossible to prove, the tales properly place Friendly in an impressive honor society.[13] Friendly's placement at Root, Clark was an early result of Frankfurter's unofficial one-man legal employment service for the firm. During his years as a Harvard Law professor, the catalytic Frankfurter placed his brightest law students in prestigious clerkships in government and top law firms. (A prevailing joke of the day was that the way to get to the Supreme Court was to go to Harvard Law School and turn left.)[14] Root, Clark was a frequent and happy beneficiary of Frankfurter's pipeline, never more so than with Friendly, who came to the firm fresh from a one-year clerkship for Supreme Court Justice Louis Brandeis. Friendly would spend the majority of his private career at Root, Clark (including the spinoff firm Cleary, Gottlieb, Friendly and Hamilton) before being tapped for the U.S. Court of Appeals for the Second Circuit.

Friendly later remembered how his early boss, the superperfectionist Grenville Clark, notoriously underused his law clerks. The stated reason was often not wanting to burden the firm's young associates. Likely a bigger factor was Clark's near-compulsive need to personally manage every detail of even the most complex cases. Or, as Friendly put it: "Like Brandeis, [Clark] was an old-fashioned lawyer who took pleasure in doing his own work; he found real joy in writing out a contract, letter, or brief, either in full or in outline, on a yellow pad on which the script always wandered dangerously away from the left margin."[15]

As a result Friendly spent more than a few lonely days as Clark's dedicated law clerk. He would routinely be on his second or third reading of the *New York Times* by midmorning, while his well-known boss was on hands and knees on the floor in his office sorting stacks of documents for a difficult case according to the specific aspect of the case each addressed. In one instance a visiting client asked whether new carpeting was being installed. "No," came the reply, "that's just Mr. Clark, one of our Partners." The close personal attention Clark devoted to his cases brought him almost unfailing success but at the cost of great personal strain during his years of practice.[16] (This strain would ultimately lead to a temporary breakdown, detailed in Chapter 6.)

Clark devoted the same close attention to developing his junior partners. Henry Friendly called him "a great chief—welcoming suggestions, appreciative of aid, considerate of other aspects of one's life, loyal in the last degree, putting his junior forward at every opportunity." Friendly also never forgot being gathered as a young associate into the warmth of the Clark family. During his first two years with Root, Clark, not yet married and new to New York City, he would often be invited out to the Clarks' home on Long Island to work with "GC" in the evening. Working on cases grew to include joining the family for meals, lively conversation, and enjoying the Clarks' young children. Decades later, on the unexpected death of Clark's daughter Mary Clark Dimond, Friendly sent a heartfelt letter of condolence to Mary's husband, Dr. E. Grey Dimond.

In it he also remembered Mary's father: "My loyalty and affection for him never ceased. I place him along with Justice Brandeis and Justice Frankfurter as the men who influenced me most."[17]

Clark became a recognized expert in railroad law, bankruptcy law, and handling large estates, but he was a generalist at heart. He took on a wide variety of cases—corporate matters; litigation involving contracts; wills; and miscellaneous controversies. That an area of practice was new to him was no deterrent. Each case was a fresh challenge, and each received his customary thoroughness and persistence, regardless of the potential fee.

Clark's mind and methods were deep rather than facile. He needed and took the time to thoroughly think through complicated matters, considering every angle, every argument, and each potential counterargument. He made sure his ironclad briefs not only were right but also looked right: he understood that readability and ease of absorption mattered. His admittedly tedious process nearly always led to a better and more complete, if not lightning fast, result. One Root, Clark partner said, "It took him forever to make up his mind, but I never knew him to be wrong." Fellow attorneys also remembered Clark for his "bulldog tenacity." One frustrated opponent lamented, "He prepares like a scientist and hangs on like a leech."[18]

Early in the firm's history Clark demonstrated this tenacity, and not a little chutzpah, in what became a fabled story in the legal and society circles of the day. The case involved collection of deficiency judgments from foreclosure proceedings. It was hardly a profitable venture since few were ever collected, but the firm was young and the partners took what work they could get. One judgment involved a notorious stock speculator named Hoadley who had already made and lost several fortunes. The slippery Hoadley and his wife had a townhouse on the Hudson River with a tunnel through which they could escape from their creditors to their yacht anchored nearby. One evening Henry Mayer, then a Root, Clark office boy and sometime warrant server (later a successful labor lawyer), got a tip that the Hoadleys were holed up in a swanky downtown hotel. When Mrs. Hoadley, bedecked in a long white opera cape, stepped into her chauffeured car, she was confronted by the intrepid young Mayer and a terrified deputy sheriff who had been summoned to serve an arrest warrant. Mayer tells the Hollywood-ready story from there:

> I nudged the deputy sheriff but he was too scared to execute the warrant. . . .
> When he still held back, I literally pushed him into her arms and announced she was under arrest. When she began to create a scene I suggested we all return to the Hoadley suite in the hotel. We did

so. When I found [Mr.] Hoadley there, I told him he was under arrest too. At first he tried to bluster his way out of his predicament. Then he went to the phone.

In short order, William J. Flynn, then head of the US Secret Service and a friend of Hoadley's, appeared. He was followed by Hoadley's lawyer, Bainbridge Colby, who later became Secretary of State under Woodrow Wilson. Colby, who was drunk, became a little drunker when Hoadley, a good sport, ordered rounds of drinks to be brought up to the suite.

The deputy sheriff, who was scared, brought the sheriff's then counsel [George] Olvany over pronto. Olvany later became a [New York] supreme court judge and head of Tammany Hall.

I was overwhelmed by all this talent so I sent for Grenville Clark, who showed his imperturbability by sitting down, opening a newspaper, and calmly announcing that he would give the Hoadleys one hour to raise the $10,000 they had to pay or go to jail. Colby said he was going to rejoin Judge Cohalan at the Metropolitan Club and have him vacate the warrant of arrest. Mr. Clark told him to go ahead and be damned.

Though Colby was in his cups, he still had sense enough to realize he had met his match and he had Hoadley send [his banker] out to raise the . . . cash at 3:00 in the morning. When the cash arrived, Mr. Clark reached out and took it. That started a donnybrook. Olvany said the money belonged to the sheriff (he was right). Mr. Clark said he would like to speak to me in the hallway. When we got outside, he handed me the ten thousand-dollar bills and said: "Run like hell, Henry." And run I did, down ten flights of steps and a couple of miles to my home. . . . I stuck it under my pillow and slept not a wink that night.[19]

These early stories conjure up a kind of Wall Street Superman (even the name and mild-mannered exterior of the Caped Crusader's alter ego, Clark Kent, fit). Clark certainly looked the part: a strapping six feet tall, broad shoulders, and a handsome patrician face with a full brow, alert expression, and the impressive square jaw that always jutted slightly forward. Even the distinctive purple birthmark on his left temple somehow added flair. Clark also had an unmistakable physical confidence forged in early scrapes with neighborhood toughs, the rough boys at Pomfret, and his general athleticism and boxing prowess. Combined with an equally brawny mind, ferocious powers of concentration, an apparent lack of fear, and a willingness to do literally whatever it took to get the job done, Grenville Clark could be daunting.

Lawbreakers sometimes learned this dramatically. In a bankruptcy case the firm was handling, Clark suspected a certain shady individual would attempt to remove hidden assets from a storage building on New York's Lower West Side. Clark's solution was to wait all night with a nervous young associate in a decrepit old loft building. Around dawn a truck arrived and Clark's suspicions were confirmed. As the first truckload of goods left the premises Clark stationed his associate to block the rear escape exit, sprinted up a full flight of stairs, and confronted the startled perpetrator with a fully prepared summons. The man and his accomplices were indicted and convicted of criminal fraud.[20]

Clark's founding partner and lifelong friend, Elihu Root Jr., summed up the raucous early days at the firm's silver anniversary dinner in 1945: "[There] were great battles. I remember bursting into the office one afternoon and crying to [young associate] John Korner, 'How is it, John?' and his responding, 'Very bad! Mr. Clark has sent for his stick!'" Clark's understated response: "I suppose these stories don't grow *less* lurid with time." Later in the speech he conceded, "We did have a big time with the American Oil Cloth Co., where we represented innocent Quaker stockholders against as tough a crowd of New York swindlers as one can imagine, and had to bust open a safe to get some records. [Root] says I did it and that he got me out of trouble by a tremendous argument in Court; so it must be so."[21]

Of course not all of Clark's methods were quite so macho. He was also a master of gentlemanly persuasion. A young associate remembered with awe his senior partner marching into the office of Chase Bank president Winthrop Aldrich. Clark came on behalf of E. W. Clark, a financial company owned by his Philadelphia relatives that had a complaint against the banking behemoth. Clark sat down across the table from the most powerful banker in New York, who happened to be a personal friend. Clark took out an elaborate brief covering every facet of his client's complaint and said: "Winthrop, you and your bank have gravely wronged my clients. I have here a printed complaint to be filed tomorrow if necessary in federal court in New York." He outlined the details of the case and suggested, "I think you should, as one gentleman to another, make a settlement of this matter without forcing my clients to go to court, for you and your bank have done them a grave injustice." Clark left the complaint for Aldrich to review, and before long a substantial settlement was quietly reached, including a tidy fee for Root, Clark.[22]

Many of Clark's cases clearly activated his ready sense of morality and rightness of cause. Some, on the other hand, were not quite so public spirited. A prime example Clark always remembered with slight embarrassment occurred almost literally in his own backyard. In 1929 a group of

Clark's super-rich Long Island neighbors asked him to represent them in a self-serving protest of the path of the new Northern State Parkway. The parkway's most direct and logical route would have cut through portions of several of their baronial Gold Coast estates, which were clustered around the carefully insulated village of Old Westbury. These were homes "identified by black-and-gold signs bearing such names as Morgan, Whitney, Winthrop, Grace, Garvan, and Phipps." Rerouting the parkway to avoid their properties would greatly increase the cost of the publicly funded project. Clark, with tolerant amusement, called the protesters "the world's most private-spirited community." But he took their case and won it; for years the parkway's resulting sweeping southward curve was known as the Clark Bend.[23]

A closer look at the parkway incident reveals Clark's willingness to use bare-knuckle tactics, his effectiveness at both front- and backroom persuasion, and his readiness to take on entrenched powers. The parkway's mastermind and champion was the powerful New York park commissioner and urban planning czar Robert Moses. For decades Moses harnessed the corruptly effective Tammany Hall machine to create an unprecedented urban infrastructure in New York City and the surrounding boroughs. His fifty-year legacy of building bridges, expressways, pools, parks, and housing developments continues to define the nation's largest and most vibrant city. Moses was not shy about his accomplishments or enriching himself through them; according to the biographer Robert Caro, Moses "built himself an empire [and] lived like an emperor."[24] He typified a favorite Clark expression: "Too much ego in his cosmos."[25] Grenville Clark had many friends but could enjoy the occasional well-placed enemy; taking on Bob Moses undoubtedly stirred his competitive juices.

Moses had long enjoyed a blank check from New York governor Al Smith. Fortunately for Clark and his neighbors the parkway case came up shortly after Franklin Roosevelt had replaced Smith in Albany. Moses and Clark first faced off over Roosevelt's desk. Then they followed the beleaguered new governor down to Warm Springs, Georgia, where FDR took treatment for his polio-crippled legs. The author Gerald Dunne says Roosevelt "must have felt like a rat caught between two mastiffs as the champions squared off."[26] The fight continued, and Moses seemed to be winning until Clark discovered evidence of inappropriate concessions Moses had made to relatives and other powerful landowners along other sections of the parkway. (Coincidentally these were the same concessions Clark sought for his clients.)

Well aware 1930 was an election year, Clark sent his old friend the governor a letter threatening to go public with the revelations. The letter had its desired effect and within days a suddenly conciliatory Moses offered a compromise, which Caro later described as an "unconditional surrender," doing permanent damage to Moses's reputation.[27] The unusually personal nature of the parkway fight was brought home one night at the family dinner table. During a ferocious thunderstorm a flash of lightning was followed by a great clap of thunder, prompting Clark's young daughter Mary, then nine or ten, to innocently ask, "Did Bob Moses do that?"[28]

As chair of the city bar's judiciary committee, Clark also challenged New York's entrenched patronage system. Clark and his good friend, fellow lawyer, and committee member Charles C. "CCB" Burlingham kept up a courtly but steady pressure on Governor Roosevelt and his successor, Governor Herbert Lehman, to nominate judicial candidates on the basis of their legal credentials. Obvious as that seems, the prevailing system instead involved selecting from a short list of acceptable candidates prepared by each political party. The governors were undoubtedly influenced, if not always thrilled, by the pair's relentless assistance.[29] Their efforts were a preview of Clark and Burlingham's much more intense and confrontational 1937 engagement with President Roosevelt about his court-packing plan (see Chapter 8).

In what he counted among his most important legal contributions, Clark founded the Bill of Rights Committee of the American Bar Association and was its first chair, serving from 1938 to 1940. The committee weighed in on Supreme Court cases involving important Bill of Rights issues—freedoms of speech, religion, and assembly, among others. Convinced that these fundamental American freedoms were at constant risk from politicians and a distracted public, Clark and his committee filed amicus, or friend-of-the-court, briefs to clarify the often complex constitutional and other legal issues involved. Later Clark turned his formidable legal and organizational talents to advancing civil rights for African Americans during the battleground years of the early 1960s. The bulk of Clark's extracurricular energies, however, would be devoted to the project that defined his last three decades: his mammoth campaign to promote world peace through limited but enforceable world law.

Clark retired in 1948 after nearly forty years of active law practice to devote full time to his increasing public service efforts. In 1954 both he and Elihu Root Jr. were invited to become "of-counsel" to a spinoff firm formed by some of Root, Clark's best lawyers: George Cleary, Leo Gottlieb, Henry Friendly, and Melvin Steen. Clark enjoyed playing the elder statesman, although, according to the biographer Gerald Dunne, "Clark made it clear that his relationship to the new firm would . . . be more form than substance." He would remain in Dublin working on public causes, and "there was no need to supply him with an office and secretary."[30] Root and Clark continued as of-counsel until their deaths in 1967.

In sum, Clark revered the law and relished practicing it. He devoted immense energy to Root, Clark and its subsequent iterations, and he derived lifelong satisfaction from seeing the fledgling firm grow in size and reputation to become one of the nation's largest and most respected legal establishments. At a firm dinner toward the end of his career Clark encouraged his younger colleagues to follow suit: "We took all our cases with desperate seriousness, yet got a lot of fun from them and many a laugh—win or lose. May this spirit always continue."[31]

In 1959 the American Bar Association awarded Clark its highest honor, the ABA Medal for "conspicuous service to the cause of American jurisprudence."[32] The medal had been awarded only twenty-three times in the bar's eighty-one-year history. Previous awardees included Elihu Root Sr., Oliver Wendell Holmes Jr., and Charles Evans Hughes Jr. A fundamentally modest man, Clark accepted the many honors and awards he received graciously but always with a touch of discomfort and an eagerness to get the spotlight off himself. This one was special, and an especially fitting capstone to a lifetime of dedicated and effective service to the law.

CHAPTER 3

Domestication
Clark the Family Man

The only thing more meaningful to Grenville Clark than the law was his family. On November 5, 1903, Clark's twenty-first birthday, he met the love of his life, Fanny Pickman Dwight, at a dance in Boston. Fanny was a poised, attractive, cultivated young woman who had attracted many suitors (Felix Frankfurter later admitted to having a major crush on the future Mrs. Clark).[1] But the tall and handsome Grenny Clark carried the day. After a six-year courtship as single-minded and results driven as any of Clark's legal cases, the couple wed on November 27, 1909. Their affectionate and committed marriage lasted until Fanny's death in 1964.

It would be difficult to overstate Fanny's influence on Grenville Clark's life. They were an indivisible team, and she was a formidable person in her own right. Fanny Pickman Dwight was born and raised in Boston, a descendant of the intensely New England Dwight and Silsbee families, who had been in Massachusetts since 1630. Both the Silsbee and Peele families (Fanny's maternal grandmother was a Peele) were Salem shipping people. Prominent and successful merchants, they were among the original China traders going around Cape Horn in wooden schooners to bring silks, china, and spices from the Orient to the West. They moved into the Connecticut Valley, where they were judges, military commanders, and even one president of Yale. Fanny's grandfather prospered in business, founding the Pepperell Mills in Maine, but lost his fortune in the economic panic of 1873.[2]

The Civil War generation of Dwights included Fanny's father and his five brothers. Like Grenville Clark's forebears they were staunch Unionists, and all saw active service in the war. The family's brightest star was Fanny's uncle Wilder Dwight, who was already a successful lawyer and rising statesman when the war began. Wilder served with distinction before dying at Antietam. With him and badly wounded in that battle was his good friend Oliver Wendell Holmes Jr. The fathers of the two young soldiers together searched through the carnage for their fallen sons. (The senior Oliver Wendell Holmes, a famous physician, professor, poet, and author, wrote of the incident in "My Hunt After 'the Captain,'" published in *Atlantic Monthly* in 1862.) Fanny inherited Wilder Dwight's sword and "a remarkable and touching letter to his mother, stained with his blood, which he wrote while dying on the field."[3] Fanny's strong feelings about the Union and her Yankee antipathy to citizens of the South continued throughout her life.

Although the Dwight family fortune had been lost a generation before Fanny was born, its dignity and social prominence remained. As did some nice real estate. Fanny's grandmother bequeathed the family's 350-acre farm in Dublin, New Hampshire, to Fanny's mother who in turn passed it down to Fanny. From the time she was two years old, the Dwights spent half the year in Dublin and the other half in Boston. The youngest of three siblings, Fanny grew up salmon fishing in Canadian rivers and took a lifelong delight in horticulture. Both experiences were largely the result of her close ties to her elegant and prosperous Hunnewell relatives, who maintained magnificent gardens on the shores of Wellesley Pond, opposite the long-standing college of the same name. Fanny and her first cousin Louisa Hunnewell were lifelong best friends. (The Clarks' youngest daughter would be named Louisa, as would be a future granddaughter.) [4]

Other family friends and acquaintances included William and Henry James, Rudyard Kipling, and the Dublin summer regular Sam Clemens, aka Mark Twain. The avant-garde cigar-smoking poet Amy Lowell was an occasional tutor at Dublin. Despite this A-list social network, and in marked contrast to Grenville's lavish upbringing in New York and Burlington, Fanny's family lived in genteel but relatively modest circumstances in Boston and Dublin. Her father was in the cotton brokerage business, while her mother studiously scrimped and saved, sewed and mended, and warned her children not to be so extravagant as to buy a magazine on the long train trip from Boston to New Hampshire each summer. These were formative influences on Fanny, who probably would not have minded one daughter's description of her as "the last Puritan."[5]

Fanny had little formal education but became highly self-educated through a combination of native intelligence, natural curiosity, and voracious reading. In addition to learning history and staying abreast of current affairs, she became fluent in German and grew to be a recognized expert in ornithology and horticulture. She also became a proficient painter, taught by George de Forest Brush and Abbott Thayer. Fanny was also a graceful skater, a good fly caster, and—her Dodsworth-challenged husband notwithstanding—an excellent dancer.[6]

Once married, Fanny ran an effective household and was the perfect counterpart for her domestically unskilled husband. A daughter noted "the talents of the two were remarkably complementary. He could barely drive a car, much less change a tire. She was the family engineer, architect, decorator, gourmet food provider, farmer, landscape designer . . . garden designer and horticulturist." As was customary, Fanny had primary responsibility for the children's education and upbringing. She saw to the cooking, shopping, gardening, domestic staff supervision, and all other aspects of household management. She fully ran their several homes, including land and livestock. Interestingly, and perhaps unusually, she was also actively involved in the family's business and financial matters. She brought to the marriage a small inheritance and the Dublin home and property but also maintained her own bank accounts, investment accounts, and the like.[7]

Fanny largely controlled the Clarks' social life, which, while deliberately outside the high-society whirl, did include frequent entertaining of family, friends, and her gregarious husband's many business and professional associates. A 1928 list of "Persons to invite to house some time" contains more than 300 names—friends, business partners, relatives, and others. Entries are coded as to whether they had been invited sometime previously or had been invited within the last two years; a subset of perhaps seventy-five were those to be invited first. (In a darkly humorous follow-up Clark updated the list in 1961, with dramatic slashes of his fountain pen marking through and noting "deceased" or otherwise incapacitated would-be guests. A stickler for detail, he tallied each page and ran final totals, noting that thirty-three years later, 75.4 percent of the original invitees were now dead.)[8]

Fanny was an excellent cook and gracious hostess. One regular weekend guest recalled decades later the thickness of the homemade cream spooned onto fresh-picked berries at the Clark breakfast table. It was but one example of Fanny's meticulous attention to the most minute detail and the pleasure she could derive and produce from "the small things as well as the great."[9]

Fanny worried a great deal about her family's health. Frugal though she was, she spared no effort or expense for doctors. One daughter felt this was excessive, verging on hypochondria, but Fanny's miserable childhood memories of raw Boston winters and the constant colds and ear infections that eventually dulled her own hearing were real. It is also easy to forget the lethality of common infectious diseases in the early twentieth century; indeed meningitis would claim a Clark daughter at the age of seven. Fanny's task was not an easy or an intermittent one, given her need to monitor her children's health and the constant hawk-like care she dedicated to her hard-charging husband, who was prone to making excessive demands on his limited health reserves. Above all, Fanny was a devoted wife to her adoring husband. A daughter summarized:

> [She] maintained a very close relationship with my father and had surely a genuine and intense interest in all aspects of his career. I think they shared every detail of his legal activities, his activities as a fellow of Harvard College later on, and all his various public efforts, their triumphs and disasters through the years. I am certain she read everything he wrote and she made room for secretaries and office areas in the house readily as he grew older. They shared a mutual concern for public affairs and political and international events and they both read a good deal. . . . Above all, my mother was at home, and . . . [when] my father from a trip or excursion he would tour the house and grounds calling until he found her.[10]

After their marriage in 1909 Grenville and Fanny lived in two different apartments in New York City before settling into a townhouse at 216 E. Seventy-second Street on Manhattan's Upper East Side. Their first child, Eleanor Dwight Clark, was born in 1915, followed closely by Mary Dwight Clark, or Mary D., as she was permanently nicknamed, in 1916. Two years later, in 1918, came the only son, Grenville Clark Jr.; after an eight-year gap (that included a stillborn son) the youngest daughter, Louisa Hunnewell Clark, completed the family in 1925.

Grenville Clark also enjoyed his friends. He maintained an array of close collegial friendships throughout his life and always made time for fraternal activities, whether social, professional, or recreational. His enthusiasm was reciprocated. Elihu Root Jr. shared an anecdote, which began (as did so many) with: "One evening at the Harvard Club . . . someone proposed the offhand question to a group of alumni, 'Suppose you were lost in the Arabian Desert, running out of water, running out of ammunition, and the Arabs were hostile. Who would you like to have appear on the horizon?' Four men instantly and simultaneously responded, 'Grenny Clark.'"[11]

They chose well. Whether facing hostile desert tribes or New Jersey street brawlers, it was good to have Clark on your side. His early law partners described him as "a man utterly without fear," citing with gusto the "famous battle in Trenton." In the early Root, Clark days a trolley line to the courthouse in Trenton went down a fairly narrow street, where horse-drawn drays continually snarled traffic. One morning, on Clark's way to argue a case at the courthouse, several drays full of workers were blocking the trolley tracks. As the story goes: "Words were exchanged;

a fracas ensued, and the athletic Clark performed so valiantly that the street was soon cleared and the conductor rang the bell to get his passengers back aboard. Clark was still engaged with the few opponents who wanted to see it out to the last man. 'It was a most perplexing situation' [Clark] later reported to his partners. . . . Should he finish the fight or get on to the courthouse? He resolved to do both. He put more steam in his punches, beat off the opposition, then sprinted to catch the disappearing trolley."[12]

Vacations could also be zestful. In 1903 Clark and three college friends spent the requisite summer in Europe after graduating from Harvard. They met up in Venice and promptly decided to see how fast they could get from sea level to the highest point in Europe. The challenge took them to Zermatt, Switzerland, on the Swiss-Italian boarder, and the towering Breithorn peak just to the south. The winning time is lost to history but not the snapshot of the grinning foursome atop the snowy summit, Harvard sweatshirts accessorized with hand-knotted rope harnesses and a pickaxe. They did not ignore culture, although they nearly missed it in at least one case. En route to the railway station on the group's final day in Paris, Clark realized they had forgotten to go to the Louvre. Panic hit, then inspiration: He instructed the taxi driver to drop them off at the vast museum's front entrance and drive around to meet them at the back. The young men sprinted through the grand corridors "as fast as they were able," with masterworks of the ages silently witnessing the spectacle. Outside they rejoined their cab, caught their train on time, and were able to say that they had indeed "been to the Louvre." (Adventure trumped culture the following year—the group went big game hunting instead.)[13]

A natural athlete and outdoorsman, Clark enjoyed the full range of sports, from country club staples such as racquet games and golf to rugged hunting expeditions in the Rockies and salmon fishing in Canada. He also made frequent duck-hunting outings to the family's marshland at the mouth of Lake Champlain. These often involved sharing a cramped duck blind for hours with his good friend John Dickey, the president of Dartmouth. Dickey later noted: "The fact that Grenville Clark was a large person in all ways was manifest to anyone who shared a duck-blind with him. Physically it was a tight fit, but the conversation was capacious."[14] On these outings the state of education and national and world affairs were as much targets for the two broadly engaged men as the overflying fowl.

Clark kept the undeveloped marshland to use for private hunting. It was not far from where his brother Julian, immobilized by childhood polio but a remarkably vigorous man, lived on the Cannon family's Burlington estate. (In another demonstration of Clark's ability to fight for private as well as public good, he methodically and at times ingeniously resisted attempts through the years to make the marshland part of a government reserve, as was increasingly the fate of adjoining parcels.)[15]

Clark was also at home indoors. He belonged to several gentlemen's groups, including an elite dozen who called themselves simply the Dinner Party. The Dinner Party was organized by Clark's great lawyer friend Charles C. Burlingham. The group met monthly at a New York restaurant or club to discuss issues of the day. Their invitation-only membership later included John Harlan, then Clark's junior partner. Another recurring men's event was a group of Harvard alumni from Clark's class of 1903 who met each year on the eve of Harvard's commencement exercises. Attendance was virtually a blood pact, with no regrets allowed and absolutely no outsiders, either—whether presidents, Supreme Court justices, or some other variety of dignitary.[16]

Clark maintained membership in a number of private social clubs: the Century, Knickerbocker, and Harvard Clubs in New York; the Somerset Club and Harvard Club in Boston, plus Saint Andrew's Golf Club in Hastings-on-Hudson, New York, and the Piping Rock Club on Long Island for golf and recreation. These exclusive gathering places were useful. For people seeking to advance their social status, membership's unspoken bond afforded access and/or introductions to an otherwise well-guarded level of society. For the already arrived—like Clark—the clubs offered the comfort and camaraderie of relaxing among like-minded, or at least similarly circumstanced, people. The clubs offered dining, lodging, gentlemen's sports such as billiards or darts, handball or pool, and a genteel place to hold meetings or just relax over a drink. The clubs could ease life's details with concierge services like cashing checks and making travel or theater reservations. They could also prove handy during minor emergencies, as in the following classic story, told by Clark's colleague Lyman Tondale:

One summer night when [Clark] was alone at his Manhattan townhouse, the doorbell rang. There was a telegram to sign for. He had been about to go to bed and was wearing no slippers and a nightshirt. As he signed for the telegram he was unaware he had allowed the door behind him to snap shut. Clark had no key, so he found himself in the small vestibule where he was not about to spend the night. He unsuccessfully explored the front of the house to see if he could gain entry, then walked to the curb to hail a taxi. The first few cabs were wary of what they saw, but at last a taxi stopped and asked, "Where to?" Mr. Clark directed that he be taken to the Knickerbocker Club. Arrived at the Club he asked the doorman to pay the fare, and almost but not quite succeeded in dashing through the entrance hall to the elevators unseen by any members.[17]

The clubs were part of an undeniably privileged world, one that fit Clark like a well-tailored suit, his own egalitarian bent notwithstanding. The Knickerbocker and Clark's other clubs, and the cosseting they provided, were simply a continuation of his Pomfret, Porcellian, and otherwise fully elitist upbringing. And given the option, especially when locked out on the streets of Manhattan in your nightshirt, why not take advantage?

CHAPTER 4

Public Service Provocateur
The Plattsburg Camps

In 1914 world events reached out and compelled the thirty-two-year-old Grenville Clark to help ready the United States to enter World War I, should its participation become necessary. To that end he created, organized, and led the Plattsburg Officer Training Camps, which became synonymous with his name. The camps were a civilian-driven, purely voluntary, military training program held in intensive four-week sessions at an army training site in Plattsburg, New York.[1] Their purpose was to prepare concerned American business and professional men for military service, on their own time and at their own expense, should the United States be forced into the Great War then raging in Europe. Against long odds the Plattsburg camps were an extraordinary success and became an important part of the U.S. war effort in World War I. The widespread influence of the Plattsburg Idea, as a range of civilian-led training efforts came to be known, profoundly changed thinking about U.S. military preparedness in the first half of the twentieth century. The Plattsburg movement also left a lasting mark on Grenville Clark, shaping his response to future public emergencies, domestic and abroad.[2] Here is how the remarkable Plattsburg story unfolded.

The opening decade of the twentieth century had been largely peaceful and prosperous for the United States. In 1912 Woodrow Wilson was elected president. Eloquent, intelligent, and utterly patrician in appearance and demeanor, the former Princeton president looked straight out of Clark's posh prep school circles, though he was in fact a southerner of relatively modest means. Regardless, Wilson well fitted the national mood and spirit.

Across the Atlantic, however, simmering tensions on the Continent were about to explode. On June 28, 1914, a Bosnian nationalist assassinated Austria's Archduke Ferdinand and his wife in Sarajevo, setting in motion a treaty-triggered chain of military mobilizations and declarations of war. Within weeks the map of Europe went from its historic bouquet of sovereign nation-states to angry swaths of territories whose control shifted between the Central Powers and the Allies. In a war that the historian David Stevenson aptly calls cataclysmic and a political tragedy, a combination of unstable alliances, diplomatic and political miscalculations, and complex treaty obligations pitted the early Central Powers of Germany and Austria-Hungary against the Allied forces of France, Great Britain, and Russia.[3]

Only one major power was left on the sidelines. An ocean away the United States wanted no part of the ugly business Americans felt was not their own. Reflecting the strongly isolationist instincts of the nation, President Wilson was resolute, even stubborn, in maintaining American neutrality. Few observers anywhere, least of all the early participants in the war, expected it to become the protracted conflict it ultimately did. ("Home by Christmas!" went the enthusiastic cheers as British troops headed for the front in August. German troops were even more optimistic, promising mothers, wives, and sweethearts they would be back "before the leaves have fallen from the trees.")[4]

Leaves fell, Christmas came and went, and instead of coming home the two sides battled their way to a blood-soaked stalemate. The fiercely entrenched fighting dragged into 1915 and then into 1916. Still, Wilson maintained that the war was not a real threat to the United States. He argued to at least one of his army advisers that even if the Germans won, they would surely be too exhausted "seriously to menace our country for many years to come."[5] The president also weighed legitimate concerns about the domestic implications that choosing sides would hold in a nation of immigrants drawn from literally all the involved countries (including 11 million of German or Austro-Hungarian descent). Neutrality felt prudent, and safe.

Besides, the United States had plenty of problems of its own. The long and bloody Mexican Revolution threatened to spill across the border, just as the nation was knitting the still-new states of New Mexico and Arizona into the fabric of the union. There was also unaccustomed new colonial territory in the faraway Philippines, acquired in the still-recent Spanish-American War, to administer. Underlying it all were vivid memories of the upheaval and loss—600,000 losses—sustained during the Civil War. Just two generations later those wounds remained deep and raw for northerners and southerners alike.[6] The idea of making that awful sacrifice for some other country left most Americans cold.

No matter the reasons for neutrality, nor how sincerely they were held, Wilson's stance was wholly unacceptable to Grenville Clark. Clark was convinced that the United States would be forced to aid the Allies—

and sooner than later.[7] To do nothing to prepare the anemic U.S. military
for even the possibility of war was irresponsible and dangerous. Just how
small was the U.S. Army at that time? In 1914 General Leonard Wood, the
army chief of staff, gave reporters a striking image: America's combined
mobile forces, even if increased by the 25,000 soldiers he was requesting,
"could be seated in the Yale Bowl at New Haven, and still leave a third
of the seats vacant." Even worse was the nation's deplorable lack of readiness. Wood again put it bluntly: "We, with a fake humanity based on
profound conceit and ignorance, [would] send our [untrained] people to
war to be slaughtered like sheep."[8]

Clark agreed. But what could a young civilian lawyer do? He had an
idea and sought the counsel of a family friend, Theodore Roosevelt:

Dear Mr. Roosevelt: November 19, 1914

I have had a little scheme in my head for the last month or two
that I should like very much to have your opinion about. . . .

I have in mind to get organized a small military reserve corps
comprised of young businessmen, lawyers, etc., who would go
through a very light training to fit themselves to be of some use in
case of any real national emergency. . . .

The plan would have in mind two general objects—first,
actually to give the men who would join the organization some
sort of familiarity with military matters, so that they would
be of some . . . use in any emergency; second, to furnish an
example by showing that some of us at least recognize the lack
of preparedness of the country for any emergency and our
willingness to take some positive step, however unimportant
itself, to remedy the situation.

If this has the slightest interest for you I should very much like
to talk to you about it and see what you think. I could come to
see you in New York almost any time you could spare me a few
minutes.

Very truly yours, Grenville Clark[9]

The full seven-page letter carefully laid out how Clark's "little scheme"
might work: the number of men (150–200), their ages (25–45), the financing (the men would be "of sufficient means" to carry their own expenses),
and likely training components (physical drills, weapons handling, tactical and military strategy, etc.) He detailed potential training site loca-
tions, funding sources for materials and supplies, and obtaining military

instructors. As in his legal briefs, Clark considered and addressed in turn each element of the problem. Roosevelt was probably on the phone to Clark as soon as he read it; no reply appears in the file. But from start to finish the old Rough Rider enthusiastically supported his young friend's call for direct citizen action. Even with such high-level endorsement, preparedness remained a tough sell. The nation had been skeptical of large standing armies and a powerful military since its inception. The defense model that had emerged up to 1914 had two prongs: a small regular army for ongoing national security needs, with state run militias (roughly equivalent to today's National Guard) to be mobilized in the event of a larger threat. According to the military historian John Chambers, Americans harbored widespread resentment toward even the small existing U.S. Army, which "suffered not simply from neglect . . . but from outright public hostility."[10] After the cessation of the Indian wars in the 1870s, the army's unenviable major roles had included the post–Civil War occupation of the South, and strike busting in northern labor disputes—thus was public antipathy to the army democratized.

The regular army and the National Guard were periodically supplemented by volunteer citizen brigades, most famously Theodore Roosevelt's Rough Riders in the Spanish-American War sixteen years earlier. Clark's initial Plattsburg idea fell most closely into the volunteer camp, although the movement's ultimate goal became universal military training and obligatory service on the Swiss model.[11] Wherever it fell within the military spectrum, the Plattsburg project's uphill battle for American public approval soon received an unsolicited boost from the Germans.

On Friday, May 7, 1915, the world was stunned when a German U-boat launched a torpedo attack on the British ocean liner *Lusitania*, killing 1,198 of the 1,962 passengers aboard. The victims were virtually all civilians—men, women, and children, including 124 Americans. At a time when wars were largely fought according to conventional rules, the act was as shocking as it was provocative. Elihu Root Jr. later recalled that dark time and Clark's instinctive resolve: "On the Sunday after the *Lusitania* was sunk, Mr. Clark and I went up to St. Andrews to play golf. I can remember that we were too angry and too horror stricken to play. We spent our time talking. Mr. Clark felt that inaction was intolerable."[12]

Clark could picture the horrific scene all the more vividly, having been a passenger on the grand Cunard liner just seven years earlier. ("Dear Papa: . . . The ship is astounding, every luxury you can imagine," wrote the son in a compact, meticulous hand on fine linen stationery with *RSM Lusitania* embossed next to the regal stamp of the Cunard Steamship Company Ltd.) Much more important, the attack underscored to Clark the urgency of the impending threat. On Monday morning he gathered fifteen other young lawyers at his Root, Clark office. They drafted and sent a petition to President Wilson urging him to respond with appropriate forcefulness. They sent a copy to the press: "The undersigned citizens of New York express their conviction that national interest and honor imperatively require adequate measures both to secure reparations for past violations by Germany of American rights and secure guarantees against future violations. We further express the conviction that the considered judgment of the nation will firmly support the government in any measures, however serious, to secure full reparations and guarantees."[13]

Clark's close contemporary, Theodore Roosevelt Jr., signed first. The president made no immediate response, but the petition appeared in the New York press, where it aroused considerable interest. The next day, May 11, fifty more concerned friends joined the original group for a luncheon at the Harvard Club to "talk over the *Lusitania*." A few days later an even larger meeting resulted in the Committee of 100, who pledged to "educate ourselves and . . . the public on the international issues and our duties with respect thereto."[14]

These young members of the Yankee elite in many ways defined the Plattsburg movement. Raised to be future leaders of government, business, and society, they had been drilled practically since birth in the concept of duty. They also shared with Clark the means and ability to get things done. Their fathers and grandfathers were captains of industry, presidents of banks, owners of railroads, and, in at least one case, president of the United States.[15] Even more relevant, most were also sons, nephews, and/or family friends of former Rough Riders. (Theodore Roosevelt Jr. was only ten when he decided he would become a Rough Rider like his adored father.)[16] With sterling educations, access to power at the highest levels, and the concrete example of a citizen-soldier's campaign, these men were ready to act and expected to be heard.

The young lawyers' case lacked one important element: how to fit Clark's civilian training camp idea into existing military training operations. Army support would be critical to bring the plan to fruition. Clark studied the issue and soon came across an article about a military training camp for college students the army was planning to hold in Plattsburg, New York, that summer. The similarities to his businessmen's training idea were uncanny: a volunteer program, paid for by attendees, a brief but intense training regimen conducted in partnership with the army. Clark quickly gathered Theodore Roosevelt Jr. and Philip Carroll, who had been working with Clark on the plan, at Delmonico's restaurant in lower Manhattan. They agreed the college camp was the perfect model for their proposed camps.[17] Philip Carroll agreed to approach the project's head, General Leonard Wood, commander of the army's Eastern Department, at his headquarters on Governor's Island in New York Harbor.

Wood was a larger-than-life character, by 1915 already a newspaper hero from his stint as army chief of staff, his participation in the Spanish-American War, and his role in the occupation of the Philippines. His fame and his ego were huge. Born in New Hampshire, Wood graduated from Harvard Medical School and joined the army in 1885 as a contract surgeon. The very next year he was part of the regiment that captured the Apache chief Geronimo, with the young Wood leading part of the campaign on a long and dangerous expedition through hostile Indian territory. He was later awarded the Congressional Medal of Honor for valor. Wood also served as personal physician to presidents Grover Cleveland and William McKinley.[18]

When the Spanish-American War broke out in 1898, Wood helped organize and lead the all-volunteer Rough Riders. The cavalry brigade would become the stuff of legends, further enhancing Wood's celebrity and promoting his collaborator, close friend, and second in command, Theodore Roosevelt, to fame and the presidency. When the war ended, Wood stayed in Cuba and became military governor of the island. Tapping his medical background, he oversaw impressive strides in Cuba's medical and public health systems.[19]

In a career redux Wood served in the Philippine-American War in 1902 and then stayed on as governor general of the islands' Moro Province until 1908. Wood's time in the Philippines included a major blot on his record, what came to be known as the Moro Massacre. In 1906 Wood ordered American and Filipino troops to "capture or kill" a band of 600 rebelling Moros, a collection of native tribes in the province. Those troops ultimately pursued the fiercely fighting but lightly armed natives into a volcanic crater and gunned them down en masse. Fifteen Americans died and all 600 Moros, including many women and children. Public uproar was immense. Mark Twain wrote an especially scathing satirical essay about the massacre that was widely circulated in the press.[20] Wood's career survived, and in 1910 he became the army's chief of staff.

When Clark encountered him in 1915, Wood's chief passion had become training and developing young soldiers. His was a persistent and often lonely voice for preparedness, and he was increasingly frustrated by what he perceived as a lack of attention, vision, and understanding of military matters by the Wilson administration.[21] Wood was not only in harmony with the message of Clark's group but had much in common with the messengers. The younger men were a generation behind Wood, but they traveled in the same circles. In many cases the general knew their fathers.

They also shared an affinity for (and membership in) the venerable Harvard Club on Forty-fourth Street, where Wood had been going "two or three times a week since assuming command of the [Army's] Eastern Department the previous summer." Months before Clark's group approached the general, future Plattsburger and then-secretary of the Harvard Club Langdon Marvin had attended Wood's stirring lecture there on preparedness. On the bill along with Wood were Harvard president Lawrence Lowell and Franklin D. Roosevelt, then a young assistant secretary of the navy. In the audience, undoubtedly mesmerized, were Grenville Clark and Theodore Roosevelt Jr. Years later Marvin cited Wood's "strictures about personal service and personal preparedness" as formative influences as the businessmen's camp idea took form.[22]

When Philip Carroll approached General Wood on behalf of the Committee of 100 in May 1915, Carroll expected and found a ready audience for Clark's idea. The general went right to the point, elaborating on the army's inadequate condition and noting that what the military would soon need most, and find hardest to locate in a hurry, were competent junior officers. The officer problem was paramount, Wood said: "To send untrained troops into the field is manslaughter, but to dispatch troops with untrained leaders is murder in the first degree."[23]

Wood, like Carroll, Clark, and their friends, took the *Lusitania* attack as a moral as well as a military outrage. If it had a silver lining, perhaps the attack would awaken American citizens to the need for national service. And it was surely not lost on the wily doctor-soldier that a well-publicized camp attended by the sons of the country's most influential families could help jump-start that awakening. Wood made the younger men a deal: if they could come up with a hundred volunteers, the War Department would provide the officers, equipment, and training materials, and they could use the same training site as the new college camps, an army training post in Plattsburg, on the western shore of Lake Champlain in upstate New York.[24]

With Wood's blessing and ground rules in hand, Clark and company began official recruiting for their businessmen's training camps in late May. The gung-ho team canvassed their offices, clubs, homes, and social gatherings and quickly passed the hundred-volunteer threshold. Momentum continued to build and by mid-July, they were receiving fifty to one hundred application cards per day.[25] Wood was delighted and dispatched two of his aides, Captains Halstead Dorey and Gordon Johnston, to work with the civilians full time.

Recruitment remained highly selective and was done primarily by personal contact. While Clark and his friends canvassed their various circles, General Wood and others made speeches around the country to well-screened groups of "the best and most desirable men." Commercial advertising was deliberately held to a minimum. This was both to control the size of the initial training camp and to keep out curiosity seekers, dilettantes, and other undesirables. As Clark put it: "Experience shows that men who respond to such publicity . . . are not the type we want to get, but men . . . of the type who want a cheap summer vacation."

The attention to selection paid off, and the quality of response was as impressive as its quantity. The Plattsburg camp's carefully targeted recruits were among the nation's top talent; they certainly represented its top families. (The Wood biographer Hermann Hagedorn quipped: "The [social] butterflies of Newport and Bar Harbor complained that life was desolate, since the best of their young men were at Plattsburg.") Wood himself wrote that he highly doubted "if there ever assembled in a camp of instruction in this country as highly intelligent [a] body of men or one more thoroughly representative of all that is best in our citizenry."[26] Delancey K. "Lanny" Jay was a prime example: a direct descendant on his father's side of John Jay, a Founder and the first chief justice of the U.S. Supreme Court, and, on his mother's side, of John Jacob Astor. Jay was one of Clark's closest friends and instrumental in the Plattsburg effort.

Twelve hundred enthusiastic participants assembled for the first Businessmen's Training Camp, held at Plattsburg from August 8 to September 6, 1915. The men included former and future members of Congress, business leaders, judges, and ambassadors. Some were also current office holders of note, such as the young and handsome mayor of New York City, John Purroy Mitchel. Joining Mitchel were his police commissioner, Arthur Woods, and a dozen of NYPD's finest. Mitchel's presence guaranteed daily publicity for the camp, much as the serious young man tried to ignore the constantly hovering reporters. But what journalist could resist story lines like "Mayor of New York Pulls K.P. Duty," "Lowly Patrolman Puts Commissioner Woods through His Paces," or "Cavalry Sergeant Drills Polo Players and Steeplechasers on How to Curry a Horse?" The press had a field day, but the Plattsburgers, as the trainees were called, were too busy and/or too exhausted to care. (They early on nicknamed themselves "TBMs"—tired business men.)[27]

Per Clark's original plan the men were "of sufficient means" to pay their own expenses, beginning with $30 on arrival for a basic issue of supplies, including a canteen, poncho, eating utensils, and pup tent. Next came a brief medical exam and assignment to a company and battalion. Army officers supervised the training, which was intense. Daily drills began at 5:45 a.m., with calisthenics, rifle practice, and classroom sessions in the morning. Afternoons, the men were divided into specialized instruction areas in cavalry, signal corps, engineering, or artillery. Evenings featured talks by General Wood around the campfire beside the lake. A recurring theme was service and that "no one has the right to think that there is anything voluntary in the discharge of his [military] duty to the country."

Despite the regimentation, a certain amount of creativity was involved. The experimental and audacious Motor Machine Gun Battery was a prime example, the brainchild of Raynal C. Bolling, Plattsburg recruit and general solicitor for U.S. Steel. Bolling, a former officer in the National Guard, led seventy men over roads and fields in lumbering steel-reinforced cars, trucks, motorcycles, and even a custom-built armor-plated superdreadnaught that reportedly weighed eight tons fully loaded. The Motor Machine Gun men bought and souped up all these vehicles at their own expense.

Like Bolling, other members of the Motor Machine Gun Battery were straight out of the Social Register. Philip Carroll, Elihu Root Jr., Langdon Marvin, and John Milburn Jr. were among those representing some of New York's most prominent and established families. The much heralded equalizing aspects of military training and service—the socially healthful mixing of classes and races—did not get much of a test with this group. One New Yorker noted: "All the best families seem to have been drafted into a machine gun platoon. Socially, it has already been a tremendous success, as people like myself are already going around apologizing for not being there."[28]

Most aspects of the camp, however, were quite democratic. Tent assignment was by order of arrival; no advance reservations were taken for bunking with buddies. Men accustomed to layers of domestic staff cleaned latrines and took their turn on K.P. duty. Trainers impressed on them the importance of camp sanitation, an emphasis that resulted in large part from Wood's experience in the Spanish-American War, where death from disease outnumbered combat deaths 9 to 1 (2,620 typhoid fever deaths, the vast majority in stateside training and staging camps, versus 280 battle fatalities. Most soldiers who died never set foot on foreign soil.)[29]

At Plattsburg the average day was more than nine hours long, and those hours were packed. Watching the well-heeled civilians take on this load with diligence and gusto proved illuminating to the regular army officers responsible for training them. General Wood's aide-de-camp, Captain Halstead Dorey, was perhaps surprised to find himself writing a year later:

The prime reason for the success of the camps is the magnificent spirit of the men who go to them. The effect upon us regular officers has been one of great encouragement. Here were eighteen hundred men who showed us not only by word, but by deed, by sacrificing a full month of their vacations and also at some expense, that they looked upon our profession as something more than a survival of a medieval custom. It is an inspiration to have these men working right shoulder to shoulder with us, doing the same sort of work and wanting to learn all they possibly could in the short time they had.[30]

The inspirational performance Dorey observed was in many ways a reflection of the camp's civilian founder, and the Plattsburgers knew it. As hard as Clark tried to keep a low profile, the men couldn't resist an occasional shout-out. A half-embarrassed, half-amused Clark privately shared with his wife: "As I was walking down another company street today someone set up a yell—'the man who thought of it all!' A number of people set up a yell but I have endeavored to keep absolutely in the background which is no trouble, everyone being too busy to bother about anything but their work."[31]

The camp's highlight for the recruits and regular soldiers alike was a ten-day hike up to Rouse's Point (dubbed "Souses Point" for its heavy-drinking locals) near the Canadian border. (So near that in one instance the men accidentally crossed the international demarcation line and tried to engage the Canadian border police in a mock battle, thinking they were other Plattsburgers.) The strenuous hike in full uniform, strapped with a heavy pack in the blazing summer heat, combined with the overall rigor of the program prevented several high-profile men from attending for health reasons. The young and otherwise healthy Franklin Roosevelt apologized to Wood that "an [emergency] appendectomy prevented any fifty-mile maneuvers for the next few weeks." Douglas Johnson, a professor at Columbia, was sorry that "with a weak heart, he could only march 25 miles a day." And cutting right to the chase, Edmund James, president of the University of Illinois, said he "would like to attend but thought it would kill him."[32]

Wood wrote in his official report that during Plattsburg's four-week session "the men covered the ground ordinarily covered by our recruits in 4½ months and they received more hours of actual training than is received by the average militiaman in an enlistment of three years." The rigorous program and its Spartan ethic appealed to the men. It was a chance to prove to themselves and the world that their pampered lives had not made them irretrievably soft. Speaking like a physician, Wood predicted the "tonic of regimen" would do the men good, and apparently it did.[33] Forgotten, at least temporarily, were psychosomatic complaints like indigestion, tension headaches, and especially insomnia, as the men fell into the soundest sleep of their lives after days filled with honest exertion. And the physical benefits were not the only or even necessarily the most important ones. A lot of the men, like Clark, were athletic by nature and stayed fit through leisure sports and other activities. Plattsburg was much more than an extended squash clinic or camping trip.

The historian Michael Pearlman has speculated that going to Plattsburg was part of a larger, more quixotic, quest by the elite New Englanders. As descendants of the Puritans, Pearlman suggests, they carried a special burden in the psychic conflict between their strict Protestant upbringing, which promotes frugality, moderation, and "scarcity capitalism," and their large fortunes, grand homes, comfortable lifestyles, and the "pernicious effects of luxury." One recruit likely spoke for many when he wrote: "We all feel instinctively that the life of ease and luxury of the present generation is wrong, it is destructive of moral and physical fiber, it tends to degeneracy. Nearly every man who goes to Plattsburg goes with the knowledge that he must give up all the comforts and conveniences of life and endure hardships and I believe that he does so freely and readily as a kind of silent protest against the easygoing life he ordinarily leads."[34]

Pearlman also hits on larger themes, like the hollowness of perpetual indulgence, glorification of war, and lasting influence of pervasive dogma. But Clark had little time (or inclination) to unravel the complex motivations of the men who attended the camp. He was a pragmatist at heart, or a pragmatic idealist, as his longtime friend John Dickey aptly described him. Whatever combination of psychosocial factors brought each man to camp was far less important than the fact that he came. If some carried complex inner struggles, subliminal inclinations to glory, or even heroic delusions, it seems that the army, the country, and the Allies were fortunate, at least in this case, that they did.

And the record seems clear that the primary motivation for Clark and the majority of his fellow Plattsburgers was duty and a personal sense of obligation to serve. Duty and service were recurring themes for these men from early childhood. If they also enjoyed the fellowship and camaraderie at camp, and were stimulated by doing something tangible toward a larger cause, fair enough. To a man they were convinced a potential emergency was at hand and felt compelled to do something about it.

That conviction was underscored midway through camp by a second deadly German submarine attack on an unarmed civilian ship off the coast of Ireland. On August 20, 1915, as Clark and the other men took rifle practice and cavalry drills, a German U-boat torpedoed and sank the British White Star Line's *Arabic*, a passenger liner, not far from the site of the

Lusitania attack in May. This time forty people were killed, including two Americans.[35] In response President Wilson extracted a promise from the German government that it would not attack another unarmed passenger ship without warning. For the United States the *Arabic* Pledge, as it came to be known, brought the country one step closer to war by forcing Wilson to respond when the Germans violated their pledge and resumed unrestricted submarine warfare the following year. For the Plattsburg trainees the *Arabic* was simply further evidence of what they saw as the inevitable participation of the United States in the widening war.

Just five days later, on the eve of the inaugural camp's much anticipated ten-day hike, former president Theodore Roosevelt was on hand in full Rough Rider regalia to watch his three sons (Archie, Kermit, and Ted Jr.) perform their regimental review. The occasion also served as a kind of public closing ceremony. After dinner Roosevelt gave a characteristically exuberant speech to the crowd, swelled by visitors to nearly 4,000. General Wood had cautioned his old friend to avoid any overtly partisan remarks that could jeopardize the camp's standing (read: funding) with the Wilson administration, which was still lukewarm on the program at best. Wood himself had done a good job of keeping politics out of the camp thus far, no easy task given the overwhelmingly Republican pool of recruits, the military setting and mission, a war intensifying daily in Europe, a neutrality-seeking Democrat in the White House, and Wood's own pugnacious personality. But he did try, largely successfully, up until this night.

Where Wood had succeeded at playing down politics, his guest speaker cheerfully failed. Roosevelt belted out one of his trademark swashbuckling, hyperpatriotic speeches, by turn praising the Plattsburgers for their hard work and acknowledgment of duty, and then hurling insults at "professional pacifists, poltroons, and college sissies who organize peace-at-any-price societies." He didn't name President Wilson, but Roosevelt might as well have as he condemned those who "treat elocution as a substitution for action . . . rely on high-sounding words unbacked by deeds, [which was] proof of a mind that dwells only in the realm of shadow and shame." The insults got even more creative when a little dog wandered into the act. The pup rolled over on its back in front of the firelight, and TR quipped, "That's a very nice dog and I like him . . . His present attitude is strictly one of neutrality."[36]

The crowd ate it up, and if Wood winced a little, what more could he have done? It was Roosevelt. The celebratory program finally ended, and Wood drove his old friend to the train station. There TR took advantage of a train delay to deliver some even more inflammatory remarks about "the powers that be" to the crowd of reporters that had gathered.

The speech and impromptu interview were all over the papers the next day, and shortly afterward Wood received the dressing-down he had expected from Secretary of War Lindley Garrison.

However irritated Wood may have been with Roosevelt (and TR had promised to behave), the general had even less patience with the Wilson administration. In his terse response to Secretary Garrison, the general acknowledged responsibility and assured future compliance but offered no apology. Roosevelt learned of Garrison's reprimand to Wood and leapt back into the fray. He wrote an open letter to the press: "I am, of course, solely responsible for the whole speech," wrote the former president. He signed off with a fresh jab: "If the Administration had displayed one-tenth of . . . the energy in holding Germany and Mexico to account for the murder of American men, women, and children that it is now displaying . . . to prevent our people from being taught the need for preparation to prevent the repetition of such murders . . . it would be rendering a service to the people of this country." Garrison fired back, and the testy public exchange continued for days before eventually dying down.[37]

Although the incident got a lot of play in the papers, it had virtually no effect on the men at camp or on their enjoyment of the culminating ten-day hike. For most the hike was the best part of camp. Finally they could put theory and technique into practice as each battalion staged full maneuvers arrayed against a mock enemy. The men also inhaled the exhilaration of intense sustained exercise in the ruggedly beautiful setting, a 180-degree change from daily lives centered around posh Wall Street offices and urban clubrooms.

With a knack for seizing the psychological moment, Grenville Clark gave a stirring speech midway through the hike. The tall, broad-shouldered young lawyer must have looked all the more imposing in full uniform in front of the fire, his jutting jaw punctuating each sentence, as he addressed the men in earnest, urgent tones under the stars. And his rare formal address would have carried added weight, since he had deliberately stayed in the background for most of the camp, leaving the spotlight to General Wood. On this crisp September night Clark made the most of his moment and, according to one recruit, expressed "better than anything I know the spirit of most of the men at Plattsburg."

In his speech Clark praised the men for what they had accomplished but made it clear the mission was far from finished. To the civilians and officers alike, Plattsburg "was not conceived [solely] as an emergency measure" but rather to become part of "a permanent, sane and sound and reasonable military system for the United States." He cautioned the men to never "become [just] a talking organization" but rather to work "along lines of action and not of agitation." He exhorted them to continue their own training and encourage others to be trained, "until by the very force of actual demonstration and not of words this country as a whole is convinced of the necessity of our idea." Back at base camp Wood underlined Clark's words by challenging the men to go home and "act as missionaries for national defense in their home communities."[38]

And so the first Plattsburg Businessmen's Training Camp came to a close. It had been a success by virtually any measure. Many men who attended would count it among the fondest and most meaningful experiences of their lives. The Plattsburg experiment also impressed the army, the public, and even the Wilson administration with the caliber of the recruits, the quality of the highly concentrated instruction, and, later, for the results the Plattsburgers would achieve in the war. Grenville Clark, General Wood, and the other organizers had reason to be pleased. But they had no time to celebrate—a second camp with 600 recruits (mostly overflow from the huge response to the first call) was scheduled to begin on September 8, just two days after the first one ended.

The second 1915 Plattsburg camp was virtually identical to the first (save for the lack of a high-octane Roosevelt speech). That made 1,800 disciples initiated during the project's first year. Three other unaffiliated training camps on the Plattsburg model were held that summer, one each at the Presidio in San Francisco, American Lake in Washington State, and Fort Sheridan in Illinois. While not achieving as uniformly high results as the original, they were evidence the Plattsburg Idea was spreading. In New York Clark worked closely with Wood's staff on Governor's Island and gave lectures to citizens, conducted weekly drills, and organized special training corps for specialized civilian groups. These included newspapermen (200 of them, in arms) and the NYPD's captains and inspectors. Clark and Wood's staff created a correspondence course in military tactics that had more than 1,700 participants by year end. There were also plenty of social gatherings—reunions, luncheons, dinner meetings, and the like, held by various regiments, battalions, or smaller groups.

In late 1915 the businessmen's camps merged with the previously separate college training camps. It was a natural partnership, with so many shared goals. Clark's primary ally with the student camps was Henry S. Drinker, president of Lehigh University. A strong advocate of student military training, Drinker had worked closely with Wood in setting up the 1913–15 college camps that had initially drawn Clark's attention. (Those camps would ultimately evolve into the present-day Reserve Officer Training Corps program.)

The student camps drew wide support for their perceived physical, moral, and civic benefits. The idea was that discipline, hard work, patriotism, and sense of duty would prevent ever-corruptible young men from slacking off or going astray. Drinker enthusiastically joined forces with Clark, Ted Roosevelt, and Philip Carroll to convince other universities to participate in the program. By the end of 1915 Princeton, Yale, Harvard, and Cornell were also on board.[39] It had been a big year for Clark, Wood, and the Plattsburg preparedness movement. But with the war in Europe drawing ever nearer, much remained to be done.

CHAPTER 5

Wartime: Building on Plattsburg

As 1916 opened, Grenville Clark was determined that the success of the previous year would continue. The trial period was over, the Plattsburg camps had worked. Now it was time to reproduce their results as widely and as quickly as possible. To many observers, including Clark, America's entry into the war grew more inescapable with every news bulletin. The Plattsburgers would not rest until a comprehensive military training program to prepare for the impending call-up was national policy.

Clark devoted nearly all his time that fall and winter to nationalizing the Plattsburg philosophy and program. He secured office space across the hall in Root, Clark's building at 31 Nassau Street and in February 1916 formally launched the Military Training Camps Association (MTCA) as the legal and organizational vehicle to carry forward the Plattsburg mission and message.[1] Clark took his usual one step back from the limelight and served as the MTCA's secretary; Robert Bacon, former secretary of state and U.S. ambassador to France, agreed to be its first chair.

Besides running the actual training camps, the MTCA had an important political advisory role to play. Its first challenge was to get federal recognition, expansion, and funding for the Plattsburg camps included in the 1916 defense bill, which had just begun to ricochet around Washington. This would not be an easy task. As the war intensified in Europe both the advocates of preparedness and pacifism dug in. Even Clark's considerable powers of persuasion would be sorely tested.

The defense debate the MTCA had just entered was not new. Heated arguments about the proper role and structure of the military date to the country's founding. Early Americans, distrustful of Europe's large professional armies, deliberately left the standing national army small when drafting the Constitution. The original colonies were also fairly distrustful of each other, and the militia system—with each colony fully in control of its own forces—was the perceived solution to preserving their independence. But the resulting lack of coordination, cohesion, and other difficulties involved in yoking thirteen and more separate militaries during an emergency caused problems from the beginning. America's first commander in chief, George Washington, called for a larger, more unified, and more professional army until his death.[2]

Gradual modifications had been made. When Leonard Wood took over as chief of staff in 1910, the U.S. Army was slowly shifting from a "small, loosely organized collection of garrisons left over from the Indian Wars into an efficient, centrally controlled professional structure on the European model." The spiritual leader of Wood and other preparedness advocates was Emory Upton, whose 1904 *The Military Policy of the United States* was strongly critical of "democracy's reluctance to finance a defense establishment in peacetime, the unreliability of state militias, and the average citizen's ostrich-like ignorance of military realities."[3]

The nemesis of the preparedness camp was William Jennings Bryan, Woodrow Wilson's first secretary of state, who famously proclaimed in December 1914: "The President knows that if this country needed a million men, and needed them in a day, the call would go out at sunrise and the sun would go down on a million men in arms." To a career soldier like Leonard Wood, who had trained thousands of men and knew how long it took, Bryan's showboating made him "an ass of the first class." Wood missed few opportunities to ridicule both the man and his remark. Yet Bryan spoke for the majority of citizens, who remained strongly opposed to the war and considered any significant increase in the military a move in the wrong direction. Clark and his friends entered this difficult and protracted fight in 1916.

The stakes couldn't have been higher for the brand-new MTCA; the new defense bill would largely determine the future of the camps for training both college students and businessmen. Henry Drinker understood the power of proximity and suggested to Clark that they "stay down at Washington all winter and put this thing through." Clark agreed. He raided his Root, Clark law office and dispatched the young and capable Lloyd Derby to temporarily relocate from New York and be a daily presence in Washington. (Derby had connections of his own: his brother Richard was married to former president Roosevelt's daughter Ethel.) Clark and Drinker, meanwhile, split their time between the nation's capital and their New York and Pennsylvania offices. The trio dubbed themselves the Three Musketeers.[4]

In Washington, Clark and perhaps the Fourth Musketeer, Phil Carroll, testified repeatedly before Congress, met with virtually every senator and representative, and even had a private meeting with Woodrow Wilson. In addition to educating and persuading policy makers of the logic of a federal military training program, they sought to assure legislators that the MCTA was made up of neither warmongers nor militarists.

If America was going to be dragged into a war already unprecedented in its lethality, they argued, it faced a moral imperative to raise, train, and equip a decisive numbers of troops. Increasing numbers of legislators agreed in private, but the majority of the population outside Washington was still so strongly isolationist that a vote for preparedness remained politically difficult.

The contentious fight lasted all the way through the spring, but Congress passed the 1916 Defense Act on June 3. The measure included federal recognition and funding for the military training camps and established two new entities to oversee the camps. The Officers' Reserve Corps (ORC) took on the administration of the Plattsburg camp, while the Reserve Officer Training Corps (ROTC) took over the college training camp program that Leonard Wood had begun in 1913. The *Literary Digest* called the act "at least a step in the right direction—as long a step as a Democratic Congress could be expected to take."

With that step taken, Clark and his team geared up for the 1916 training camps. Much like the original Plattsburg camps in structure, the new camps would enable many more citizens to attend and from a much wider range of backgrounds. The MTCA also actively persuaded employers to give their employees paid leave to attend the camps. Even Wilson pitched in during a Memorial Day address and challenged business leaders to do their patriotic duty and "give the young men in their employment freedom to volunteer" for the training camps. Many employers cooperated. Another new and somewhat surprising ally Clark recruited in 1916 was the labor leader Samuel Gompers, founder of the American Federation of Labor (AFL). While Gompers did not formally join the MTCA, he and Clark worked closely and harmoniously, and Gompers remained interested in and sympathetic to the work of the MCTA. (When war came, Gompers and the AFL actively supported the war effort with the intertwined goals of boosting morale and not striking while also raising wages and expanding AFL membership.)[5]

In all, more than 16,000 recruits would attend the newly named Regular Army Instruction Camps in 1916—four times the number from the previous year. That number would have been far higher, perhaps 50,000, were it not for the major military distraction in the Southwest. In March 1916 the Mexican revolutionary Francisco "Pancho" Villa led a surprise cross-border raid into New Mexico, killing seventeen Americans. It was the first foreign attack on U.S. soil since 1812. The raid prompted the mobilization of nearly three-quarters of the country's National Guard units to secure the border. The regular army had to coordinate that entire mobilization, plus take over the duties of active guard units, on top of trying to prepare for the major European war that the country was still trying to stay out of. The army's resources were stretched so thin that the 1916 training camps were briefly slated for cancellation, but Clark and other irate MTCA members protested loudly, and most were soon reinstated.

At the 1916 camps new recruits were joined by an estimated 85 percent of the original Plattsburg attendees, who came back for the second year, entering at the rank they had achieved in the 1915 camps. The alumni were increasingly being taught how to lead, in keeping with the officer-training focus of the program. They prepared for the army's ORC examination; if they passed, they became eligible to become an officer, anywhere from second lieutenant on up to a major. Nearly 600 civilians took the ORC exam at Plattsburg that year, achieving "very satisfactory" results.

Perhaps the biggest and most important difference in the 1916 camps was that the elite recruits now shared tents and duties with an influx of "clerks, salesmen, groups of sponsored employees, the unknown Browns, Kelleys, Olsons, and Smiths." The camps were finally realizing their idealistic goal of "heating up the melting pot," as Wood liked to say.[6] As Wood's hardworking aide, Captain Dorey, put it: "That was what we tried to teach at Plattsburg, perhaps more than anything else. There were no Jews nor Gentiles, Catholics nor Protestants, no men from Yale, nor Harvard, nor Columbia, no men from Illinois nor Missouri. They were simply good Americans, trying to prepare themselves to defend their country should their country ever need them."[7] Dorey may have painted slightly too rosy a picture, but the Plattsburgers' belief in the democratizing and Americanizing benefits of universal service was sincere. And unlike the original Plattsburg camp, a great deal of class mixing did occur, certainly more than in most of the men's civilian lives.

Once the war began, the semiexperimental integration of at least some minorities into the overwhelmingly Anglo-Saxon Protestant army expanded, and Theodore Roosevelt's sweeping declaration—that "the military tent, where all sleep side by side, will rank next to the public school among the great agents of democratization"—was at least in part borne out. During the war one of Grenville Clark's brightest young legal protégés, Robert P. Patterson, later a federal judge and ultimately secretary of war, would lead an army infantry regiment in New York's multiethnic Seventy-seventh Division, which become famous as the Melting Pot Division. The Seventy-seventh's jaunty marching song bragged: "The Jews and the Wops / And the Dutch and Irish Cops; / they're all in the Army now." Patterson's World War I memoir notes that his "wartime association with doughboys named Czak, Wogatzke, Lo Bono, Breitweiser, Lehmkuhl, and Finucane confirmed his faith in the democratic bonding derived from shared military obligations."[8] Patterson's close and class-transcending ties to these men and others like them continued throughout his lifetime.

Glaringly absent from this democratic mix, however, were African Americans. Before 1917 black citizens were discouraged from attending the camps, although plans existed for a separate camp, should sufficient numbers apply, which did not happen.[9] Unconscionable as that is, the creators of the Plattsburg camps could perhaps be forgiven in light of the time and circumstances. The U.S. Army was still segregated, and the camps tried to mirror army policy wherever possible to expedite the merging of the camps into the regular army once the overarching goal of national service became a reality. Clark and the other organizers were fighting formidable odds to get the training camps approved and funded for recruits of any color. Whether he should have, or could have, done more at Plattsburg, Grenville Clark's willingness to fight for civil rights and social justice would be increasingly demonstrated throughout his life, including taking a major role with the NAACP in the 1960s. At Plattsburg the single-minded focus on the urgent task at hand, preparing an unprepared nation for an imminent world war, superseded all other considerations.

Racial inequality was far from the only problem at the 1916 camps, especially early on. Major challenges came on many fronts: assimilating so many new recruits, administering two new federal programs (ORC and ROTC), the reduced number of army supervisors because of the Mexican border call-up, and trying to figure out and implement the nuances of the brand new Defense Act of which they were suddenly a part. Even Mother Nature threw a curveball with unusually heavy summer rains that turned the camp at Plattsburg into a huge mud hole. But conditions improved, and in the end most participants agreed that the 1916 camps were a success like their predecessors.

Other areas of the military watched what was happening at Plattsburg and tried their own versions of the training camps. By the end of the year the services had established a Naval Plattsburg, an Air Plattsburg, a two-week training course in military medicine for medical students, and a special instruction course for the New York Police Department. There was also a well-attended Youth Plattsburg for 1,200 boys younger than eighteen. As a young assistant secretary of the navy, Franklin Roosevelt argued bluntly for the public education value of the training camps or, in this case, training cruises: "Really, the fundamental trouble with those poor idiots who make harangues against the Navy and preparedness in general [is] they simply lack education. If one could take them individually and show them the real facts with their own eyes they would stop handing out untruthful hot air."[10]

As 1916 drew to a close, the MTCA had accomplished much and built a solid reputation among people on both sides of the preparedness divide. Clark decided the time had finally come to call openly for universal training. He prepared a formal endorsement to the organization's charter resolving that "the object and policy of [the MTCA] is to bring about a system of universal obligatory military training and equal service for the young men of the United States under exclusive federal control, and that this policy be publicly announced and followed as the policy of this organization."

"Exclusive federal control" was a big departure from the signature civilian leadership and selective recruitment of the original Plattsburg camps, although becoming part of the 1916 Defense Act had been a step in that direction. The MTCA membership would have to vote to approve this major milestone at its next meeting. To beef up attendance Clark set the meeting date for the Friday before the annual Harvard-Yale football game.

In addition to understanding the power of camaraderie and esprit de corps, Clark knew how to throw a party. Members were invited from across the country, along with their wives. The organization held a business meeting on Friday, November 24, and on Saturday the group took buses to New Haven for the big game. A block of tickets on the fifty-yard line awaited. (Alternatively, members could go with General Wood to West Point for the Army-Navy game.) On Sunday everyone was treated to a cruise around New York Harbor in Mayor Mitchel's police boat, followed by a reception on Governor's Island, where members enjoyed "a first rate flying exhibition" by Philip Carroll. (Carroll had become an enthusiastic aviator and was largely responsible, along with Raynall Bolling of the Motor Machine Gun Corps, for establishing Air Plattsburg, which was instrumental in the eventual establishment of the military's air corps as an independent unit.) More than one hundred members from twenty-five states attended, and most brought their wives. Clark summarized the weekend as a great success that would "have important results that do not show on the surface in the way of making everyone pull together and stimulating interest."[11]

The MTCA membership easily approved the universal training amendment and likely would have, even without football and flying exhibitions. But was there something inherently contradictory about this new strategy? The historian J. Garry Clifford points to "a certain paradox" in the members' push for universal training, while they themselves were a strictly voluntary organization. "The Plattsburg method seemed different from the Plattsburg Philosophy." The pacifist camp surely saw the group's saying one thing and doing another as evidence of its hypocrisy. Was this bait-and-switch or some other slick tactic by a bunch of New York City lawyers?

Yes and no. The best explanation is that the evolution of the Plattsburg strategy was the result of pure pragmatism and an astute gauging of public (and presidential) readiness, or unreadiness, to accept something so inherently unpalatable as compulsory training and/or service. Convinced of its necessity, Clark made sure that his practical objectives at every step were attainable. In 1915, and well into 1916, open endorsement of compulsory training would have killed the training camp movement instantly. In Clark's words: "The civilians have got to be educated up to it gradually."[12] The MTCA succeeded with its more aggressive and controversial strategy in 1917 largely because Clark's prudent early efforts had resulted in demonstrable success.

In Washington this patience and restraint was paying off as Congress, reflecting slowly shifting public opinion, gradually became more willing to consider universal training. This shift owed much to the MTCA's relentless public education crusade, first and best through the working example of the camps themselves but also through speeches, articles, and other efforts to reach as many citizens as possible. Lieutenant General S. B. M. Young was much in synch with the MTCA when he said: "It has been my experience that it takes about fifteen or twenty minutes to convince any thinking and reasonable man that Compulsory Military Training is the only safe and sane principle upon which to base a Military Policy." Naturally with members of Congress it took longer. Clark, Wood, and other MTCA members testified repeatedly before Congress during a six-week period in early 1917 as the legislators considered various versions of a compulsory training bill. The MTCA also began publishing the aptly named journal *National Service*, "Devoted to the Cause of Universal Military Training." The first issue came out in February 1917.

Meanwhile the MTCA recruited and planned for the 1917 training camps "just as if conditions were normal." The 1917 camps were to feature two new special programs—one (segregated) for African Americans, and one for major league baseball players (postseason, in October). Those plans were scrapped when the United States formally entered the war on April 6, but ongoing efforts, including the winter training sessions (held inside armories) and the popular military correspondence course, continued apace, now under the formal direction of the War Department.[13]

The MTCA's newly aggressive push coincided, not accidentally, with the crashing course of the war in Europe. On January 31, 1917, the Germans resumed unrestricted submarine warfare, effectively forcing President Wilson to make good on his 1915 threat to enter the war if they violated their previous pledges.[14] Reluctantly the United States severed diplomatic relations with Germany on February 3. Later that same month news broke of the infamous Zimmerman telegram, a coded message from Germany to Mexico intercepted by British intelligence. The communiqué proposed that Mexico go to war against the United States, thus limiting America's impact in Europe. In return Germany would help Mexico reconquer its lost territory in Texas, Arizona, and New Mexico. Mexico declined, but the boldness of the covert attempt right on America's southern doorstep squelched any remaining hopes of neutrality.

Wilson continued last-ditch efforts at a diplomatic solution well into March. But knowing the long odds of a negotiated peace at this late date, the president, his War Department, the army's general staff, and other key advisers simultaneously scrambled to create a war plan that addressed questions of policy, strategy, and funding, as well as to compose the all-important formal public announcement. The president's long-awaited war message was scheduled for April 2 before a joint session of Congress. In addition to formally asking Congress for a declaration of war, Wilson would announce immediate steps to be taken, military and civilian. This included how to raise the soldiers needed. The approach Clark and the MTCA had been advocating—a national draft— was by now widely acknowledged—within the military, the War Department, and increasingly among Wilson's advisers—to be the only realistic method to rapidly assemble large numbers of troops. Days before the scheduled address, however, friends in the War Department alerted Clark that while the president still planned to request expanding the army to 500,000 men, he had abandoned the call for a draft.

Alarmed, Clark ignited the MTCA's ever-widening network. Telephone switchboards lit up across the continent. Letters, telegrams, and phone calls urging the adoption of universal service were soon inundating the White House and congressional offices from across the nation. Clark again set up camp in Washington, D.C., taking a suite at the strategically located (and powerfully frequented) New Willard Hotel on Pennsylvania Avenue just a block from the White House. Perhaps the effort was persuasive; President Wilson's historic April 2 message not only called for the expected troop increase to 500,000 but also added the long-sought explicit endorsement that the new troops "should, in my opinion, be chosen on the principle of universal liability for service."[15] Relief surely merged with quiet dread at the now-official reality of entering the bloody war.

Congress issued an official declaration of war on April 6, 1917. (The vote was not unanimous, but it was a convincing majority: 82–6 in the Senate; 373–50 in the House.) Next it passed the wartime Selective Service Act on May 18. Containing nearly everything the MTCA sought, the act authorized the president to recruit the regular army and National Guard to full war strength, permitting him to draft 500,000 men immediately and another 500,000 when he deemed appropriate. It was a victory for the Plattsburg Idea in every way except that the compulsory service provision was only temporary, authorized for "the period of the existing emergency." This intent was unequivocal, the law's very title proclaiming: "An Act to Authorize the President to Increase Temporarily the Military Establishment of the United States." It was not an unimportant point to Clark and the MTCA, who urged a more permanent service mandate, but at least the urgently needed national troop call-up and training program were now in motion.

How much influence did Grenville Clark and the MTCA have on passing the Selective Service Act? They certainly were not alone in calling for conscription. Once Germany resumed submarine warfare, Wilson was under increasing pressure from White House military advisers, the armed forces leadership, and from Europe. And at some point he and his inner circle undoubtedly read the bitter tea leaves for themselves, as attempt after attempt at mediation and his much hoped-for negotiated "peace without victory" failed. Clark's modest judgment years later belied the probable influence of the Plattsburgers' fight: "It would be going a little far to say that the training campers' activities had much to do with the President's recommendation for universal service . . . but one can never tell. The agitation certainly did no harm and may have done considerable good."

Agitation did harm one key member of the Plattsburg team. On March 24, just one day before Clark received the tip from the War Department, General Wood was reassigned, in reality demoted, by having his Eastern Department chopped into three separate commands, of which he could keep one. Given a choice of the Philippines, Hawaii, and Charleston, South Carolina, Wood defiantly picked Charleston, to remain as close to his former base as possible and not be out of sight—and out of mind—overseas, even though the other two areas were larger, more important commissions. Clark surely deplored the public slap at the dedicated and decorated career soldier, even though Clark had had his share of run-ins with the prickly Wood in the past two years, but there was nothing to be done. The two original Plattsburg leaders remained in regular communication through the war (much of it, not surprisingly, consisting of ongoing sniping by Wood about the Wilson administration).

What led to Wood's abrupt reassignment? There is no one incident or final showdown to point to. The best answer seems that the general and the president, both stubborn men with nearly opposite views on virtually every issue, had simply reached an impasse. Wood, a career soldier, obeyed orders, but he had also been relentless in his condemnation of the president's lack of action on preparedness, among other things. Having spent a professional lifetime in the U.S. military, which holds civilian control of the armed services sacrosanct, the general knew he was crossing the line with his ongoing public harangues against the president. But he seemed incapable of reeling himself in. In typically plain words he asked: "As a soldier I am supposed to risk my life in the service of my country. Should I not be willing to risk my commission?"[16]

But even if Wilson, as commander in chief, was justified in pulling rank, the timing made no sense. The irony of the president's sidelining General Wood at the exact moment Wilson was adopting Wood's position on universal service is striking. Not to mention the questionable wisdom of dismantling a crucial command on the eve of entering a major war and busting down (in military jargon) the army's leading authority on manpower just before an unprecedented national troop call-up. Why Wilson, an outspoken proponent of diplomacy, could not find a way to make peace and take advantage of Wood's abundant talents and experience is as puzzling as it was unfortunate.

Grenville Clark couldn't worry for long about Wood's de facto demotion. Beginning in mid-April Clark focused his attention and energies on the new officer training program and tailoring the existing Plattsburg protocol to achieve it. It was Clark's first experience working closely with the lumbering and inefficient government bureaucracy. He groaned to Fanny, "Everything is so *slow*. They take *too long* to get around to things." But he plowed through the red tape and inertia, until the army finally crafted a comprehensive plan for officer recruitment and training to begin May 8. Sixteen Plattsburg-style officer training camps would be located throughout the country with 2,500 men at each. The camps used existing army facilities: Plattsburg; Fort Benjamin Harrison, Indiana, and Fort Sheridan, Illinois, each would host two camps; and Forts Niagara (New York), Meyer (Virginia), McPherson and Oglethorpe (Georgia), Logan H. Roots (Arkansas), Riley (Kansas), Snelling (Minnesota), and Leon Springs (Texas), as well as San Francisco's Presidio, would hold one camp each. The camps would last three intensive months, with each broken into infantry, artillery, cavalry, and engineering units.

The daunting task now at hand was to recruit and process 40,000 officer candidates to fill these camps, and to do so in just three short weeks. The MTCA rescued the understaffed army administration in carrying out the nearly impossible assignment, and by May 15 a grand total of 46,000 men had reported for duty at the sixteen training camps across the country. The men ranged in age from twenty-one to forty-five and came from a variety of backgrounds. They naturally included the vast majority of the primed and ready 1915 Plattsburg alumni. These elite originals were joined by enthusiastic regular fellows from around the country, many from the 1916 camps. Ninety-days later more than 27,000 men graduated as officers and received commissions as first and second lieutenants, captains, majors, and even one lieutenant colonel and two colonels.

Throughout the process of incorporating the civilian-run camps into the U.S. Army, Clark worked closely with Adjutant General Henry McCain and his staff. To further facilitate his role as liaison between the army and the MTCA, Clark took and passed the officer examination, drily noting, "My showing was not brilliant." His showing was apparently good enough, however, and the newly minted Major Clark was formally assigned to the adjutant general's command center in Washington beginning mid-May. It was a perfect placement, as the office was responsible for all recruitment and training efforts, on which Clark had arguably become the nation's leading authority. Clark was charged with overseeing the continuation and expansion of the training camps and other manpower issues. He also developed and implemented a rating scale as a standardized system for selecting candidates for commissions, developed the Committee on Classification of Personnel, served as executive officer (second in command) to the adjutant general, and organized the popular Students' Army Training Corps (SATC—the wartime version of the former and future ROTC).[17] Clark was soon promoted to lieutenant colonel and later received the Distinguished Service Medal for his wartime contributions.

During his time in Washington, Clark characteristically bumped up against established policies and procedures and at times against direct superiors. A prime example occurred over an issue Clark and other Plattsburgers regarded as sacred, the principle of not commissioning officers without training. (Awarding a certain number of direct commissions as plums was common at the time.) Upon learning that General McCain planned to award a handful of direct (untrained) commissions, young Clark stormed into his commanding officer's office: "[I] worked myself up to a white heat and gave [McCain] some straight talk, [that] breach of faith, loss of lives [would lead to the] everlasting discredit of the War Department." McCain relented, prompting Clark's more or less magnanimous summary statement to Fanny: "I don't think Mc[Cain] ever means badly; only not quite big enough and needs a rod stuck up his—to stiffen him occasionally."

While Lieutenant Colonel Clark served in McCain's office, his civilian leadership role continued. Clark assisted with the MTCA's brimming slate of activities, including providing inspection reports to the secretary of war on each officer camp and divisional cantonment (temporary quarters); continuing to publish *National Service;* and managing the now 1,300 MTCA branches that had sprung up around the country. These branch offices performed a range of important auxiliary duties. They sponsored Liberty Loan (bond) drives, organized home defense battalions, offered preliminary military instruction for newly drafted men, and generally served as local information bureaus for the army. The MTCA also helped to find and enlist specialists in areas in which the army found itself lacking—technicians, mechanics, electricians, even motorcycle drivers. The massive reach of the civilian organization in each case enabled its "splendid response . . . to meet the immediate emergency requirements."[18]

While Clark performed dual roles in Washington, his Plattsburg cohorts were dispersed throughout the war effort. Many, including Clark's early collaborator Theodore Roosevelt Jr., were shipped directly to the European front. Ted's June 17, 1917, letter to Clark has a nostalgic ring and reflects their shared ambivalence about what they had and had not accomplished during the tumultuous last two years:

Dear Grenny:

Just a line to say good-bye and good luck. Am sailing for France almost immediately. It has been great fun working together for the last two years. It must be just about two years ago this time [Philip] Carroll, you and I lunched at Delmonico's and originated the idea of the Plattsburg Camps.

A great deal of water has flowed through the mill since then, but it makes me feel glad to believe that not all of our work was entirely useless in trying to get this country started on the right road . . .

Affectionately, Theodore Roosevelt [Jr.][19]

Nineteen hard-fought months after the United States entered the Great War, the final armistice with Germany was signed on November 11, 1918. (Adding a touch of poetry to years of carnage, the armistice took effect at 11:00 a.m., "the eleventh hour of the eleventh day of the eleventh month"). With the war ended, and world leaders gathered in Paris to hammer out the Treaty of Versailles, Clark received a warm commendation letter from Secretary of War Newton Baker: "The Plattsburg movement, personnel work in the army, and the Students' Army Training Corps is a record of accomplishments scarcely paralleled by any other officer in this great world war."

Clark's performance at the adjutant general's office and the resounding success of the Plattsburg camps led to the first of many attempts to draft him into government service. In 1918 Franklin Roosevelt was one of many to endorse Clark for a newly created position, assistant secretary of war. Nothing came of it, but FDR's letter to Langdon P. Marvin, a mutual friend and the officer in charge of the selection process, is both a warm endorsement and an early glimpse of the future president's inimitable, engaging style:

> Dear Lang: You can be sure I will do everything possible to boost the suggestion of Grenny Clark for one of the new assistant Secretaries of War. He would be a corker, and more than that he deserves it.
> Always sincerely yours,
>
> Franklin D. Roosevelt[20]

If the press and the public had started out lampooning the Plattsburg project as an Ivy League Eagle Scout camp, the snickering was replaced by real and well-deserved respect when the Plattsburg men persisted and became soldiers of widespread distinction in the war. Many of the original recruits were killed, including the former New York mayor John Purroy Mitchel, the Motor Machine Gun Battery and air corps enthusiast Raynall Bolling, and Robert Bacon, the former ambassador to France and first MTCA chair. Many more were badly wounded, including Clark's close friend Delancey K. "Lanny" Jay, who would never fully recover from his war wounds. Robert P. Patterson and five of the men in his Melting Pot Division were awarded the Distinguished Service Medal after a near-death skirmish with German forces along the Vesle River in 1918.[21]

Theodore Roosevelt Jr.'s bravura performance as a soldier would exceed even the massive expectations attached to his legendary name. One commanding officer he particularly impressed was General George Catlett Marshall, the future army chief of staff and a man not given to flowery speech. Marshall wrote to Roosevelt after the war: "With absolute honesty I will tell you that my observation of most of the fighting in France led me to consider your record one of the most remarkable in the entire AEF [American Expeditionary Force]. . . . I consider your conduct as a battalion commander . . . among the finest examples of leadership, courage, and fortitude that came to my attention during the war."

Marshall, almost apologizing for his effusiveness, added: "I do not believe I have ever before indulged myself in such frank comments of a pleasant nature to another man, but I derived so much personal satisfaction as an American from witnessing the manner in which you measured up to the example of your father."[22]

In the end the improbable idea that large numbers of American business and professional men would choose to undergo military training on their own time and at their own expense to prepare for a war the country was trying to stay out of was a remarkable success. By the time U.S. forces went abroad in 1917, more than 16,000 officers had been trained through the camps; by the war's end the total neared 100,000. An estimated 80 percent of those who commanded U.S. troops in France had passed through the Plattsburg camps. A French military historian called it a "military miracle" that so many trained officers were produced so quickly.[23] The rigor and effectiveness of their concentrated training earned the Plattsburg officers the proud nickname "90-Day Wonders."

Their success was a testament to skillful organizing, determination, grit, and above all the power of an activated citizenry to come through in a time of crisis. The Plattsburg experience also left a permanent imprint on its civilian organizer, Grenville Clark, who would find himself leading numerous future citizen campaigns for public causes. For now, however, his work was done. It was time to "get loose of Washington," and Clark did precisely that.[24]

CHAPTER 6

Suburbia, Breakdown
and Recovery

After the war Grenville Clark turned his attention back to his temporarily sidelined law practice and his young and growing family. The Clarks returned to their Seventy-second Street townhouse in Manhattan but soon found themselves spending more and more time on Long Island. Finding the then-bucolic suburb suited Fanny's love of gardening and the outdoors, and seeking a country home environment in which to raise their children, the Clarks in 1920 bought a weekend getaway place on twelve acres just a few train stops from Manhattan on the Long Island Rail Road (LIRR). The property was located at 193 I. U. Willets Road, now in Albertson, although it was then considered part of East Williston; Clark referred to it simply as "E.W." throughout his lifetime. In 1924 the family moved to E.W. full time, keeping the Manhattan townhouse for periodic city stays and midweek use when Grenville was working from his Wall Street law office.

The home was located in Long Island's fabled Gold Coast region but couldn't have been more different from the lavish mansions and estates modeled after European fortresses and French chateaux that give the North Shore its posh reputation. For specific and pragmatic reasons the Clarks chose a modest clapboard house a stone's throw from the Oyster Bay branch of the Long Island Rail Road: Fanny wanted "town water" and hardwood floors, and Grenville wanted to be able to walk to the train.[1] The place filled the bill, and the Clarks made it their primary residence for the next two decades. (Theodore Roosevelt's Sagamore Hill home in nearby Oyster Bay is described in similar terms: modest yet comfortable, not ostentatious, a real family home—all, of course, relative to the neighborhood.)[2]

The Clarks enjoyed Long Island and it suited them well. They had good friends living in the area, the elegant Piping Rock Club indulged Grenville's passion for golf and his other sporting enthusiasms, and the children attended excellent schools nearby. And, in keeping with his original request, Grenville Clark's commute to Wall Street involved a fifty-yard walk from his breakfast table to the railroad tracks, where he hailed the LIRR train with a red flag tucked into a box mounted on a pole next to the track for that purpose.

A tradeoff for this proximity to the train was the hazard of frequent grass fires started by sparks thrown from the locomotives' coal-burning engines. Sometimes the fires would race past the plowed firebreak around the Clarks' property and come menacingly close to the home, providing high excitement for the Clark children. Undaunted, Fanny continued her transformation of the place from twelve acres of sandy scrubland into a garden oasis, bringing in boxcars full of topsoil, plants, trees, shrubs, and flower species from around the world. (On Fanny's death in 1964 Clark donated the property to the Brooklyn Botanic Garden. Now owned and operated by the Town of North Hempstead, the Clark Botanic Garden is open to the public year round. A hidden treasure in the now densely populated environs, it is still an easy fifty-yard walk from the Albertson LIRR station, although you can no longer hail the train with a red flag.)

While fully enjoying Long Island's charms, the Clarks were determined not to let its conspicuous affluence spoil their children. According to a daughter, "while they had close individual friends among them, both my [parents] were wary of the super-rich and went to great lengths to insulate their children from their influence." A prime example was this daughter's visit to the home of a schoolmate from a well-known family that embodied the reasons for the Clarks' concern. When the Clark girl came home "prattling about being taken over to the racing stable where the grooms brought out the yearlings for us two ten-year-olds to see, I was never allowed to go there again." And it was no accident that at the close of each school year, the children were immediately "spirited away to New Hampshire, well away from the summer delights of Long Island's North Shore Gold Coast."[3]

Summers in Dublin, New Hampshire, were not exactly a hardship. The Clarks' much-loved Outlet Farm was a 350-acre retreat that had been in Fanny's family for three generations. (The name Outlet was for a nearby opening in Dublin Lake that feeds into a rocky stream). Long a thriving summer colony for artists and writers, the small village of Dublin (population 675 in 1950) is where Fanny in her youth came in contact with many of the creative lights of her generation, including the poet Amy Lowell, the painters Abbott Thayer and George de Forest Brush, and the iconic American humorist and writer Mark Twain. Twain found Dublin "bracing and stimulating" and spent two full summers there in a rented farmhouse (along with three rented kittens) dictating to his early biographer, Albert Bigelow Paine. Twain came to Dublin on a tip: "I remembered that Abbott Thayer had said . . . the New Hampshire highlands was a good place. He was right—it is a good place."[4]

Celebrities aside, Dublin was a quintessential New England farming village whose mostly rural inhabitants had been carving a living from the rocky soil at the base of the area's tallest granite peak since the mid-1700s. Outlet Farm's rambling red brick–and-wood country house nestles in an idyllic spot on Dublin Lake at the base of Mount Monadnock. Clark loved "our mountain, Monadnock," and enjoyed telling visitors that its name came from an Indian word meaning "mountain that stands alone."[5] (Monadnock's impressive mass does thrust itself up from the ground, peculiarly independent of other peaks or any mountain chain, not a bad metaphor for the man who lived at its base.) Perhaps Dublin's most well-connected gentleman farmer, Clark took refuge at Dublin when he needed to decompress from his relentless activity, and he did so with increasing frequency through the decades.

Later in life Clark's love of Dublin was reciprocated in a postcard of the town from the late 1950s. The printed caption reads, "Aerial View of Dublin School, Dublin, N.H.," and notes that "Dublin has attracted prominent citizens, writers, and artists: President Taft and Grenville Clark; Mark Twain and Amy Lowell; Abbot Thayer, George de Forest Brush and more." An amused Clark scrawled in the margin: "Am I supposed to be an artist, or writer, or 'prominent citizen'? Or *what?* G.C."[6]

Wherever Clark was, he took great pleasure in his domestic life and spent as much time with his family as his demanding schedule allowed. Clark kept a fully functional home office and frequently conducted both legal work and his ongoing public service efforts from Long Island or Dublin. Clark's need for time at home, and his overlapping obligations in New York, Washington, Cambridge, and Dublin, made him a moving target for his loyal longtime secretary, Genevieve Maloney. Miss Maloney, as she was always called, would gather up important documents and meet her busy boss wherever she could catch up with him—at his various homes or on a train, even occasionally at the formal Root, Clark office on Nassau Street. Her office calendar was nearly as dizzying as his.[7]

Grenville Clark was a thoroughly enthusiastic husband and father. His keen appreciation of nature and bent for teaching made the unspoiled spaces around Dublin the perfect classroom in which to pass down the basics of outdoorsmanship. In a junior version of Plattsburg's ten-day hike, Clark had his children camp for several nights in a row, rain or shine, on the "40 acre lot up on the ridge" of his beloved Mount Monadnock. By day they hiked and surveyed the surrounding countryside from their elevated perch, where they were encouraged to imagine it as Cortez might have seen it centuries before (although why the usually precise historian selected Cortez, who is famous for conquering the Aztecs in present-day Mexico, is hard to say).[8]

With their father as an expert field guide, the Clark children picked wild blueberries, collected in tin pails tied to the waist, and found local rocks, frogs, and other treasures to bring home for further scientific investigation. At night they built bonfires from brush gathered on the mountain slopes and enjoyed on-the-spot astronomy lessons. Clark taught the children to identify stars, planets, and the constellations, and to understand why they changed position in the night sky. He coached his daughters, not just his son, in all manner of sports, from golf, tennis, and other racquet games to horseback riding, using a bow and arrow, and marksmanship with a shotgun, rifle, and pistol. (Daughter Mary D. would later shock unsuspecting midwestern sportsmen, when the proper New England lady shucked her white gloves and beat them all at target shooting in rural Missouri.)[9] Summer meant golfing, swimming, fishing, canoeing, and sailing. With winter came "fancy skating," skiing, tobogganing, and long cross-country treks on snowshoes—they missed virtually no sporting possibility.

Both parents emphasized academics, and Grenville Clark was at the ready to personally tutor his children on topics from the most basic to the esoteric if he detected a lack of basic knowledge. One daughter vividly recalled an impromptu lecture he gave on a cruise ship, about differentiating the three branches of the U.S. government. The lesson was seared permanently, practically verbatim, into her memory. The child who, say, tossed an ancient Greek phrase into a conversation to show off could expect a sharp follow-up question: "Is that all the Greek you know?" It wouldn't be for long.[10]

Supplemental civics lessons included periodic trips to Washington, D.C. Like countless other schoolchildren the Clark offspring were brought to the nation's capital to observe the hub of government first hand—where law and politics, deals and ideals, daily collide. Like other children they explored the Smithsonian's wonders, toured the major government buildings, and perhaps chased each other around D.C.'s imposing marble monuments. Unlike most children, however, the Clarks' Washington visits included private calls on senior senators and cabinet members with whom their father might be working on a high-level project, and lunching in the Supreme Court dining room with family friend Felix Frankfurter. When the court was not in session, the Clarks would visit Justice Benjamin Cardozo at his D.C. apartment. A handwritten note confirms:

A visit from the Clark family will bring me pride and pleasure.
. . . I shall be at my apartment—which serves me also as an
office—both morning and afternoon.

Benjamin Cardozo[11]

A visit to the home of the recently retired justice Louis Brandeis was another highlight of the children's extracurricular civics agenda. One spring break even included a private call on President Franklin Roosevelt in the Oval Office, which surely made for a hard-to-beat summer vacation essay back at school.

The Clark children's summers included vacationing in Canada with the Supreme Court legend Charles Evans Hughes, whom Clark jokingly called "Old Brushface" because of his famous bushy white whiskers. They met Admiral Richard Byrd, who spent two summers in Dublin preparing for his expeditions to Antarctica. The incessantly talkative poet Robert Frost was a frequent visitor. Frost would hold forth in the Dublin living room well into the night, requiring the senior Clarks to take shifts listening to him. The family knew well the top educators of the day—Presidents Lowell and Conant of Harvard, Harold W. Dodds of Princeton, and John Sloan Dickey of Dartmouth were all close friends and regular visitors. The dashing young Robert Maynard Hutchins and his wife, the novelist Maude Hutchins, made a big impression when they stopped in on their way to reinvent the University of Chicago.

The great variety of people who passed through the Clarks' homes and lives also included governors, ambassadors, and influential journalists—the two-time Pulitzer Prize–winning writer, editor, and political analyst Walter Lippmann was a good friend. The Clarks lunched regularly with Edith (Mrs. Theodore) Roosevelt at the former president's Sagamore Hill estate in nearby Oyster Bay. In fact all the Theodore Roosevelt clan were friends of the Clarks.' A postwar trip to London included dinner with British Prime Minister Clement Attlee, who in later years came to be Clark's close friend and strong collaborator on world peace through world law. One daughter's favorite celebrity moment was encountering Albert Einstein at a meeting of intellectuals gathered by her father at Princeton to work on "the peace problem," as Clark always called it. The young girl had the unusual opportunity to rescue the brilliant scientist from falling down a hotel's narrow scullery stairwell—a memorable experience among so many others.[12] From presidents to prime ministers to Albert Einstein, the children of Grenville Clark received an expansive liberal education.

The family's after-dinner rituals often included Grenville Clark's reading aloud to the children: *Uncle Remus,* Kipling, Sir Walter Scott, and especially Shakespeare, all were rendered with dramatic flair, complete with outrageous accents and full emphatic gestures. Or he would regale the young people with tales of his own adventures—grizzly bears he encountered on hunting trips in the Rockies, or mischievous anecdotes from Pomfret School or Harvard days. The family also played parlor games, including Fanny's childhood favorite of charades in front of the nearly constantly burning low fire in the living room.

The Clarks celebrated holidays with enthusiasm and mountains of gifts—Grenville Clark was an irrepressible gift giver, often to the chagrin of frugal Fanny. Apparently he was also a last-minute shopper. Daughter Mary recalled that each Christmas Eve, presumably on her busy father's way home from Wall Street, "Abercrombie and Fitch . . . was assaulted by him in remarkable style." A short LIRR ride later, the top-coated Santa would burst through the front door loaded with gifts. Louisa, the youngest child, was in charge of writing the annual family "Christmas epic," recounting in rhyming verse the year's adventures by all Clarks. These ran several legal pages and were read aloud with all the children piled onto their parents' bed on Christmas morning on Long Island.[13] Another Christmastime ritual was reading Dickens's *A Christmas Carol* aloud before the fire on Christmas Eve, with Père Clark's voice becoming increasingly unsteady as the story neared its poignant ending. (Mary D. carried on that tradition, reading the holiday classic aloud to her own family on Christmas Eve. Every year she cried.)[14]

The Clarks took regular vacations together, within America and around the world. In addition to the annual summer stretch in Dublin, they took regular jaunts to the former Cannon estate in Burlington, Vermont, where Grenville's brother Julian still lived, and to Boston to spend time with Fanny's family. The family enjoyed lengthy cruises to the Caribbean, South America, Scandinavia, and Russia, and winter escapes from bitter New England weather to country club resorts in Florida and Arizona.

But even as seemingly charmed a life as the Clarks' does not come without some measure of sorrow. Grenville and Fanny's second decade together was wrenched by a double tragedy. In November 1922 their beloved first-born daughter, Eleanor, contracted meningitis and died at age seven. In cruelly rapid succession came a stillborn son, Dwight, in 1923. A sensitive and deeply caring man, the stricken Grenville Clark wore a black mourning band on the arm of his business suits for a year.

The children's deaths came during an already sobering time for the nation. In January 1919 the seemingly invincible former president Theodore Roosevelt had died in his sleep of a blood clot to the lungs. The grief provoked among TR's national, and even international, army of followers was intense and sustained. For Clark it was a personal blow; Roosevelt had been a close friend and early mentor. One historian called TR's death "a prelude to the disappointment and disillusionment that pervaded practically all of America in the years immediately following the World War."[15]

There was also a lingering malaise from crushed hopes for a lasting peace after the 1919 Paris Peace Conference. Instead of resolving past differences after World War I, the conference produced the Treaty of Versailles, which actually created new ones by carving vast conquered territories of the defeated Ottoman Empire into colonies (euphemistically called mandates) for the victors, sowing seeds of sectarian conflict in the Middle East and North Africa that reverberate to this day.[16] In a final blow to the exhausted, embittered, and increasingly invalided President Wilson, his own government would ultimately reject his cherished League of Nations. (Unlike most of his conservative contemporaries, and in a foreshadowing of his later work for world peace, Grenville Clark was a strong supporter of the league.)[17] Across the country the wartime boom had collapsed, and in its place came riots, strikes, and the red scare. And though no one yet knew it, things would only get worse, much worse, as the superheated stock market boom of the mid-1920s set up its spectacular 1929 crash into the Great Depression.

Through it all Clark maintained his relentless work ethic. He vigorously practiced law, took on another term as chair of the MTCA, and even added to his load the chair of the New York City Bar Association's important Judiciary Committee. He had no buffer to absorb life's regular accumulation of stresses, let alone the crushing grief of losing two children. In 1926 the burdens proved too great, and the man of granite began to crack. Described by Clark's physician and close friend, the eminent cardiologist Paul Dudley White of Massachusetts General Hospital, as having an "extraordinary interdependence of mind, body and soul," Clark in this case was unable to counterbalance an anguished soul and exhausted body even with his usually indomitable force of mind.[18] The forty-two-year-old Clark suffered a nervous breakdown, capping an unrelenting state of mental and physical exhaustion.

The treatment protocol for nervous disorders in the 1920s was some variation of the rest cure. Clark was prescribed a full year at a sanatorium in Kerhonkson, New York. (Here as elsewhere, wealth smoothed the edges—Clark was able to move his entire family and staff into a house on the Kerhonkson grounds for the duration of his stay.) There is little record of his time there; we can judge only by results that it was a success. It speaks to both the skill of the medical staff and the grit of the patient that Clark enjoyed the bulk of his remarkable career after this significant event. Even at a physical ebb Clark was still making friends. His doctor at Kerhonkson, Andrew Foord, and one of his fellow patients, Edward M. Day, a Hartford attorney, remained in close contact through their lifetimes. With a nod to the episode and the dark events leading to it, Clark summarized in a midlife autobiographical sketch for Harvard that "in my family life, I have been fortunate beyond measure. Our share of illnesses and sorrow has been far outweighed by our blessings."[19]

Clark returned from Kerhonkson to a hero's welcome at Root, Clark in 1927. His relieved and protective partners attempted to mitigate his bent for overwork by assigning him his own law clerk. This was none other than the young and shining legal talent Henry Friendly, fresh from Harvard Law School and a year's clerkship with Supreme Court Justice Louis Brandeis. (Friendly would go on to a top legal career on the bench of the U.S. Court of Appeals for the Second Circuit.) As noted in Chapter 3 the attempt was a spectacular failure and Clark immediately resumed his exhaustive personal work habits. While making Friendly a lifelong friend and admirer, Clark continued to drive and manage his myriad cases, projects, and activities virtually single-handedly.

Among Clark's diverse legal clients in the 1920s were beer brewers and distilleries seeking relief from the 1920 Volstead Act, which instituted Prohibition. The moment the measure took effect, the livelihoods of brewers and distillers came to a virtual halt. Clark was never a big drinker, but he instinctively opposed Prohibition because he saw its sheer unenforceability and the related spike in criminal activity from bootlegging, speakeasies, and other illegal enterprises as poisonous to public respect for the law. It created scofflaws. That it also circumvented personal responsibility, which was unwise, attempted to legislate morals, which was impossible, and turned mobsters into celebrities, which was distasteful, were likely secondary factors.

An unintended consequence of Clark's Prohibition stance was losing a potential presidential appointment in 1930. President Herbert Hoover was seeking a nominee for U.S. attorney for the Southern District of New York, a major post recently vacated by Charles Tuttle in his unsuccessful bid to become governor. (Clark's law partner Emory Buckner held the position before Tuttle, in 1925–27.) When word leaked out that Grenville Clark was the leading candidate, enthusiastic articles endorsing his appointment appeared in the *National Business Review* and the *New York Times,* and letters of congratulation poured in from associates and friends. Clark was ambivalent. In a letter to one friend he admitted, "I am not doing anything whatever to get appointed because it is just exactly even money whether I would like it or not. Every possible argument is against it except that I have a slight hankering to do a tour of public service."[20]

Clark had been selected at least in part because he was the ideal candidate to depoliticize the appointment, given the growing public discontent with the Republican administration amid the worsening Depression. Clark was listed in the 1930 *Who's Who* as a Republican, but he was not seen as closely linked to the Hoover administration. Yet there was no escaping politics. Early in his discussions with the president, Clark alerted Hoover that he (Clark) was on record as opposing Prohibition—in correspondence with George Wickersham of the National Commission on Law Enforcement and Observance. Wickersham had asked Clark to investigate "the industrial alcohol situation," meaning how to ensure that approved industrial alcohol manufacturers did not produce illegal liquor on the side. As Wickersham had requested, Clark's response outlined the basic framework in which the distilleries operated in regard to Prohibition. It also made clear his distaste for the law: "I believe that the effort to continue prohibition is contributing more than any one thing to lack of respect for the law and the many evils arising from that. . . . I think the minority in opposition is and will continue to be so great that the present law is unenforceable and a breeder of corruption to an extent outweighing the benefits which it brings."[21]

Without recanting or equivocating, Clark assured Hoover that his views were private and would not interfere with his duty to carry out all laws of the land. Clark had raised the issue simply so that the president would not be caught off guard if it came up in what was likely to be a thorough vetting process. Hoover, a Quaker and unyielding supporter of the Eighteenth Amendment, with much of his political support coming from the "drys" in the House and Senate, blanched at the possibility that his dwindling political base would hold Clark's anti-Prohibition stance against the president. The administration dithered for months, while the gossip uncertainty generates splashed through the press. It was an unwelcome intrusion and unaccustomed embarrassment to the very private Grenville Clark. When the impasse continued, Clark withdrew his name from consideration, citing outside obligations. A cordial but brief acknowledgment from Hoover closed the chapter:

My dear Mr. Clark:

I have your kind letter of October 23rd. I quite understand the situation that has arisen. I am in hopes we can press you into public service at some other point.

Yours faithfully, Herbert Hoover[22]

While the aborted nomination did not appear to leave Clark with an unquenched thirst for political appointment, a less publicized near-miss with the Hoover administration did cause him serious reflection in later years. This was a personal appeal in 1931 from Henry L. Stimson, then Hoover's secretary of state, who had previously served as secretary of war under William Howard Taft. Stimson was a generation older than Clark, and the younger man had long admired Stimson's distinguished public record and steady straightforward personality. Clark described Stimson's unique request in a 1943 letter to his son:

Dear Grenny [Jr.]:

You mentioned recently wanting to become "as well-educated as possible on the war in general." I think your ideas on it for two years and more have been very mature and good but here are some notes for what they are worth.

I was reflecting that after all, in the past 5 years especially, but for 30 years before that, I've had exceptional chances to size up what was going on the world over—at least for a non-official person, and maybe that's no handicap, since the official people sometimes get cramped up a little just because they are official.

In 1931 when [Stimson] was Secretary of State under Hoover, he got hold of me and gave me a big talk about how world events would develop and asked me to take a mission of four years as an Assistant Secretary of State (special title for the purpose) and stay in Russia and then China two years each—objects—to pay them special attention and to get information.

He had a definite theory—that Germany and Japan were the rising, dynamic powers; that because of U.S. aloofness (isolationism), we knew and cared little about Russia and China, who would be our badly needed allies in the global war to come; and so we must try to know them more and get on better terms with them; that we ought to do something unusual to this end, such as he proposed.

He really had a long view ahead and I've sometimes wished I'd taken that on; declined mostly on account of your mother's health and bringing up the family, all then at school.[23]

The letter went on to carefully analyze the war from Clark's decidedly not "cramped up" perspective as an intimately involved outsider. Stimson's prescience was startling in retrospect, as events unfolded during the next two decades almost exactly as he had predicted. This was well noted by Clark, whose confidence in Stimson's observations and judgment never wavered. As it happened, the two men would get their chance to work closely together a decade later, when Stimson led the War Department during World War II and recruited Clark to be his private adviser. (See Chapter 10.)

In both "near-nomination" cases it is interesting to speculate on where a working relationship between Clark and Hoover might have led. As one historian notes, although their politics and policy ideas were quite different, they shared some strong operational tendencies: "Hoover's reputation as the Great Humanitarian for saving starving civilians in WWI (Committee for Relief to Belgium) operated much as Clark's organizations did—like minded elites volunteering for a good cause and avoiding public office. If Clark had accepted Stimson's offer to be assistant secretary of state, he might have become a Hoover acolyte."[24] Clark himself did not appear to engage in such speculation, other than to tuck both incidents into his mind (and files) and press on.

CHAPTER 7

Full Speed Ahead

The 1930s brought one of Grenville Clark's longest-running and most personally meaningful service roles. In 1931 the loyal Harvardian became a Fellow of Harvard's virtually unseen yet extraordinarily powerful seven-member board known simply as the Corporation, or, as Clark described it, "that curious self-perpetuating body composed of the President, Treasurer and five Fellows, which was created by Act of the General Court in 1650 and still acts under that unamended Charter."[1] A completely private entity, the Corporation literally owns and manages Harvard. Board members are appointed for life; together they choose the university's president and govern virtually every aspect of university business. The Corporation has no outside supervision, reports to no one, no records of meetings are released, and no discussion transcripts are made available.[2] Erwin N. Griswold, former dean of Harvard Law School and at one point U.S. solicitor general, recalled: "When I returned to teach in 1934, Mr. Clark was already an eminence grise. He was one of that august body, the Harvard Corporation, which Harvard professors know exists and which they understand, deep in their hearts, is a rather beneficent group. However, they are not only mighty, but remote, and there is very little contact with those who are carrying on the day-to-day activities of the university."[3]

Clark took his Corporation duty seriously and devoted substantial time and energy to it for nearly twenty years (1931–50). He pointed out that, contrary to some largely honorary boards, "membership on the Corporation is no sinecure, especially for a non-resident of Boston. The long meetings twice a month are only part of the duties, which include the study of documents, conferences, and correspondence. One is rewarded, however, by the consideration of a great variety of problems that is in itself a liberal education, by congenial associations and by a sense of participation in the important work of maintaining a great University free from coercion of any description."[4]

Clark's reference to "freedom from coercion" was deliberate and specific. He made perhaps his most important contribution to Harvard, and to education, as the Corporation's unwavering voice for academic freedom throughout his tenure. He spoke out loudly against requiring professors to take loyalty oaths when Massachusetts in 1935 joined twenty-one states that were attempting to soothe prewar jitters by enacting loyalty statutes. These oaths often seemed harmless enough on the surface—written vaguely, requiring teachers to swear general loyalty to America, the Constitution, and the laws of the land. Yet, as Clark pointed out, "[they] represent an infringement of civil liberty which is all the more effective and hard to eliminate because [they are] cast in a plausible and innocuous form." Other such statutes were quite direct, such as this one from the District of Columbia: "I further state, without reservation and for the purpose of obtaining payment of salary otherwise due me, that I did not at any time during [previous and current career span] in any school of the District of Columbia or elsewhere teach or advocate Communism."

Clark and other educators were incensed—how could America's youth fully understand their own form of government, let alone learn about the world, with no mention permitted of its major competing political ideology? His response spoke for many: "These laws are vicious, not [only] because they are unfair to teachers . . . [and] few teachers are in an economic position to be heroic . . . or [to] their students [by depriving them of knowledge], but [mostly] because they are unfair to the country in that they strike at the most fundamental requirement of all in our democracy—the training of an informed, active minded, and discriminating electorate."[5]

Harvard's president, and Clark's friend and supporter during much of his time on the Corporation board, was James B. Conant. This may have involved some measure of gratitude, as Clark was reportedly instrumental in Conant's election. When A. Lawrence Lowell retired after an extraordinary twenty-four-year presidency in 1933, such was the respect Clark had earned in only two years as a Corporation trustee that he was also a candidate for the position. The story goes (unconfirmed because of the secrecy surrounding Corporation decisions) that the vote to elect Clark or Conant to be president of the seven-member group was tied at 3–3 when Clark himself cast the deciding vote for the other man. Although the two had disagreements through the years, at least one serious (see Chapter 13 for discussion of the Arnold Arboretum controversy), they grew to deeply respect and enjoy each other. The Conants spent regular weekends at Dublin, and Conant was the first to encourage Clark to write up his ideas on world peace.[6]

As Clark embarked on his long service on the Harvard Corporation board, he was also organizing another public service campaign, this time in the realm of economic policy. With the spectacular collapse of the stock market in 1929, the rapidly deepening Depression, and the Hoover administration's laissez-faire policies doing little to ameliorate the national misery, the man who created the Plattsburg camps felt compelled to once again apply direct citizen action.

In 1931, the depths of the Great Depression, Clark cofounded the National Economy League (NEL) with Archibald Roosevelt (son of Theodore), former president Calvin Coolidge, Admiral Richard Byrd, and Charles Evans Hughes Jr., among others. Their battlefield was the thorny problem of federal finances, their mission to balance the federal budget and restore stability to the financial system. The NEL's primary focus was on reported abuses in the veterans' pension system. Veterans' claims were already consuming nearly half of all government revenues and were slated to increase rapidly in upcoming years. Department audits found that a majority of the disabilities claimed were not connected with actual war service but rather were the result of illness and injury not related to combat.[7]

Clark and the other NEL members were convinced that the illegitimate claims discredited veterans' reputations and consumed precious federal dollars urgently needed elsewhere. Their conviction traced to Plattsburg and its central tenet of each citizen's obligation to serve the country. Members of the NEL rejected the idea that veterans should get special entitlements for what should be every citizen's moral, societal obligation. It was a tough argument to make, given the dire economic straits of most of the claimants, and tougher still to be making it against veterans—the one group that by definition had in fact served in the nation's defense.

That nearly all NEL members were recent World War I veterans, several with combat-related injuries, muted some criticism. Still, as establishment men of wealth and privilege, they made perfect archvillains cast against the bent and impoverished pensioners, described by one writer as "unemployable, middle-aged men whose government pittances were their sole resource against utter destitution."[8] A haunting editorial cartoon in the Veterans of Foreign Wars' *Foreign Service* journal depicted a firing squad made up of society men in top hats and tails taking aim at three enfeebled veterans, one each from the Civil War, the Spanish-American War, and the World War. The veterans' gazes are calm but stern. The tall broad-shouldered executioner, seen in profile closest to the viewer, is labeled "National Economy League" and bears more than a passing resemblance to Grenville Clark and his well-heeled NEC cohorts.

The struggle was a miserable one and Clark took no pleasure in it. But driven by principle and what he saw as economic necessity, he and

Herbert Lake, "Some Call This Economy," *Foreign Service*, April 1933. Courtesy Veterans of Foreign Wars.

his fellow NEL members vigorously protested the proposed 1932 veterans' bonus bill, a measure that would have speeded up payment of a congressionally mandated service bonus to World War I veterans. Originally delayed until 1945, the one-time bonus, an award of approximately $1,000 per service member, would instead be paid immediately. In the spring and summer of 1932 thousands of desperate veterans and their families marched on Washington in what came to be known as the Bonus March. They camped in a makeshift shantytown not far from the White House, quickly dubbed Hooverville to shame the president.

At the time the American Legion, Veterans of Foreign Wars, and other organizations were lobbying to further liberalize veterans' pensions and health care benefits, which would nearly double the already unsustainable annual payout to veterans from the Treasury. The beleaguered Hoover had vetoed a similar measure in 1930, calling it "a radical departure . . . [giving pensions] to men who have incurred disabilities . . . [with] no relation to their military service." Clark wrote Hoover a supportive letter, agreeing that "real economy is virtually synonymous with a radical cut in the billion a year for veterans."[9] The NEL and the Hoover administration were not alone in trying to control costs related to veterans. The Democratic presidential candidate, Franklin Roosevelt, was also opposed to the bonus bill and was busy crafting what would be unprecedented national economic measures once he was elected. The bonus bill passed in the House but was rejected in the Senate 76–19.

The NEL undoubtedly influenced the Senate vote as well as the large reductions in veterans' payments that became part of Roosevelt's 1933 Economy Act, but it was not a victory to savor. Despite the administration's best intentions and many promises, the act's draconian cuts harmed thousands of veterans and their families, including many with legitimate benefit claims. In later years Clark's feelings about his NEL efforts were decidedly mixed. After World War II he fully supported the GI Bill, saying, "In view of the difference between soldiers and civilians in the second world war, I would never again oppose anything in reason that the veterans want."[10]

However he and the future would judge the NEL, it offered a natural segue for Clark to work closely with the new president on economic policy. Franklin Roosevelt had campaigned vigorously on a promise to rein in the wasteful spending of the former Republican administration, and he tapped Clark to help him do it. Clark took on the assignment and with Alphonse Laporte, a New York banker, wrote the brief that would become the Economy Act of 1933, one of the most successful pieces of Roosevelt's famous Hundred Days.[11]

To squeeze in a briefing on the act, the president asked Clark to arrange to sit next to him at (yet another) upcoming dinner at the Harvard Club. Clark agreed but club politics interfered. Thomas Lamont, a JP Morgan bigwig and former president of the club, had already claimed the prized dinner seat next to the president. After thirty minutes of getting "a terrible earache" from Lamont ("He has been telling me how to run the country. I think I know as much about it as he does"), the exasperated FDR abruptly ended the conversation, called Clark over to take over Lamont's seat ("Why are you not sitting next to me?"), and their briefing proceeded.[12]

Clark recalled both the president's enthusiasm for the act ("I agree with you 100% and you don't have to argue it to me") and his novel idea to spread the word to the public using a relatively new medium, the radio airwaves. FDR sounded out his old friend, saying: "I must get it to the people, for it will be a very drastic law. Look here, nobody has used the radio very much, and I think I'll try that. What do you think?" Clark had no doubt Roosevelt would be a natural, having since youth observed his easy charm and ability to connect with an audience. Clark answered, "I think you would do that very well."[13]

On March 12, 1933, Roosevelt delivered his first (of thirty) now iconic fireside chats over the radio and proved Clark correct. In his uniquely genial yet convincing style, FDR reassured the American people that the beleaguered U.S. banks were safe and outlined the provisions in his Economy Bill. The address was a huge success, and the bill passed Congress in just forty-eight hours. "The President was naturally pleased," Clark recalled. "[He] said kind things to me, including, in substance, 'come see me whenever you want to and let me have your views.'"[14]

Clark did regularly share his views with the president on a host of topics, as he undoubtedly would have even without an invitation. Clark was enthusiastic about one of Roosevelt's favorite New Deal programs, the Civilian Conservation Corps. The CCC was an ambitious plan to put 250,000 young unemployed men (aged eighteen to twenty-five) to work in reforestation and development of the national parks and forests. Roosevelt and Clark, though different in many ways, shared a love of nature and an almost zealous faith in human potential and the possibilities of social progress. To them the CCC was a home run. It promised "mental, moral, and physical" benefits to its mostly poor urban participants, many of whom rarely, if ever, escaped their gritty and polluted environs; it also reduced unemployment and made possible bold public improvement projects. The nation's parks would blossom, roads would be built out west, and thousands of young men at risk of becoming "despondent idlers" in overcrowded cities would be transformed into hardworking citizens who would "return to their homes . . . with a better chance to meet the various problems of life."[15]

Clark wanted to take the program even further. He had never given up on some form of national service and envisioned a CCC that was both universal and incorporated a military training aspect. He approached Roosevelt about merging the CCC with the ongoing post-Plattsburg training camps, the CMTC (Citizen Military Training Camps). This was in part to address the concern that despite the CCC's great popularity, the concentration of urban poor in its work camps might inadvertently stoke a potentially dangerous "proletarian spirit." The combined program Clark proposed would in contrast be a "national adventure" combining both upper- and lower-class youth in an "indissoluble unit against social disintegration."[16] It was a public works version of Theodore Roosevelt's dog tents of democratization.

The CCC would also thus "be merged into the greater effort of imparting an education for citizenship of the country's youth," thereby keeping "awake the American instinct for the frontier and the joy of overcoming the obstacles threatening the future of the country through a common effort."[17] Clark wanted all of America's young men to have grizzly bear stories from the Rockies to tell their children in front of the fire some day. The president endorsed the idea wholeheartedly. Franklin Roosevelt tried hard to make the CCC a permanent institution in the late 1930s, but neither Congress nor the public would support it as anything more than a relief measure. The CCC survived in some fashion until 1943, when it died of attrition. Clark and Roosevelt were deeply disappointed that their combined and permanent program never came to pass.

While Clark was advising the president, leading the NEL, and serving on the Harvard Corporation, he was also fully reengaged as a lawyer. In the early 1930s the firm now named Root, Clark, Buckner, and Ballantine was finding its stride. (Buckner had returned to the firm in 1927–28 after his stint as U.S. attorney.) Each of the four partners had areas of particular expertise, but the entire organization worked together as a much more integrated team than was usual in large Wall Street firms. The caseload was steady and growing when in 1934 Emory Buckner, sixty-one, unexpectedly suffered a major stroke from which he never fully recovered. The inimitable irreplaceable Buckner was not only the firm's star litigator, he was also its chief organizer, administrator, business promoter, and a name partner. As when Clark was away for his rest cure at Kerhonkson, the remaining partners fielded but felt the increased load. John Harlan, then a young Root, Clark associate, eventually stepped in to fill Buckner's role as lead litigator. When Buckner died in 1941, he was remembered at a large firm dinner and in an op-ed tribute in the *New York Times,* and he was later the subject of a worthy biography by Martin Mayer. In a posthumous tribute to Buckner, Elihu Root Jr. said that while he and Grenny Clark might have had great fun practicing law, without Buckner the firm would never have grown into the powerhouse it did.[18]

The firm carried on, and Clark continued to pull his share and more. Among his many specialties, Clark had become a recognized expert in the then-dominant field of railroad law. He appeared regularly before the all-powerful Interstate Commerce Commission, arguing cases ranging from rate setting to railroad securities investments to shareholder returns on various line projects. Henry Friendly, who worked with his senior partner on many large and complicated railroad rate and reorganization cases, later noted: "It must be hard for young lawyers today to comprehend an era when the ICC [Interstate Commerce Commission, which regulates the railroads] was spoken of simply as 'The Commission' and an argument before that body was treated almost as seriously as one before the Supreme Court. I doubt that anyone, Brandeis included, ever made better arguments before 'The Commission' than G.C. did in these cases. What was impressive, beyond his command of the facts, was his moral force. Commissioners might disagree with him, and did, but they could not fail to respect his complete sincerity."[19]

Clark also had some interesting individual clients, including Lucius N. Littauer, multimillionaire glove manufacturer, who was also a five-term U.S. representative from New York, a Harvard alumnus, and Harvard's first football coach.[20] When Littauer retired from his many other roles to become a full-time philanthropist, he hired Grenville Clark to arrange the substantial estates of Littauer and his wife, Flora. The mighty task included wills, trusts, and a separate charitable foundation (Clark and Felix Frankfurter served on its board) as well as the administration of a whopping $2 million gift to Harvard to establish a new graduate school for public administration. It was a record-high donation for any university at the time, intended to realize Littauer's vision of "a school for a new professional governing class" under the auspices of his cherished alma mater.[21]

Execution of the generous gift proved tricky. When Littauer pledged the money in 1934, five long years into the Depression, both client and attorney expected the economy to turn around soon. Instead the nation's economic misery dragged on, and the value of Littauer's estate continued to plummet, severely complicating the making of the gift's final install-ment payment of $850,000, which was scheduled in 1937. Clark managed the delicate negotiations between his client, Littauer, and the Harvard Corporation, on which he served. It required every ounce of his skill and diplomacy to secure the remaining funds, as pledged, without the uni-versity or the Corporation's seeming ungrateful to the sensitive donor. Clark spoke to this point in a 1938 letter to Felix Frankfurter: "I think per-haps [Littauer] thinks Harvard has been rather businesslike in the mat-ter of extensions [of the final payment], but he does not quite take into account that Harvard made commitments both as to the building and sal-aries and program [for the new graduate school] on the faith that all the money surely would come in."[22]

The pledge was eventually fulfilled and Littauer's dream of a gradu-ate school for public administration at Harvard became a reality in 1937. Clark remained on the Littauer Foundation board to help direct its other charitable giving, frequently to worthy Jewish causes, and also helped his increasingly enfeebled client resolve some tricky estate claims from circling relatives after Flora's death.[23]

As Clark's legal and professional reputation continued to grow, he was increasingly sought for positions in government. A tempting exam-ple was a 1934 offer to join FDR's National Steel Labor Relations Board, a newly created three-member committee to mediate labor disputes, oversee voluntary arbitration of labor claims, and "maintain industrial peace with justice."[24] It was an important role during those volatile years of massive labor unrest—sit-down strikes, lock-ins, and violent clashes between workers and management, as grim economic times further frayed already-strained relations. Clark considered the offer seriously but in the end declined. His preference was still to work behind the scenes.

LeGrand Bouton Cannon, Grenville Clark's maternal grandfather and strongest early influence, circa 1880.

Grenville Clark as a small boy, circa 1885.

Clark with classmates at Pomfret School, Pomfret, Connecticut, 1895. Clark is front row, center, holding the "99" sign.

Clark with the Porcellian Club, Harvard, circa 1901. That's Clark in the back row, far right, using his index finger to make a point as he vigorously lectures another member.

Clark with Harvard classmates on Alpine peak, summer 1903. Clark, hatless, is at right with a rope knotted around his waist.

Clark, big game hunting, 1904. Family photo albums identify the location only as the Northwest.

Portrait of Clark as a young man, circa 1904.

Fanny on her wedding day, November 27, 1909.

Grenville and Fanny Clark as newlyweds, 1909.

Clark in uniform during World War I, circa 1917.

Clark at law firm desk, circa 1920.

Root, Clark office dinner at University Club of New York, 1921.

The first three Clark children, Mary D., Eleanor, and Grenville Jr., 1921. Eleanor, center, would succumb to meningitis just one month later.

Clark, recuperating at Kerhonkson, New York, 1926.

Clark, playing golf with daughter Louisa on Long Island, 1931.

Clark clowning on vacation at Ribault Club, Fort George Island, Florida (off Jacksonville), circa 1933.

(Above) Clark and FDR in audience at Harvard tercentenary, 1936.
(Below) Harvard Corporation board, 1945, front row, left to right: Dr. Roger I. Lee,
Clark, James B. Conant; back row, left to right: Paul Cabot, Charles A. Coolidge,
William L. Marbury, Henry L. Shattuck.

Clark at Dartmouth to receive honorary degree, 1953. Clark is fourth from the left in the back row, just behind President Eisenhower.

Clark, at right, with Earl Warren, left, and Felix Frankfurter, center, at Supreme Court, circa 1962.

Clark at home, 1963, while being interviewed by Mary Kersey Harvey.

Clark, right, arriving in Vermont to go duck hunting with John Dickey, November 1964.

Clark, mentoring students in Dartmouth's "A Better Chance" college prep program, 1964.

Clark, speaking at Dublin Conference, 1965.

CHAPTER 8

Taking on the President: Grenville Clark, Franklin Roosevelt, and the 1937 Court-Packing Battle

Although the families of Grenville Clark and Franklin Delano Roosevelt had been "friends for generations," as Clark once casually put it, their personal and professional relationship through the years was complicated. Generally cordial, frequently collegial, occasionally conspiratorial, Roosevelt and Clark had such utterly different personalities—and methods of operating—that a certain amount of tension between the two was probably inevitable. Clark captured his ambivalence about FDR in his contribution to a 1953 commemorative booklet for the fiftieth reunion of their Harvard class: "Although I was by no means a consistent follower of our eminent contemporary, [our close association as law clerks] led in later life to many exchanges of view during his 16 years as Governor and President."[1]

Frustration often marked the interactions of the two men, for both the congenitally straightforward Clark and his mercurial, equivocal, sometimes deliberately opaque, friend. FDR in most matters preferred to lead from behind, to let events unfold and see where public opinion ended up on a given issue, before announcing his own position. If Clark found this erratic, even inadequate, leadership, Roosevelt felt that Clark failed to give appropriate weight to political realities, something that, as an elected official, Roosevelt dared not do. FDR once snapped to an aide, "Grenny Clark . . . could not get elected to Congress in any district—North, South, East or West."[2]

In his later years Clark was asked about declining various offers to join FDR's administration. His response was a good summary of their relationship: "Yes, he asked me to become head of the National Labor Relations Board before the war . . . [and] once or twice said, 'Why don't you come on in with me? You can have almost anything you like and we will go along together.' [But] I used to say to FDR, in essence, 'I appreciate what you say, but disagree with you on so many things, and our approach is sometimes so different, that it would never work.'"[3] Still, the practically primordial ties between the two men remained largely intact, and they stayed in regular and cordial communication until their friendship struck an iceberg over an extraordinary, and extraordinarily divisive, issue.

In 1937 Clark and Roosevelt's relationship ruptured when Clark was unable to abide FDR's so-called court-packing plan. On the heels of his landslide reelection in 1936 Roosevelt attempted to circumvent a conservative, obstructionist bloc within the Supreme Court that was dismantling, piece by piece, his congressionally passed, publicly supported New Deal recovery programs. He proposed to enlarge the court from nine to fifteen justices, with the transparent goal of obtaining a favorable majority through new appointees more sympathetic to his agenda. The president did not frame his plan candidly, however, and claimed that the court was overworked and that it needed additional justices to help it stay abreast of its important duties. Clark was alarmed, even though he supported Roosevelt and much of the New Deal and agreed that the obstructionist court was a real problem. He was convinced that the president's plan was reckless and would set a dangerous precedent. Clark considered the court-packing fight a full-fledged constitutional emergency, and many scholars since have agreed. The incident itself, and the citizen action campaign Clark organized to meet it, merit a closer look.

FDR's proposed "reorganization of the judiciary"—forever after known as his court-packing plan—was announced on February 5, 1937, just weeks after Roosevelt's second inauguration. It came as a shock to virtually everyone, having been conceived in secrecy by its chief draftsman, FDR's attorney general, Homer Cummings, and the president. Although couched within a larger program to improve the efficiency of the entire judiciary, the plan was immediately recognized for what it was—a shot across the bow of the "Nine Old Men" on the Supreme Court.[4]

What motivated Roosevelt? The 1937 court could be considered remarkably hostile to his new programs. It is not unusual for the Supreme Court, with its lifetime appointees, to mirror the political landscape in which it was forged, sometimes long after the rest of the country has moved in a different direction. But this ultraconservative court, a product of the regulation-averse boom years of the 1920s, seemed out of touch with the country to an extreme. As just one example, it had repeatedly used the Fourteenth Amendment's "liberty of contract" clause to cancel such basic social protections as child labor laws and minimum wage provisions for impoverished working women. Harold Ickes, FDR's secretary of the interior, lashed out at the infamous decision to strike down New York's minimum wage laws in the 1923 case of *Adkins v. Children's Hospital:* "The sacred right of liberty of contract again—the right of an immature child or a helpless woman to drive a bargain with a great corporation. If this decision does not outrage the moral sense of the country then nothing will."[5]

Worse, this was the Fourteenth Amendment, originally written to secure full civil rights for former slaves, yet it had never once been applied on their behalf. Instead it was repeatedly and distortedly construed to protect corporations and exploitative employers.[6] Nor was this merely "differing opinions on economic philosophy," as some would make it out to be. It would be unimaginable for the 1937 court to have used the Fourteenth Amendment for its intended purpose. For example, Supreme Court Justice James C. McReynolds—FDR's cantankerous nemesis on the court who joined in the *Adkins* decision—was a notorious and unapologetic racist. His young law clerk in 1937, John Knox, received the following advice-cum-warning when McReynolds felt Knox was getting too friendly with McReynolds's African American servants:

I do feel this is the time to speak to you about one thing. I realize you are a Northerner who has never been reared or educated in the South, but I want you to know you are becoming much too friendly with Harry [McReynolds's valet]. You seem to forget he is a negro and you are a graduate of Harvard Law School. And yet for days now it has been obvious to me that you are, well, treating Harry and Mary [the maid] like equals. Really, a law clerk to a Justice of the Supreme Court of the United States should have some feeling about his position and not wish to associate with colored servants the way you are doing. Of course you are not a Southerner, so maybe it's expecting too much of someone from Chicago to act like a Southerner, but I do wish you would think of my wishes in this matter in your future relations with darkies.[7]

Against this racially and politically charged backdrop, the president's bill proposed to dynamite the court's conservative roadblock by having Congress authorize the president to appoint as many as six additional justices, one for each sitting justice who was older than seventy, had served at least ten years on the court, and had not yet announced retirement. Conveniently this included FDR's most steadfast opponents on the bench, the staunchly conservative Four Horsemen: Justices George Sutherland, seventy-five; Pierce Butler, seventy-one; Willis J. Van Devanter, seventy-eight; and James C. McReynolds, seventy-five. Inconveniently it also included the court's liberal lion, Louis D. Brandeis, the oldest member of the court at eighty-one, and Chief Justice Charles Evans Hughes, a moderate who was seventy-five. The remaining justices included the other two progressives: Benjamin J. Cardozo, sixty-six, and Harlan Fiske Stone, sixty-four. The youngest justice, Owen Roberts, sixty-one, was the crucial swing vote.

A lifelong student of American government, Grenville Clark understood that the president's plan to enlarge the court was not unconstitutional—the Constitution does not specify the number of Supreme Court justices, and it fluctuated several times in America's early history. (Because the document did not specify the number of justices, Congress determines how many should sit on the court; the number of justices has remained at nine since 1868.)[8] The fatal flaw of Roosevelt's plan was its inherent deception. Because he chose not to address directly the true problem of the ideological, reactionary justices, FDR appeared to be making a naked power grab, disingenuously blaming justices' age for a largely imaginary judicial backlog. Roosevelt's claim that the justices were too old to keep up with their workload, and that he was merely adding a younger, fresher justice for each older, overburdened one, rang false. When Chief Justice Hughes delivered a rare public statement that the court was not now, and had not in recent memory been, behind on its docket, the administration was forced to admit it had made a mistake and abandon that line of argument.

Despite the president's presumed mandate from his overwhelming 1936 election victory and huge Democratic majorities in both houses of Congress, opposition to his court-packing plan quickly emerged on several fronts. His previously solid support among fellow Democrats in Congress showed immediate cracks, particularly among southern moderates and fiscal conservatives who were increasingly uncomfortable with the dizzying pace of FDR's reform legislation, the heavy debt financing of the new programs, and the growing concentration of power in the White House. The president also strained his formerly warm relations with some of his strongest supporters in labor and agriculture by not consulting leaders of those powerful groups before making his startling public announcement. He encountered strong opposition from the right, naturally, including former president Hoover and conservative business groups that were as hostile to the plan as they were to virtually everything FDR did.[9]

Opposition from the Supreme Court itself came in the form of a crafty move. Justice Owen Roberts, who had been the crucial fifth vote striking down FDR's early New Deal legislation, suddenly, silently, switched sides in the midst of the controversy. ("The switch in time that saved nine" went the inevitable quip.) With not a word about court packing, Roberts began voting with the liberal and moderate bloc in support of New Deal programs, tipping the court's rulings in the administration's favor on legislation remarkably similar to that which he had formerly voted against. (Most famous was the 1936 case *Tipaldo v. Morehead*, the decision that reversed *Adkins* on state minimum wage law; it was followed by a domino-like series of others.) Justice Roberts's unexplained reversal effectively removed the rationale for the president's bold solution by apparently eliminating the problem.[10]

Despite these layers of opposition, defeat of Roosevelt's plan was anything but assured. The president was enormously popular, politically skillful, and the real pain being inflicted by the Depression lent sympathy to his goal, if not his method. Perhaps no one was more alert to the complexity of the challenge than FDR's old friend Grenville Clark. Clark's role in the court fight is largely absent from the public record, mainly the result of his deliberately discreet modus operandi. But lack of coverage does not equal lack of impact.

When news of the president's court-packing plan broke in February, Clark went to work. He contacted Charles "CCB" Burlingham, the New York lawyer who was his friend and coagitator for judicial independence in the Empire State for more than a decade. Since the late 1920s the pair had been taking on New York's entrenched patronage system for selecting judges, first with then-governor Franklin Roosevelt and later with his successor, Herbert Lehman. Now the stakes were much higher, and Clark and CCB would be squaring off against the president of the United States. But the core issue was unchanged: judicial independence had to be protected. Clark and CCB created the National Committee for Independent Courts; CCB agreed to serve as committee chair.

Clark and CCB soon recruited 250 lawyers, business leaders, journalists, academics, and other men from around the country who also opposed the president's plan. An important feature of the committee was that membership was limited to those who had actually voted for Roosevelt, even though filling the group with hostile anti-FDR conservatives would have been easy. The absence of a partisan attack argument cut the legs off White House opposition at the outset. This shrewd suggestion came from a Republican ally, Senator Arthur Vandenberg of Michigan, who pointed out that "the greatest handicap for the proponents of the President's Supreme Court scheme, at the moment, is their lack of a 'Liberty League' [a vitriolic splinter group of conservative Democrats opposed to the New Deal] at which to shoot. We must see to it no such target is provided."[11]

Strategic recruiting and other tactical maneuvers notwithstanding,

Clark and his fellow committee members were fervent about protecting judicial independence. Most were lawyers, and they took the ideal of a nation of laws personally. At stake for these men was nothing less than preserving America's independent judiciary—the cornerstone of democracy. A member from Texas wrote: "By environment, temperament and heredity, I am a Constitutionalist of the straightest sect, and my humiliation is deepened when I observe so many of the Southern Senators extending their support to a measure which would undermine the only citadel of protection the South possessed in the long night of Reconstruction."[12]

Clark reached even further back than Reconstruction. He cited examples from English common law in 1616, when Sir Edward Coke stood up against King James I's heavy-handed efforts to influence England's highest court. (Coke, chief justice of the King's Bench, refused the king's imperial request to delay a hearing so that he could personally speak to the judges before the case was decided. Coke was promptly dismissed for insubordination and has been a heroic figure for judicial independence ever since.) Clark and CCB repeatedly cited Coke and other historic examples to emphasize how important, hard fought, and carefully and deliberately established was the constitutional safeguard of an independent judiciary. Committee members wrote, spoke, and lobbied with real passion that no immediate goal, no matter how sincere, was worth fissuring this democratic bedrock.

Equally dangerous were unanticipated future consequences of taking liberties with the Constitution. The members made it clear they were in no way anti-Roosevelt. By definition they had all voted for him. (Committee stationery, business cards, and literature restated the membership criteria: "A Committee of Citizens, All of Whom Favored the President's Election in 1936, and All of Whom Are Opposed to the President's Supreme Court Proposal.") In an early radio address Burlingham noted with zero malice that the president himself would be "the last man to claim that he is a great lawyer." FDR had set his sights on politics from his earliest days as a law clerk, as he had freely shared with Clark back in 1906. Giving the president an out, Burlingham suggested that FDR's attorney general, Homer Cummings, who drafted the court-packing plan, had "led [the president] into a shabby enterprise." The problem was the precedent: "I am not one of those who imagine that the President is reaching for more power to make himself a dictator. This is absurd and unthinkable. But President Roosevelt is not the last President of the United States; there will be others."[13]

Although Clark and Burlingham had been actively opposing the president's plan since its announcement in February, the first official meeting of their National Committee for Independent Courts was held May

21–22, 1937. The early core group of members from around the country gathered at the Mayflower Hotel in Washington, D.C., for a two-day session with Clark presiding. Also attending were several key senators, including Democrat Burton K. Wheeler of Montana, who would later receive much credit for defeating the president's plan.

On the first night Wheeler arrived at the Mayflower "in a blue funk," worried that the president's support was just too strong and it might be impossible to prevail against him.[14] Gradually Clark and CCB's infectious optimism, and the obvious determination of the gathered group to carry the fight, bucked Wheeler up. He briefed the brand-new committee on the court-packing plan's shaky majority support in Congress and emphasized that their assistance in lobbying individual members of Congress and maintaining public pressure through their personal, professional, and media contacts would be crucial. The men pledged their full support and mapped out a strategy. They divided the country by its nine federal judicial districts and assigned a local lieutenant to spearhead recruiting in each. They agreed to three stated goals:

- To defeat the president's proposed court-packing plan and any watered down substitutes
- To explore a constitutional amendment as the proper way to resolve the agreed-upon serious problem of an ideologically rigid and obstructionist court
- To launch a nationwide education campaign for the general public on the importance of an independent judiciary[15]

The meeting concluded, and the committee members went home to their respective districts. From there they worked their various spheres of influence through an aggressive campaign of personal visits, letter writing, and phone calling. Grenville Clark, for one, knew how to work a telephone; at one point in the 1950s his monthly phone bill was more than $1,000.[16]

Committee members also gave speeches to business groups, civic groups, women's groups, and virtually every organization that would provide a stage. The members worked through local and national media connections to encourage, write, and guide anti-court-packing editorials and opinion pieces in newspapers, magazines, and on community bulletin boards. They also made radio addresses, after FDR's enormously popular fireside chats had cemented radio as an effective public medium.

In Washington Clark established a command center at the Shoreham Hotel, led by the able Root, Clark associate Cloyd Laporte. The committee's young lawyers in Washington worked with cohorts from the American Bar Association to maintain a near-constant presence on Capitol Hill. They attended the daily hearings the Senate Judiciary Committee held on the court-packing bill. They took detailed notes on the testimony of each witness and combed them each evening for inconsistencies, omissions, or falsehoods. They researched and wrote up succinct summaries of relevant historical and legal background and provided them to Judiciary Committee members the following morning to use for follow-up questions and cross-examination.

FDR responded to the opposition mostly by ignoring, stonewalling, and using parliamentary tactics, such as having his skillful Majority Leader declare a lengthened "legislative day" during Senate hearings to limit debate. (By the rules of the Senate, senators are limited to speaking twice on one subject in a single day, which is usually the same as a calendar day. If the Senate leader recesses rather than adjourns when members break for the night, the legislative day can run indefinitely, limiting opponents' chances to speak.)

The strategy was clever, but Clark's committee had a few tricks of its own. Committee staffers and young ABA lawyers prepared dozens of amendments to the court bill, some obviously and deliberately trivial (e.g., in the section of the bill that limited the enlargement of the court to fifteen: "Strike out the word 'fifteen' and insert in lieu thereof 'fourteen.'" Next amendment: "Strike out the word 'fifteen' and insert in lieu thereof the word 'thirteen,'" and so on). Frivolous or not, by Senate rules each new proposed amendment formally introduces a new subject to reopen debate, thereby allowing each senator two more chances to speak. Clark's staff was coached in this controversial art of the filibuster by the long-serving and anti-court-packing senator Josiah Bailey, a Democrat from North Carolina.[17]

In late June the administration presented a watered-down substitute bill, the Logan-Hatch Amendment, to break the growing impasse. Its only substantive difference from the original bill was that the new justices would be added over two years instead of all at once. Laporte called it "a fraud, but it fooled some people, including three [crucial] senators."[18] Laporte was assigned to write up a detailed brief exposing the subterfuge. That brief would be instrumental in convincing the Senate to reject the amendment.

While Congress successfully mired the court-packing bill in parliamentary gamesmanship, the president mounted a charm offensive, to which he was particularly well suited. In a typically surprising and engaging move, Roosevelt invited all his Democratic friends (on both sides of the issue) to a leisurely three-day picnic, June 25, 26, and 27, at the Jefferson Islands Club on Chesapeake Bay. Vintage newsreel footage shows smiling members of Congress in shirtsleeves, playing baseball, laughing with FDR under a tree, and strolling down a pier. The president hosted 150 guests each day, including Democrats from both houses of Congress, cabinet members, and reportedly even a Supreme Court justice or two. The island resort was just fifty miles from Washington, but the relaxed atmosphere—water views, good food, cold beer, a well-stocked bar, and a relaxed and congenial FDR holding court in the shade of an old mulberry tree—achieved at least temporary harmony. The clever Roosevelt never mentioned politics and engaged in no overt arm twisting on the court bill; his guests found just a genial host telling stories, asking about families, and recalling funny anecdotes from previous times together.[19]

Revealing a darker side of the famously multifaceted FDR, Roosevelt's cohorts back in Washington worked all summer on strong-arm tactics to use against the opposition, including Grenville Clark. Roosevelt felt threatened enough by the Committee for Independent Courts (ostensibly headed by CCB, but the president understood who was its driving force) to launch a heavy-handed investigation into the personal finances of Grenville Clark and a handful of other influential opponents of the court-packing plan. The men were accused of creating illegal tax shelters through complex estate-planning vehicles and thereby robbing the Treasury of tax income. It was the president's strongest salvo yet at what he dubbed the "economic royalists" who opposed him. FDR worked in concert with his loyal Treasury secretary, Henry Morgenthau, who relished the chance to increase government tax revenues and embarrass the president's opponents at the same time. While the court fight was surely not the sole motivation for the probe and resulting tightening of tax laws for the wealthy, it was without question a major factor, and its timing was no coincidence.

Roosevelt had sent CCB a note hinting of his intentions on May 27. The thinly veiled warning was clearly intended to be passed along to their mutual friend Grenville Clark: "Under your hat, within a few weeks quite a storm is going to break over the heads of individuals who have been cheating their own government. Watch and see how many lawyers condemn them and how many lawyers condone them."[20] On July 2, just a week after the convivial Jefferson Island picnic, the promised storm broke in the *New York Times*. Clark's name led the (not-alphabetical) list of seven accused tax evaders: "GRENVILLE CLARK, member of the New York law firm Root, Clark, Buckner, and Ballantine. Credited by the Treasury official with sixteen trusts, arranged jointly with his wife for members of the family, the proceeds of some of which could be used to pay the insurance premiums and through all of which Mr. Clark was credited with a tax savings of $90,000 in one year."[21]

Among the problems with the president's public humiliation strategy was that it was illegal. Federal income tax law prohibits the release of private financial information that citizens provide in confidence to the IRS. Two top Internal Revenue lawyers resigned in protest and issued a terse press release: "Assistant Chief Counsel Russell J. Ryan and myself were unable to convince ourselves that it was proper to use the Bureau of Internal Revenue as planned in the tax avoidance and evasion investigation. Being given the choice of participating in the presentation of names or of resigning we tendered our resignations. . . . [Signed] Chief Counsel Morrison Shaforth."[22]

In contrast Clark's financial planning, while sophisticated, was scrupulously legal. A meticulous individual, Clark had cofounded the Fiduciary Trust Company years before solely to manage the financial affairs of its small roster of wealthy clients, including the Clark family. In 1931, the final year of the Hoover administration, Fiduciary's stakeholders anticipated the incoming Democratic administration's stepped-up taxation of inherited wealth. To buffer their families Clark and his friends created, and Congress approved, the generation-skipping trust, in which money can be passed down for three generations before inheritance tax comes due. The widely used estate-planning vehicle was legal then and remains legal now.[23]

With a continued absence of subtlety the administration also investigated the finances of Senator Burton K. Wheeler—the chief opponent of the president's plan in Congress. An outraged Wheeler wrote to Treasury Secretary Morgenthau: "Are you checking up on the income tax of any other member of the Senate?"[24] The final blow came when the investigation inadvertently ensnared Eleanor Roosevelt as the subject of potential tax impropriety stemming from her newspaper and radio earnings. Her activities were as innocuous as Clark's, with all her proceeds donated to charity, but the publicity was no less embarrassing. The scare tactic had backfired—the investigation fizzled and eventually was quietly dropped. The epitaph appeared in the *New York Times* on July 16, 1937, with quotation marks making an editorial statement: "EVADERS" OF TAXES NOT TO BE CALLED.

It was a week of big headlines: Just two days earlier, on July 14, a relentless heat wave, combined with a superhuman job assignment, was widely blamed for the death of FDR's congressional point man for the court plan, the popular Senate Majority Leader from Arkansas, Joe Robinson. A career politician (five-term member of the House, four-term senator, and governor of Arkansas in between), Robinson was a fiercely loyal Democrat and notorious workaholic. He suffered a massive heart attack and died in his Washington apartment; the next morning a staffer discovered Robinson's lifeless body next to his bed. Robinson had spent his grueling final weeks attempting to save the president's controversial plan with some success.[25] His death changed the court-packing equation significantly.

A special train was arranged to transport Robinson's many friends and colleagues from Washington to Little Rock for his funeral services. The day before Robinson's funeral Senator Edward Burke of Nebraska, the leading opponent of the court-packing scheme in Congress, read Cloyd Laporte's legal brief unmasking the disingenuous Logan-Hatch compromise bill. Burke asked Laporte if he could get enough copies to distribute the brief to all the members of Congress who would be aboard Robinson's funeral train the following morning. This was no small feat in the days before photocopiers, but Laporte provided the copies. He took quiet satisfaction that the Logan-Hatch bill was permanently shelved shortly thereafter.[26]

On Thursday, July 22, 1937, the president's court-packing plan was formally defeated, or, as the court-packing scholar William Leuchten- burg puts it, "unceremoniously returned to committee from which it never emerged." The vote was a resounding 70–20; the entire episode took 168 days. The leader of the plan's most quietly influential opposition group was at that moment on a North Cape Arctic cruise with his fam- ily. At a port stop in Leningrad, Grenville Clark was handed a telegram from his agent in Washington that said it all: FINISH TRIP—COURT PACKING KILLED FOR THIS SESSION. LAPORTE.[27]

There are varying interpretations of the importance of the court- packing controversy. Some say FDR lost the battle but won the war, as the court began ruling in favor of New Deal legislation and the obstruction- ist justices retired and died. During his unprecedented four terms Roos- evelt ultimately appointed nine justices—more than any other president in history.[28] Other court scholars hold that the incident was an unfortu- nate and needless scar on Roosevelt's legacy. With the laissez-faire era fading the president may well have had no need to suffer such a deci- sive public defeat. Handled better or even waited out, the problem likely would have resolved itself. In addition, the court battle deeply divided the Democratic Party, caused new fissures among previously united reformers, and undermined bipartisan support for the New Deal. It was also a significant distraction to FDR's conduct of foreign affairs as Amer- ican involvement in World War II loomed.[29] Other scholars feel that FDR emerged unscathed but only barely.

Most historians and court watchers agree the results were mixed. FDR did emerge with a more cooperative court, his remaining time in office was free from judicial meddling, and in ultimately appointing nine new justices he did leave an indelible mark on the court. Yet with this freedom came the loss of any pretense of control over anything resembling a unified Democratic Party. Wheeler in particular became a bitter opponent of Roosevelt's efforts to aid Britain and France before Pearl Harbor. The court scholar Leonard Baker credits the cross-party alliances forged by southern Democrats and midwestern Republicans during the bitter fight as the beginning of the conservative coalition that would ultimately block civil rights bills after World War II as well as any further expansion of the New Deal.[30]

Clark described the effect of the fight on his personal relationship with Roosevelt as "a breach in our relations not restored until 1940." That breach came at an especially dear cost to Clark, even though he had technically won. His early memoir collaborator, Sam Spencer, points out that it was a particularly courageous act for Clark to not only publicly oppose his longtime friend, who also happened to be president, but to do so surely knowing it would eliminate any possibility of being appointed to the Supreme Court. For all the public appointments Clark almost routinely turned down, serving as a justice on the nation's highest bench—a lifetime assignment to full-time thoughtful, intellectual consideration of weighty constitutional matters in a (theoretically) apolitical, nonpartisan environment—may have been the one government appointment he would have truly relished. It would have allowed Clark "the freedom of spirit and mind so essential to him," and in turn "his mental acuity and high competence, his gift for analysis, and his sensitivity to social needs would have made him a great justice," Spencer writes.[31]

In stark contrast Felix Frankfurter, then a Harvard Law School professor who was close to both Clark and FDR, maintained a deafening public silence on the court-packing issue although both Clark and CCB strongly urged Frankfurter to speak out. Eighteen months later Frankfurter was seated on the Supreme Court. Letters exchanged by Clark and Frankfurter one month into the court battle underscore the heated differences between the two friends in the matter. Clark wrote first, on March 4, 1937, after an apparently unsatisfactory conversation:

Dear Felix:

It really bothers me that you do not publicly express your views about the Supreme Court, whatever they are. Whatever one's opinions are, it cannot be denied that the question that has been raised is of fundamental importance. Accordingly, on such a question it is no more than normal and natural that people should expect those who are competent to speak on the subject to express their ideas. This is, of course, preeminently applicable to yourself because you have written and talked about the Court for many years with the obvious and necessary result that thousands of people assume that you must have views on the subject that would be interesting and valuable.

Thinking over what you said, I am not satisfied, to be frank, that the reasons you give for not making a statement will hold water. I don't really know what your views on the subject are but I think that is entirely immaterial as bearing on the question whether you ought to express [them].

I rather surmise that if you will put yourself through another course of self-examination, you would find yourself saying that on balance you favor the proposal. I know you must think there are some horrid things about it and that it contains great dangers, and yet, as between being for it or against it on balance I think you would probably say the latter. If this be so, I have a strong opinion you would be wrong. However I say again this is immaterial. The only real point is that, as one of the few people in the country who is known to have considered the problem of the Supreme Court and the Constitution for years past, it is really up to you to let the public, or those of them who are interested in your views, know what you think of this plan.

If I am wrong, show me! . . . The thing that is really not understandable to the average man is why, at a time like this when everyone is seeking light, you of all others should remain silent.

Yours as always, GC[32]

Frankfurter's response was immediate and typically elaborate. His most impassioned argument—that any statement he made would be misconstrued because he was Jewish—sounds a bit defensive until one remembers how rampant anti-Semitism still was in the 1930s. In the words of one historian: "People forget that in those days Jews were treated little better than Blacks," with unchallenged discrimination still widespread in hiring, housing, country club membership, and even lodging at hotels and resorts.[33] Still, history would reveal that anti-Semitism was in this case a red herring:

Dear Grenny:

Candor about delicate themes is one of the essential attributes of friendship, and yet how rarely it is exercised. And so I value very deeply the plain speech of your letter of the fourth as one more manifestation of a friendship that is very precious to me.

I wish we could have the wide berth for exchange of views on a difficult subject that only talk affords. Letters, in these hurried days, are very inadequate means for the exchange of intimate views. . . . I think to put it bluntly you are inadequate of your analysis of the situation in which I find myself in reference to the Court debate, precisely because you have left out very important considerations, and have judged the matter too much from the thing on which you are concentrating, the achievement or defeat of the President's proposal. I would do the same if I were in the arena but I am not and I have the pressure of responsibilities which are not yours, and still less those of the members of the New York Bar who are so het up as to think that the welfare of the country is at stake. Let me put it to you as briefly as I can, the reasons that move me to be silent. . . .

Fundamentally, because through circumstances in the making of which I have had no share, I have become a myth, a symbol of the Jew, the "red," the "alien." In that murky and passionate atmosphere anything that I say can be enveloped. I would be heard and interpreted by what you call the average man—the reader of the Hearst papers, the Chicago Tribune, the Legion, the D.A.R's, the chambers of commerce, I am sorry to say the "leading" members of the bar all over the place, the readers of Time, the Saturday Evening Post, etc., etc., etc., not as a man who by virtue of long years of service in the government and his special attention to the problems of constitutional law and the work of the Court spoke with the authority of scholarship, but as the Jew, the "red," and the "alien." Instead of bringing light and calm and reason, what I would be compelled to say about the work of the Court—and it is the only subject in this debate on which I can speak with a scholar's authority—would only fan the flames of ignorance, of misrepresentation, and of passion. . . .

A quiet, rustic place like Cambridge off on the siding has its disadvantages, but on the other hand, there are also some gains in the opportunities it affords for detachment. I think if you were up here and we had another long, quiet talk about it all, and you were not in the enveloping atmosphere of New York's passionate activism on the subject, you would, I am sure, at least acknowledge that a man might reasonably reach the conclusion I have reached, even though, were you in my shoes, you might act differently.

Ever yours, FF[34]

Roosevelt appointed Frankfurter to the Supreme Court in January 1939, upon the death of Justice Benjamin Cardozo. Although it is excessive to suggest a direct cause-and-effect relationship between Frankfurter's silence on court packing and his later appointment, it is impossible to imagine no connection existed. In fact private papers released after all the major parties had died confirm that Frankfurter, despite his protestations to Clark, Burlingham, and others, was not merely remaining silent but was all along secretly and actively encouraging and advising the president in favor of his court-packing proposal.[35]

As for the country, Clark's able assistant Cloyd Laporte noted: "There is still that hole in the Constitution which does not specify the number of justices . . . [but] the idea of permitting the president and Congress to use it to seize control of the third branch of the government received a telling blow in the rejection by Congress of this effort, now of evil memory."[36] For Clark as an individual, as with FDR, the court-packing incident becomes a near-footnote on a weighty resume. And the Clark-FDR relationship? It would eventually recover, and the two would be back to active collaboration well before the president's untimely death in 1945. Still, for the rest of his life Clark counted among his most important activities the 1937 crusade to keep America's court system free and independent.

CHAPTER 9

Defending Rabble-Rousers

Although the U.S. Supreme Court was safe from presidential meddling, at least for the time being, Clark still worried that Americans were "losing the feel" for their civil rights. He decided to continue the public education campaign the court fight had begun, writing, "The recent nation-wide discussion of the Supreme Court issue was not only educational in a high degree in respect to our frame of government, but also in respect to our civil rights; for hundreds of thousands were led to inquire into and perceive the relation between independent courts and the security of their civil rights."[1]

Clark knew that in order for people to protect their rights, they had to first understand them. The core freedoms enshrined in the Bill of Rights were (and are) so intrinsic to American life that few citizens could name them all, let alone define them beyond the bumper-sticker level. Determined to elevate a discussion commonly reduced to campaign slogans and election-year propaganda, Clark wrote detailed articles and pamphlets about the history, effect, and intricacies of Americans' civil liberties and the need to actively protect them. He spoke directly to the intelligentsia with "Court Help or Self Help?" which was published in the *Annals of the American Academy of Political and Social Science* in January 1938. His message was vintage Grandfather Cannon: Citizens must jealously guard their constitutional freedoms and not blindly trust in government or the courts to protect their rights. The article led to a series of six lectures at the New School for Social Science Research in New York City. They were well received. The noted journalist Walter Lippmann wrote, "Dear Grennie, I have just read your address on civil liberties with the greatest admiration and agreement. It is most exhilarating to see the whole problem put on such a high plane. My warmest congratulations. Walter." Theodore Roosevelt Jr., Clark's old friend and Plattsburg comrade-at-arms, now an executive at Doubleday, also approved:

Dear Grennie:

I thought [your lectures] were excellent.

What you voice is what I have fought for . . . when I condemned Franklin's action on the Supreme Court. Moreover there isn't a doubt but that this country is in grave danger of losing its civil liberties and representative democracy.

I don't know whether the danger is greatest from left or right—it makes no difference, because if you go far enough to the left, as witnessed by Communism in Russia, or far enough to the right, as exemplified by Fascism in Italy, governmentally you will reach exactly the same position—Civil liberty and representative democracy are dead and a tyranny or an autocracy has taken their place.

Best wishes, TR Jr.[2]

Clark also directed his message to other attorneys. He gave a ringing speech, "Conservatism and Civil Liberties," to his local Nassau County Bar Association on Long Island. It was reprinted in the nationally distributed *American Bar Association Journal* in August 1938. He opened by pointing out that the defense of Americans' essential rights had been "allowed to drift into the hands of the left" and that "Bar Associations ought to take up the question." He then took his fellow conservatives to task for being more interested in defending property rights than "the great rights guaranteed by the First Amendment, including freedom of speech, of assembly, and of petition." Calling "a little intolerance . . . as dangerous to the [political] body as a little potassium cyanide in the human body," he asserted, "it is nothing to be played with and . . . the sole security for the civil liberties of *any* of us is dependent on the firm defense of the civil liberties of *all* of us." Clark closed strong: "[There] is only one sound attitude for conservatives consistent with a real understanding of the essence of American life, namely, an attitude of firm and impartial defense of the rights of the citizen under the Bill of Rights in every case where these rights are threatened and irrespective of whether we approve or disapprove of the sentiments and policies of the persons affected."[3]

Arthur T. Vanderbilt, the outgoing president of the American Bar Association (and later chief justice of the New Jersey Supreme Court), read a transcript of Clark's speech in the *New York Times*. He immediately phoned Clark to say he had been thinking along those same lines himself and wanted to hear more. He scheduled a meeting with Clark and the incoming ABA president, Frank Hogan. After the meeting Hogan authorized a new committee of the national bar to take up the matter; Grenville

Clark was his natural choice to chair it. Clark wrote to Charles Burlingham about being more or less trapped into compliance: "Since I agitated on the subject I didn't feel in a good moral position to refuse so there I am with that on my hands."[4]

The project now on Clark's hands was quite a departure for the then-conservative American Bar Association. The new committee was named the Committee of the American Bar Association to Protect Civil Liberties Vouchsafed by the Bill of Rights, usually and understandably shortened to the Bill of Rights Committee. Clark carefully handpicked the initial membership. He first tapped fresh talent from the Root, Clark pool of associates, Cloyd Laporte and Louis Lusky. Clark also recruited established lawyers from around the country, including Douglas Arant of Alabama. Arant had worked closely with Clark during the court-packing battle and would take over as committee chair when Clark stepped down in 1940. Only one of the twelve members was not Clark's personal choice: John Francis Nylan, a prominent San Francisco attorney who represented the powerful conservative Hearst news conglomerate and had been recommended by Frank Hogan. Clark acquiesced but soon regretted it. He later recalled: "I mistakenly agreed to . . . [include] Nylan who was a dogmatic Catholic entirely out of time with the committee's purpose, made us a lot of trouble and was the sole dissenter on several of our most important decisions."[5]

The friction with Nylan illustrates one of Clark's more marked tendencies: to almost exclusively choose as collaborators for his various projects those who strongly shared his ideas and goals. The pros and cons of such like-minded associates are open for debate—synergy versus groupthink, for example—but they undeniably produced results. And Clark's range of associates and collaborators did grow increasingly diverse throughout his life. One supporter who was decidedly not like-minded was the outspoken left-wing journalist I. F. Stone. Almost in spite of himself "Izzy" Stone came to admire the establishment-born and -bred Clark, calling him "a maverick of the noblest type." Stone slyly saluted "GC" in an irreverent memorial tribute: "Grenville Clark overcame a handicap worse than poverty. He was born into the highest circles of wealth and social position. [In 1938] he performed the miracle of getting the overstuffed American Bar Association to create a Bill of Rights Committee. He used it to defend the liberties of the CIO, then still a struggling labor movement, and to help block the deportation of Harry Bridges as a dangerous Red. It took moral stamina of a high order for a man of Clark's upper class connections to do battle for such disreputables."[6]

The Bill of Rights Committee's stated purpose was to "aid in the elucidation of close constitutional issues in this difficult and controversial field" of civil rights as guaranteed by the Constitution.[7] Its primary arena was the Supreme Court, where the committee weighed in on civil rights cases involving "constitutional issues of national consequence and permanent importance" with amicus curiae, or friend of the court, briefs.

The gambit, now fairly common, was unusual at the time. Roger Baldwin, a contemporary of Clark's at Harvard who would go on to lead the American Civil Liberties Union, remembered: "In 1938 . . . Grenville Clark promptly got his new committee to file *amicus* briefs, then an unheard of procedure. Such was his prestige he could swing it. I marveled at it then and told him so, [while] expressing my doubts about continued [ABA] support [for civil liberties] if he withdrew."[8] Unfortunately Baldwin proved correct: the committee withered after Clark left it for pressing duty just before World War II. But while he remained its chair, it was a force. It filed its two most famous Supreme Court briefs in important civil rights cases: *Hague v. CIO* (1939), and *Minersville School District v. Gobitis* (1940). Each warrants a summary review.

Hague v. CIO involved the colorful Jersey City mayor "Boss" Frank Hague, who was preventing what he considered subversive or otherwise radical groups from using parks and other public places in his city. When a new labor union then called the Committee for Industrial Organization (CIO) planned to hold a meeting in a Jersey City park, Hague invoked an obscure antilittering ordinance to deny the group a police permit. He prevented CIO members from distributing pamphlets explaining the rights of citizens to collective bargaining under the National Labor Relations Act and had Norman Thomas, the Socialist Party presidential candidate who was going to speak at the CIO event, literally run out of town. The American Civil Liberties Union thereupon accused Hague of denying the free speech of CIO members and their use of a public facility. Hague retorted that a city controlled the use of its public places.

Against prevailing public opinion, with national passions inflamed by the perceived spread of communism, Clark's Bill of Rights Committee filed a stirring amicus brief insisting that free speech and assembly in public spaces are fundamental constitutionally guaranteed rights not subject to the whim of local politicians. The Supreme Court ruled in favor of the CIO, concluding, in accordance with Clark's arguments, that Mayor Hague had "deprived respondents of the privileges of free speech and peaceable assembly secured to them, as citizens of the United States, by the Fourteenth Amendment . . . and [he] could not deny the public access to tax-supported public facilities for assembly nor free speech."[9]

Minersville School District v. Gobitis (1940) involved a Jehovah's Witness family in Minersville, Pennsylvania, whose two children, Lillian and William Gobitis, then aged twelve and ten, respectively, refused to take part in the mandatory daily flag salute at their elementary school. According to the children's religion, saluting the flag was "bowing down before a graven image" and therefore prohibited by the Ten Command- ments. The Minersville School District insisted that it could compel all pupils to salute the flag and suspend them from school if they did not. The Gobitis children refused and were suspended indefinitely. Clark's committee argued against the school district's position, declaring that compulsory flag salutes are an unconstitutional infringement of religious liberty on three main grounds: Compulsory flag salute statutes override sincerely held religious beliefs; no sufficient public need exists to over- ride these religious scruples; and, the religious aspect aside, compulsory flag salutes are unconstitutional as an unjustifiable infringement on per- sonal liberty.

Although Clark was known for his slow, methodical approach, he and Zechariah Chaffee, a member of the committee, wrote the *Gobitis* brief in one intensive week at Clark's Long Island home. Chaffee was no ingénue—a Harvard professor who had written *Freedom of Speech,* con- sidered the gold standard for textbooks on First Amendment rights. One legal scholar called Chaffee "possibly the most important First Amend- ment scholar of the first half of the twentieth century." Both men consid- ered the *Gobitis* brief among the most important they ever produced.[10]

Despite their credentials and their zeal, Clark and Chaffee ended up on the losing side, at least initially. The Supreme Court ruled against the Gobitis family, 8–1, with the majority stingingly led by Clark's old friend Felix Frankfurter. Clark felt the decision was motivated by misplaced superpatriotism on the part of the immigrant Frankfurter and that the other justices had, sheep-like, followed his lead. To be fair the decision is best understood in the heightened context of the opening years of World War II, with Hitler's menace already on graphic display in Europe, even though the United States had not yet formally entered the war.

Frankfurter's opinion acknowledged as much: "National unity is the basis of national security. The flag is a symbol of our national unity, tran- scending all internal difference, no matter how large, within the frame- work of the Constitution. We live by symbols." Broadly establishing the lofty but vague national unity as his premise, Frankfurter switched into the narrow, precise language more typical of the Supreme Court to con- struct the body of his intricate decision. His reasoning was classic judi- cial restraint, a legal philosophy Frankfurter would hone and become increasingly identified with throughout his career. Judicial restraint emphasizes that the Supreme Court's role is not to determine the merits of a particular case—that is the function of the lower courts. The Supreme Court merely determines whether a contested lower court ruling is rea-

sonable within accepted interpretations and applications of the Constitution. Frankfurter, an early and active member of the ACLU, quickly
pointed out that he thought the Minersville School District *should* have
granted an exemption to the Gobitis children. But, since he found no constitutional principle that *required* such an exemption, the lower court's
ruling must stand.[11]

Clark was not impressed. He saw the elaborate opinion, of which
Frankfurter was quite proud, as a legalistic cover-up for a wrongheaded
national security goal. To Clark it ignored or deliberately circumvented a
clear violation of the Gobitis family's civil liberties as guaranteed by the
Bill of Rights. In a delayed but de facto victory for Clark, Chaffee, and the
Bill of Rights Committee, the court reversed itself less than three years
later. Clark's misgivings about Frankfurter's illiberal rulings in the civil
rights arena remained strong. Years later, after Frankfurter had retired
from the court, Clark privately offered his theory about what may have
motivated his friend:

> As to F.F., I am certainly glad that he is off the Court, for I think
> he did a lot of damage in his last ten years or so—going back in
> its origin . . . to [the *Gobitis* case] in 1940. I think his underlying
> trouble has been lack of confidence in the country, making him
> ready to uphold repressive measures as against the individual
> . . . as in any way necessary or justifiable. And I surmise that
> this was mostly due to his foreign birth and consequent lack of
> background as to the country's capacity to permit radical dissent
> and agitation and still get on all right.[12]

Clark's Bill of Rights Committee also published the *Bill of Rights
Review,* a substantial publication underwritten by a grant from the Carnegie Foundation. Clark served as editor, publisher, and frequent con-
tributor to the *Review* for many years. The periodical drew praise for the
quality of its articles and its unique dedication to restoring the feel of
Americans' civil liberties, particularly those singled out for protection
in the First Amendment—freedom of speech, religion, press, assembly,
and the all-important right to petition the government for redress. Clark
pushed for all the state bar associations and some of the big city bar associations to form similar Bill of Rights committees to reinforce the national
effort. Twenty-five or so did.[13]

In 1941, as U.S. involvement in World War II drew closer, Clark used
the Bill of Rights Committee as a platform to speak out against emergency encroachments on civil liberties in the name of national security.
Rejecting the perennial false choice between liberty and security in times

of crisis, Clark took on the popular prewar argument that the country "cannot organize [for defense] adequately without the permanent loss or great impairment of our liberties":

> Plainly this line of thought contains a destructive and sterile fallacy. It amounts to saying that a country of free institutions in a world where force is being employed on a vast scale is impotent to protect itself, and that the greater the force brought to bear against it, the more helpless a free country becomes to repel the threat. It means flatly that there is no alternative to the creation of necessary emergency powers and disciplines adequate to the situation except the permanent relinquishment of free institutions and individual liberties.
>
> We utterly deny the validity of any such alternative. We affirm the practicability of organizing the manpower, the industrial power and the moral power of our people in a way adequate to meet any threat from whatever source over as long a time as may be necessary to overcome that threat, without any permanent or essential sacrifice of constitutional liberties. A denial of this is not only a counsel of despair, it is also untrue as judged by the lessons of history.[14]

Grenville Clark was bitterly disappointed that the ABA's Bill of Rights Committee essentially died after he left it, with no appreciable lasting effect on the bar's disinclination to beat the drum for civil liberties. When Judge Henry Friendly formed an independent group to investigate the quasi-legal federal loyalty and security program in 1955, Clark did not mince words: "I think with surprisingly few exceptions that the legal profession has been much too timid and mealymouthed in the face of the long series of rank injustices which are even now going on; and that it is high time for the profession, through an independent group such as you have, to look into the whole subject very thoroughly."[15]

Even in his eighties Clark was still urging others to pick up the ball. He wrote to Irving Dilliard, legal scholar and writer for the *St. Louis Post-Dispatch*, in 1962: "As you know, the A.B.A. Committee [on the Bill of Rights] nominally survives, but, so far as I know, has become utterly inert. All the more reason, therefore, it seems to me for encouraging the state and local committees, if any still exist other than the New York one, to do something."[16] Still, Clark was justifiably proud of his work in instigating the Bill of Rights Committee and of its accomplishments in the early years under his direction. He left it only when his time became increasingly consumed by war preparedness efforts in 1940.

In a civil rights matter outside his ABA committee, Clark was approached in 1939 for the second time that decade by FDR's secretary of labor, Frances Perkins. This time Perkins sought Clark's help with the thorny Harry Bridges deportation case. Bridges, the Australian-born west coast leader of the International Longshoreman's and Warehouseman's Union, was an inflammatory figure who had powerful enemies in the steamship owners, the Daughters of the American Revolution, and conservatives in the press and in Congress, among others, because of his efforts to organize dock workers. Bridges gave incendiary speeches, distributed leftist propaganda, and led mass protests and labor strikes for higher pay and better working conditions for dock workers.

Perkins was under pressure from Congress to have Bridges deported as a dangerous alien who sought the overthrow of the United States by violence—grounds for deportation under existing immigration laws. Despite her deep personal distaste for Bridges and his provocative behavior, the conscientious labor secretary was not persuaded of either the validity of the charges or the appropriateness of the process (deportation without trial), sensing instead a campaign of expedience to boot out a rabble-rouser.[17]

Perkins asked Grenville Clark to serve as a special hearing officer to determine whether Bridges should be deported. Clark admired Perkins, and he shared her concern that Bridges's deportation under these circumstances would amount to a railroading of his civil liberties. Clark accepted the appointment but soon had to recuse himself upon learning that one of the plaintiffs, the American Hawaiian Steamship Company, was a client of his law firm. Clark did not abandon Perkins, however; he put her in touch with James Landis, dean of the Harvard Law School, whom Clark fully briefed on the case. As the special hearing officer, Landis conducted the hearings and found Bridges not deportable; Secretary Perkins affirmed Landis's findings. The case was then moved to the Justice Department and ultimately ended up at the Supreme Court, where Bridges was absolved. He became a naturalized U.S. citizen in 1951 and was a fervent supporter of the war effort; his longshoremen did not strike during World War II.[18]

While Clark was immersed in myriad professional and public service endeavors during the 1930s, his children were growing up. His oldest child, Mary Dwight "Mary D.", was off to Foxcroft prep school in the beautiful Virginia countryside, while Grenville Jr. prepped at Milton Academy outside Boston.

For the Clark family boarding schools did not mean banishment. While the children were away at school, their parents remained in close contact through regular visits, weekly (almost daily in some cases) letters, and steady communications with teachers and administrators. Grenville Clark arranged business trips to include stops at the children's various schools and wrote frequent and charming letters peppered with light news, fatherly advice, and upbeat encouragement as needed. Stationery and letterheads from business and government offices, clubrooms, and hotels around the world silently spoke to the full slate of duties he was temporarily putting aside to be a daddy. The outwardly buttoned-up Clark could be a true softie with his children. One especially touching letter offered encouragement to fifteen-year-old Mary D. during a difficult time at Foxcroft. Grenville Clark undoubtedly drew from his own memories of being a young boy far from home at Pomfret in the Connecticut countryside as he reassured his daughter:

> Dearest Mary D—We'll be fairly glad to see you home [for an upcoming break]; in fact I may hug you so hard as to squash you.
>
> Muz [Mother] showed me your letter that you were a bit discouraged. Well I don't make light of that but your troubles won't last forever or very long and there are some things to remember—the encouraging things when you feel down:
>
> 1. You're a fine, sweet girl and many people—the most discriminating ones—have recognized this, not just your adoring Pa and Ma.
>
> 2. You have an excellent head and good talents, for example your drawing shows great promise and will be a resource to you.
>
> 3. You haven't any capacity, I guess, for saying sharp things and defending yourself and probably feel helpless about slamming [verbal hazing] but I guess you inherit that from your Daddy and later on you won't regret it.
>
> 4. Miss Noland and your teachers think well of you—very well—and that means a lot.
>
> So if you feel down think of all the good things about yourself and remember that all will be well. Also say your prayers a little extra for God gives strength and cheerfulness to people who call for it. And also never forget your Daddy and Muz are right near and back of you always.
>
> Your loving Daddy[19]

CHAPTER 10

Preparedness Redux
The Draft, World War II,
War Department Service

Grenville Clark appropriately titled his private summary of 1939 to 1944 "Five Years of Crisis."[1] The global menace of the Second World War dominated those years for the Clark family, as for the world. When Germany conquered Norway in April 1940, the fifty-eight-year-old Grenville Clark was already juggling his busy law practice, the ABA Bill of Rights Committee, Harvard Corporation duties, plus personal and family obligations. But he was convinced that the United States could not avoid involvement in World War II, even though the U.S. government and citizens alike were again clinging to isolationism. With no small sense of déjà vu, he also saw clearly that, against Hitler's military machine, the small and alarmingly ill-equipped U.S. Army would face disaster in its present condition.

Isolationists had branded Clark an imperialist—and pacifists had called him a warmonger—during his Plattsburg effort. Then as now he was in fact motivated by his conviction that war was inevitable and that providing adequate manpower and proper training as soon as possible was a humane imperative for the soldiers. He was also not immune to the quiet dread felt by many that the future of democracy itself was in peril. If this seems too big a statement now, it perhaps was not then, with swastikas flying over Oslo and the seemingly unstoppable Nazis on their brutal march across Europe.

On May 8, 1940, just one day before German panzers would rain fire on Belgium and France, Grenville Clark launched a blitzkrieg of his own. In New York, at an otherwise routine luncheon with the old Plattsburg group at the Harvard Club, an impatient Clark cut short a dull discussion about planning the twenty-fifth anniversary celebration of their Military Training Camps Association. Were they not aware of the spreading emergency in Europe? Did they not recall their original mission, sparked by a similar threat twenty-five years before? Enough talk of parties and parades—was it not time once again to mobilize for action, to help prepare the country for a war that surely was coming, like it or not? Clark's challenge found a ready audience, and the luncheon marked the beginning of a relentless four-month campaign that culminated in an unprecedented U.S. peacetime draft.

Military historians have cited the resulting Selective Service Act of 1940 as "undoubtedly the most important of America's defense measures prior to Pearl Harbor."[2] Some years later Clark summarized how the frenzied four months unfolded:

> I proposed to some of the old Plattsburg group at a meeting on May 8, 1940 (after the conquest of Norway but before the big German attack in Belgium) that we advocate a peace-time selective service act. Everyone agreed and naturally appointed me to draft an act and try to get it introduced and passed.
>
> FDR was at first doubtful about supporting so unprecedented a measure, General [George] Marshall strongly opposed it upon the ground that it could not pass and would interfere with other plans of his, and [isolationist] Secretary [of War Harry] Woodring was strongly opposed to it. It was therefore most difficult to find good sponsorship in the two houses of Congress and I made up my mind that the thing to do was to get a new and strong Secretary of War.
>
> At that time, however, although I knew FDR well and had worked closely with him in 1933–1936, I was out of favor because of having opposed his court scheme in 1937. Therefore, I decided I needed a collaborator in the shape of Felix Frankfurter and put the proposition to him. He agreed and in late 1940 he and I met and made separate lists, on each of which was H. L. [Colonel Henry] Stimson's name. We soon agreed on him as our nominee, but also decided that FDR was unlikely to appoint him at his then age of seventy-three unless he had a much younger and very reliable Assistant Secretary. Therefore we made a second list on which I put Bob [Judge Robert P.] Patterson's name and we very soon agreed to the joint ticket, which within an hour FF took over to FDR.
>
> Then neither FF nor I heard anything for three weeks until on the evening of June 19, 1940 I had a phone call from Long Island from HLS [Stimson] to me at the Carlton Hotel where I was working to find the right sponsors for the introduction of the then completed draft of the Selective Service Act.

I well remember HLS's opening words which were, "Your preposterous plot has succeeded" and then he went on to say that FDR had just phoned him and asked him to be Secretary of War and when HLS replied that FDR evidently had not heard accurately of his four conditions, FDR replied, "Well, let's see," and, as HLS said, then repeated them "almost verbatim as I gave them to you three weeks ago."

FDR then said "the conditions are all accepted without qualification and I shall expect you at my office at ten o'clock tomorrow morning" and HLS then added to me, I remember, "and I shall expect to see you at my hotel at 9 o'clock."[3]

Clark's selective service effort followed his trademark process: identify a problem, round up a committee, make a detailed plan of attack, and then work that plan relentlessly through to completion. In this case completion meant convincing a highly skeptical U.S. Congress to pass the 1940 Selective Service Act, an enormously unpopular yet urgently needed national draft. Working with a dedicated group of Plattsburg alumni, Clark wrote the act and organized the National Emergency Committee (NEC) to advocate for its passage. Against long political odds he then led the NEC's exhaustive 120-day campaign to make the bill become law.

In 1940 the idea of a peacetime draft was all but heresy in the United States. The substantial public resistance to the Plattsburg camps just two decades earlier paled in comparison. The horrors of the Great War, and how quickly the brief peace that followed it was shattered, only reinforced the convictions of pacifists and isolationists. The last thing most Americans planned to stand for was having the country dragged into another bloody European conflict.

In her aptly titled book *Those Angry Days,* the author Lynne Olson chronicles the years between 1939 and 1941 and the fierce battle between the interventionist and isolationist camps about whether to enter World War II. The interventionists, who very much included Grenville Clark, were convinced that "America could no longer evade international responsibility: the times were too dire." The isolationists felt equally fervently that this was not America's fight. General George Marshall would later tell his biographer: "People have forgotten the great hostility of that time"; the young CBS correspondent Eric Sevareid described the period as bitter and heartburning. The historian Arthur Schlesinger summed it up as "the most savage political debate in my lifetime."[4]

Isolationists had been winning that debate since the end of World War I. One historian describes the 1920s postwar mood—when citizens and leaders alike "assailed the arms makers (the 'merchants of death'), starved their armed forces, adopted policies of strict neutrality in foreign affairs, and looked hopefully toward a future of lasting peace."[5] Clark and his friends were among a small minority urging caution against returning to prewar levels of unpreparedness. They were virtually ignored. In the 1930s preparedness took another hit, as the Depression ensured no money would be available for military spending or anything else. Soldiers' priority was being paid for the service they had already given (see Chapter 7's discussion of the veterans' Bonus March), not preparing for another war.

Fast-forward twenty years, and the alarming ease with which Hitler's Nazi machine was rolling over Europe made deadly clear that another global conflagration was under way. For Clark and other internationalists an enduring lesson from the first war was that being an ocean away did not guarantee America's cherished neutrality; "Fortress America" was no longer a viable position. With heightened stature on the international scene, and ever more sophisticated economic and diplomatic ties to Europe and beyond, the United States would soon have no place to hide. For the Plattsburgers it was 1914 all over again. Now in their late fifties instead of their midthirties, the men were a little grayer, a bit thicker around the middle, but their belief in citizen action was undimmed. Clark's old collaborators enthusiastically accepted his challenge and immediately launched the campaign for a selective service act.

As Clark noted in "Five Years of Crisis," the top priority was installing sympathetic leadership at the War Department. This was one of many lessons learned from Plattsburg, when Secretary of War Newton Baker had proved an invaluable ally. Clark and Frankfurter's agreed-upon candidates, Henry L. Stimson and Robert P. Patterson, were already well established on the national scene. Each had a distinguished career, a Plattsburg background, and close personal and professional ties to Clark, Frankfurter, and many members of the NEC.

Stimson was often called the Colonel, carrying his military rank from the Great War into his civilian life as a badge of honor and reminder of duty, as did many of his generation. Before and after the war he had enjoyed a notable public service career, including serving as secretary of war under William Howard Taft and secretary of state under Herbert Hoover. A lawyer by training, Stimson was a moderate Republican and a close friend of, and near-father figure to, Grenville Clark. Patterson was Clark's junior by a decade but had earned his senior partner's full confidence and respect early on as a bright young lawyer at Root, Clark. Patterson had already held important government posts, including U.S.

district judge for the Southern District of New York. Patterson was currently serving on the prestigious U.S. Circuit Court of Appeals for the Second Circuit, along with the well-known judges Augustus and Learned Hand (or Gus and B, as Clark called them in warm personal correspondence through the years).[6]

After Clark and Frankfurter had made their lists and agreed on the "Stimson-Patterson ticket," the task remained to maneuver the two distinguished (and busy) men into cabinet-level positions, one of which was already filled (by Woodring), and the other of which did not yet exist (undersecretary of war). Minor obstacles. Clark and Frankfurter agreed early on that Frankfurter, whom FDR had recently elevated to the Supreme Court, would privately lobby the president about the proposed appointments while Clark orchestrated the larger public effort. With impressive moxie Clark began by contacting Roosevelt, with whom his relations had been badly strained by the court-packing fight just two years earlier. With no mention of their past troubles Clark laid out his latest case in a polite, informative letter:

Dear Mr. President: May 16, 1940

I am presiding at a private meeting of the old Plattsburg Camp Group on Wednesday evening, May 22, at the Harvard Club. (About fifty picked men will be there—Delancey Jay, George McMurtry, Robert P. Patterson, Julius Ochs Adler, and men like that.)

We propose to debate the question of recommending and supporting compulsory military training of a sort suited to our conditions—on the idea that nothing less may suffice to safeguard the U.S. (This particular lot of men should be in a sound position to propose compulsory service, since all were in the previous war and many served with distinction.)

Assuming that we decide to support such a proposal, the question will arise whether, as a matter of timing, it is opportune to put it forward publicly at this time.

Presumably, also, we will vote to support your immediate proposals for preparedness.

I inform you of this so that if you wish to send me any comment, you may do so.

With great respect, I am

Very truly yours, Grenville Clark[7]

Roosevelt's friendly, if slightly cryptic, reply came just two days later:

Dear Grennie:

Thanks for yours of the 16th. I see no reason why the group
you mention should not advocate military training . . . I am
inclined to think there is a very strong public opinion for
universal service so that every able bodied man and woman
would fit into his or her place. The difficulty of proposing a
concrete set of measures "short of war" is largely a political one—
what one can get from Congress.
I hope to see you soon.

As ever, Franklin[8]

As Clark and Roosevelt carefully reestablished rapport, Frankfurter
applied his characteristic full-court private persuasion. The president was
receptive—Roosevelt instinctively liked the idea of Stimson as secretary
of war. A decorated soldier and proven public servant, "Harry" Stimson
had earned a level of respect that verged on reverence in Washington.
"The veriest Roman of them all," said Judge Learned Hand, an esteemed
figure himself, "a Regulus who, for his country, would be rolled down
the hill in a barrel full of spikes."[9] That Stimson was a Republican was
also a plus, as FDR had already planned to have at least two cross-party
members in his unusually mixed cabinet. (Roosevelt had also appointed
the first female cabinet member, Labor Secretary Frances Perkins.)

Concerns about Stimson's stamina at age seventy-three were assuaged
by having the young and vigorous Bob Patterson as undersecretary. (In
persuading Stimson to accept the position, Clark optimistically estimated
that with Patterson's able assistance, Stimson could do the job in just
four hours a day.) To allay any remaining health worries, Clark took the
unusual step of obtaining a private health report from Stimson's physician, a mutual friend. The report was good, declaring the septuagenarian
Colonel to be in fine health and physically up to the job. Clark passed
along the information and checked off that concern. (The understandably irritated future secretary ultimately forgave Clark for the invasion
of privacy.)[10]

A few weeks later came FDR's hearty phone call from the White
House to Highhold, Stimson's Long Island estate. Clark's "preposterous
plot" had succeeded, and Henry L. Stimson soon became the nation's fif-
ty-fourth secretary of war (Robert P. Patterson would be its fifty-fifth). The
importance of the Stimson-Patterson appointments in getting the Selective Service Act passed is inestimable. Felix Frankfurter later described it
as an example of "Cleopatra's nose"—meaning the role of contingency
in history: "If anyone tried to tell me it would have made no difference

whether [anti–Selective Service] Woodring or [pro–Selective Service] Stimson were in charge of the War Department, they might as well say that two plus two equals seven."[11]

With favorable leadership thus in place, the next challenge was to neutralize partisan opposition. Clark recruited sponsors from both parties for the Selective Service Act (SSA): Senator Edward Burke, an anti–New Deal Democrat from Nebraska, and U.S. Representative James Wadsworth, a Republican from New York. From then on the SSA was officially called the Burke-Wadsworth Bill. Clark and other NEC members also negotiated extensively with the War Department and other officials in the executive branch to iron out differences between the department's proposed voluntary recruiting drive and SSA, to eliminate the tempting compromise of beginning with an all-volunteer effort, which Clark felt strongly would end up being too little too late.[12]

Clark and his team also worked with (and on) General George Catlett Marshall, the army's chief of staff, whom Clark had noted was strongly opposed to his plan. Marshall later bristled at the suggestion that he had been opposed to the draft. Instead, he insisted, he merely had important differences of opinion with Clark about how best to achieve it: "No one had to tell me how much it was needed—I knew that years before—but the great question was how to get it. It wasn't for me to establish a reputation because I asked for selective service legislation."[13] Marshall was in a difficult position, with the American public still months away from supporting even all-out aid to the British, let alone conscription, which met with passionate resistance even during wartime. Surveying the prevailing public mood, both General Marshall and President Roosevelt deliberately stood back and allowed civilians to bring the fight for selective service legislation to Congress. Marshall described the careful timing and delicate politics involved:

If I had led off . . . I would have defeated myself before I started and I was very conscious of that feeling. [But] if I could get citizens of great prominence to take the lead . . . then I could take up the cudgels and work it out. . . . You might say the Army played politics. . . . That is a crude expression. Actually, we had regard for politics. We had regard for the fact that the President did not feel assured he would get the backing of the people generally, and in the Middle West particularly, and had to move with great caution.[14]

No doubt Marshall's concerns had validity, but Clark was convinced that the president and his chief of staff underestimated the people. Clark's National Emergency Committee began an extensive campaign to educate the public on the logic and necessity of selective service. Clark and the committee members gave speeches, wrote editorials, published articles, and worked through friends and associates around the country. To augment the in-house effort, Clark hired the talented and well-connected former *New York Times* reporter Perley Boone to coordinate an all-out publicity assault through the media and other public relations channels. Boone worked tirelessly and to great effect.[15]

Despite the extensive public relations effort, resistance to a draft remained strong. It was difficult for members of Congress to vote for the SSA even if they believed it would ultimately become necessary, as many privately did. The lobbying effort by both sides was immense. Clark and his staff "practically wore out shoe leather tracking down and button-holing Senators and Representatives."[16] They applied relentless pressure to vote for the national good, even if it meant taking substantial political heat at home. They maintained that pressure until the final moments of the formal vote count in September.

White House support for the bill was underwhelming, with President Roosevelt publicly offering only hints and ambiguities, although he had already assured Clark in his private letter of May 18 that he agreed it was needed. Understandably, in the midst of a tight reelection campaign Roosevelt didn't want the opposition to use against him his support for an unpopular program. Clark decided the solution was to persuade FDR's opponent, Wendell Willkie, to publicly support selective service, thereby taking it off the table as a campaign issue.

Willkie was a dark horse candidate who had never held elected office yet somehow emerged from the stunning 1940 Republican convention as the party's official nominee, defeating the much better known Thomas Dewey, Robert Taft, and Arthur Vandenberg. The handsome, charismatic, and unpredictable Willkie was from Indiana but lived much of the time in New York. There he was a member of many of the same professional and social groups as Grenville Clark, among them, the elite and strongly interventionist Century Group.[17] Willkie was a corporate lawyer; former counsel to, and then president of, a major utility company (Commonwealth and Southern); like Clark, Willkie was a moderate Republican with a strong internationalist bent. Unlike the majority of his party, Willkie was already leaning toward supporting the SSA but was strongly cautioned by his campaign advisers to dodge the highly charged issue.

Two days before Willkie's highly anticipated acceptance speech at a massive campaign rally in his hometown of Elmwood, Indiana, Clark sent a lengthy wire urging the candidate to use that platform to forcefully endorse conscription. Clark's advice was direct and specific: be bold, "no weasel words"; any hedging or equivocating would be "wholly inconsistent with your character." Willkie was, of course, under considerable pressure from the isolationist wing of his party to do the opposite, but skillful persuasion, coupled with his character (to which Clark so unsubtly alluded), led the Republican candidate to publicly announce his support for selective service at the August 17 rally. Formal FDR support for the measure quickly followed.[18]

Less than a month later, on September 16, 1940, the Burke-Wadsworth Bill—the first peacetime draft in U.S. history—became law. The bill passed by solid, if not overwhelming, margins (Senate: 58–31, House: 263–149). A year and four short months later came Japan's devastating surprise attack on Pearl Harbor. It was a dramatic after-the-fact endorsement of Clark's SSA efforts, which had remained highly controversial until that moment. (So controversial that an important follow-up bill in August 1941 to extend the draft period from twelve to eighteen months squeaked through the House by just one vote. Had it failed, the vast majority of Burke-Wadsworth draftees would have been back at home, and the army back to skeleton status, when the Japanese attacked just four months later.)[19]

After the war General John J. Pershing said, "Had it not been for Grenville Clark, we would not have had any training act until Pearl Harbor." According to Lewis Douglas, former member of Congress, director of the budget, and U.S. ambassador to Britain, the measure "became one of the solid foundations of our military strength. It saved many months, possibly a year, at a time when minutes were the difference between victory and defeat."[20]

Typically Clark did not attend the formal White House signing ceremony that was held with great fanfare in the Oval Office. With "movie cameras whirring and flashbulbs popping," and flanked by Henry Stimson, James Wadsworth, General Marshall, and Senator Morris Sheppard, a Texas Democrat, FDR signed the historic Burke-Wadsworth Bill into law. While Clark downplayed his role as "only minor," those close to the event knew better. Henry Stimson wrote to Clark, "I want to tell you what a fine job—in fact unique job—you have done in getting [the SSA] drafted and passed. If it had not been for you no such bill would have been enacted at this time. Of this I am certain." Personal differences notwithstanding, Marshall told a reporter at the ceremony: "Grenville Clark should have been here instead of me."[21] Following the success of his selective service effort, Clark was awarded the Roosevelt Distinguished Service Medal in 1940 by the Theodore Roosevelt Memorial Fund.

As noted, a big part of the success (and audacity) of Clark's selective service campaign was maneuvering Henry Stimson to become FDR's secretary of war in 1940. In a prime example of the axiom that no good deed goes unpunished, Stimson soon drafted his crafty promoter and trusted friend to come to Washington to help him run the war effort. As Stimson put it, "You got me into this . . . now you must come down here to help me out."[22] Clark, ever leery of a formal government role that might compromise his cherished independence, was not immediately sold on the idea. It took two increasingly insistent letters from Stimson (August 22 and September 2, 1941) and a lengthy private conference at Highhold (September 6) before Clark finally agreed to a "90 day trial trip" to Washington.[23]

Clark further conditioned his acceptance on Stimson's obtaining explicit approval of the arrangement from FDR and Marshall. Stimson agreed, and after receiving the president's blessing (Stimson's diary notes: "[Roosevelt] said he was delighted to hear of it and thought Clark would be very useful"), Stimson approached Marshall. According to Stimson, "[Marshall] was perfectly satisfied" with having Clark in the office. Noting he differed with Clark "on one matter" (he undoubtedly meant officer training), Marshall said that on others they were in accord and he had the "highest respect and liking for [Clark]."[24]

Thus was a highly unusual nominating process for a secretary of war followed by an equally unusual appointment of his officially sanctioned but oddly off-the-record aide de camp. Clark's "90 day trial" stretched into four years as Stimson's private civilian adviser, with his own office next to the secretary's at the War Department. Clark did this without taking an official position, a formal oath, or receiving pay. Clark (and Fanny) simply moved into a suite at the Carlton Hotel, and he reported for duty. Washington became the Clarks' adjunct home base from 1940 to 1944.[25]

Clark and Stimson paired well, with a strong mutual respect, admiration, and friendship that went back to the Plattsburg days. Stimson was the prototype for the elite group dubbed the Wise Men by the authors Walter Isaacson and Evan Thomas. They describe their subjects as a select handful of engaged citizens who "by breeding and training . . . duty and desire, heeded the call to public service." Stimson represented, trained, and hired many of these men: "The original brightest and best . . . whose outsized personalities and forceful actions brought order to post-war chaos." (Some historians have argued since that the new order the Wise Men created led directly to the Cold War, Vietnam, and later Iraq—all of which Grenville Clark protested or would have. Yet completely apart from that interesting and important political and policy debate, the strong public service instinct and contributions of Stimson and others like him remain noteworthy.)[26]

Stimson saw national service, military or political, as a moral duty rather than a personal choice. Like Clark, he was raised in elite New York society and enjoyed the most prestigious of educations, with his own Skull and Bones credentials from Yale fitting neatly with Clark's Harvard-Porcellian pedigree. Both were Harvard Law graduates, respected Wall Street lawyers, devoted family men, and enthusiastic outdoorsmen. They were natural and harmonious partners.

Stimson's second-in-command, Patterson, soon to have the newly created title of undersecretary of war, was a generation younger but had much in common with the Colonel. Patterson graduated second in his class at Harvard Law School. His successful legal career included a series of increasingly distinguished judgeships. A Plattsburger to the core, "Fighting Bob" Patterson became a genuine war hero in the First World War and was described by one historian as "the tough minded, hard-driving, former federal judge who served throughout the emergency [of the Second World War] and beyond, and whose contributions to victory were . . . comparable only to those of . . . General George Marshall and of the President himself."[27]

The Stimson protégés John J. McCloy and Robert A. Lovett were soon added to Stimson's dream team as assistant secretaries of war. A veteran of the first Plattsburg camp of 1915, McCloy was a successful lawyer and banker. (He would later serve as president of the World Bank, U.S. High Commissioner for Germany, chair of the Council on Foreign Relations, and influential presidential adviser, among many other roles. McCloy's biographer, Kai Bird, dubbed him "the Chairman of the Establishment.") Bob Lovett was an investment banker by profession and a skilled and enthusiastic aviator who flew with first British and then U.S. naval air squadrons in World War I. He did not attend the Plattsburg camp but would have fit right in—Skull and Bones at Yale, postgraduate study at Harvard, a father who was president and CEO of the Union Pacific Railroad. Both McCloy and Lovett considered Stimson a mentor and role model. Stimson in turn "bequeathed [to them] a complicated blend of toughness, idealism, and rationality." The Colonel called the pair his Heavenly Twins or (fondly) Imps of Satan, depending on his mood.[28] In Stimson's memoir *Active Service in Peace and War*, co-written with McGeorge Bundy, the Patterson, McCloy, Lovett trio is described as follows:

> These . . . were "sixty minute players" in a team to which many others were added for special purposes at different times. All were men in the prime of life, the forties and fifties. All had been conspicuously successful in private life. . . . All of them came to Washington at serious financial sacrifice. None of them had ever been politically active, and none had any consuming political ambition. All were men of absolute integrity, and none were small minded

about credit for his labors. [They] were Republicans, but none ever aroused partisan opposition. They were civilians, but they earned the unreserved confidence of the Army. All of them were whole-hearted in their loyalty, but none interpreted loyalty as merely a duty to say yes, and Stimson often trusted their judgment against his own.[29]

Stimson called it the best staff he ever had.[30] Clark undoubtedly agreed.

Not everyone at the War Department shared Stimson's love for his exuberant and influential new team of civilian advisers, especially its peculiarly unofficial team captain, Grenville Clark. The seeds of George Marshall's irritation were planted early on, as telephone calls from Clark and other "previous Plattsburg men" twice interrupted the general's first briefing with the newly appointed war secretary at Stimson's Highhold estate. These were advisory calls, as Marshall explained to his biographer: "Grenville Clark . . . [was] one of those leaders who wanted [Stimson] to change things instantly the minute he got in position as secretary of war." With the subsequent appointment of Bob Patterson ("[another] Plattsburg graduate," Marshall tersely noted) as undersecretary of war, "the whole set-up was then to restore the Plattsburg movement immediately and in quantity."[31] Marshall and Clark had managed a fragile harmony through the selective service campaign, mainly because they shared the ultimate goal. Yet despite Marshall's official nod of approval for Clark's coming on board, friction between the two men remained and would only increase.

In 1941 Marshall and Clark got into a pitched battle about officer training. In a rare public display of temper Marshall threatened to resign because of Clark's undue influence at the War Department. The conflict began once it became clear that the Selective Service Act was (miraculously) going to pass. The War Department and Marshall's general staff worked feverishly on its myriad components and implementation. Officer training was prime among these, especially to Clark, who felt the army was compromising all-important officer quality with an overreliance on National Guard and army reserve candidates. In the anemic interwar years the quality of these units had grown spotty as their prestige and funding had dwindled—men were often poorly trained, and many were of questionable caliber and motivation. Clark strongly encouraged Stimson to get rid of the "dead wood" and set up as quickly as possible Plattsburg-style training camps for a freshly recruited 30,000 "picked men" from the civilian population.[32]

Stimson was simpatico, and Marshall was incensed to learn that his boss was leaning toward a civilian-based training program that Marshall had already rejected. To Marshall, Plattsburg was fine, even noble, in its time. He had actively participated on the army side of the original civilian training camps. But that had been a unique situation. Marshall, now in charge of the entire army, had a very different plan, one centered on the core military policy of promoting from within. Officers were supposed to earn their stripes. The general was also working with limited resources and felt it was imperative to control the rate, and thereby the quality, of officer training, especially early on. And beyond the particulars of policy and procedure, the chief of staff of the United States Army must have found it infuriating to have the secretary of war taking the advice of a civilian lawyer and Harvard Club chum over the general's own.

In his official biography Marshall admits to "bluntly [telling] Secretary Stimson that he must decide whether he intended to follow the views of his Chief of Staff and the General Staff in military matters or listen to Grenville Clark and other civilian advisors." Full interview transcripts released later capture Marshall's frustration more vividly: "I think I got a little sarcastic and said, 'You get a Plattsburg man and run it to your own satisfaction.'" In both accounts Marshall came to regret the incident as unbecoming conduct on his part: "As I say, I think this is a rather reprehensible attitude for a member of the government at a time like this, particularly when he's a military member, when he's a career man—but nothing else would stop the thing."[33]

Reprehensible or not, the general's ultimatum did indeed stop the thing. Stimson was startled but managed to reassure Marshall that he would "not have him unduly worried." They worked out a compromise on officer training, which at least Stimson later felt "was a better [solution] than any of them anticipated." The compromise plan was a series of Officer Candidate Schools (OCS) for men selected from the ranks after a minimum six months of service. Officers would not be recruited directly from the civilian population, à la Plattsburg. As Patterson's biographer noted, the OCS emphasis on "demonstrated leadership within the Army, and on entry into the officer corps at lower grades, conflicted sharply with the Plattsburg ideal of selection based on civilian educational and professional criteria," Clark's "picked men."[34] Clark lost that round to Marshall, but no one was keeping score. There were far too many other emergencies to contend with.

As the war intensified and drew ever nearer, antiwar passions grew correspondingly more urgent. Senator Burton K. Wheeler, the Montana Democrat who had been Clark's ally in the court-packing fight, was a staunch isolationist who had already publicly accused the administration of planning to "plow under every fourth American boy." Wheeler enjoyed being a constant irritant to the Roosevelt administration and had a penchant for taking on entrenched power. Early in his career Wheeler had gone up against the mining giant Anaconda Copper Company to seek better working conditions for miners, although the company dominated Montana politics. He survived numerous heavy-handed attempts at reprisal by "the Company" and its well-oiled cronies in Washington. Wheeler ultimately chaired a Senate investigation of Anaconda. A novel written about the young idealistic senator's inspiring fight against corruption later became the Hollywood classic *Mr. Smith Goes to Washington*, with the Wheeler character memorably played by the actor Jimmy Stewart.[35]

In the spring of 1941 Wheeler enraged Clark and Stimson by publicly predicting that the United States would be occupying Iceland in late June. Wheeler released his statement just as U.S. forces were at sea, preparing to augment and relieve British forces in Iceland. Stimson, who did not believe in clairvoyance or coincidence, publicly accused Wheeler of leaking classified and sensitive information to deliberately jeopardize a military operation.

Clark meanwhile undertook an investigation of the officers he felt were responsible for the leaks to Wheeler and other isolationists. Then Clark took it a step further and pressed for the prosecution of Wheeler and others under the 1917 Espionage Act. Clark wrote and circulated a substantial legal brief on the law and wrote to Felix Frankfurter: "I have worked up a memorandum of what I consider to be a pretty clear violation of the Espionage Act by Senator Wheeler and General Robert E. Wood [national chair of the strongly isolationist America First Committee], and probably by several others whose identity I don't know. I have written a memorandum of fact and law to Acting Attorney General Biddle suggesting a careful investigation."[36]

The heavy-handed investigation seems a departure from Clark's strong belief in protecting civil liberties, but context was everything. In the surreal eighteen months since Clark had gathered his Plattsburg colleagues at the Harvard Club, Hitler's Germany had conquered Poland, Denmark, Norway, Luxembourg, the Netherlands, Belgium, and finally France. In June 1941 the Wehrmacht plunged into the Soviet Union; most U.S. experts predicted that Russia would fall within three months. Britain, the only Western power still free, was increasingly desperate. Italy had joined the Axis powers under its fascist dictator, Mussolini. The European war had spread to North Africa, the Mediterranean, and the oil-rich regions of the Middle East. On the other side of the world imperial Japan's aggression was intensifying against China, with Japan occupying French Indochina and threatening oil-rich Dutch and British possessions to the south. (World War II had begun for Asia in 1937, three full years before Hitler invaded Norway, but the war in Asia received a fraction of the press coverage devoted to the European front.)

To Clark and others close to the war effort, citizens remaining isolationist in the face of the global threat were misguided, misinformed, or obtuse. But for Wheeler, or any professed public servant, to make inflammatory public statements while acutely aware of the alarming war news pouring into Washington was, in Clark's view, a dereliction of national duty as well as a potential legal breach. Freedom of speech did not extend to leaking classified military information in wartime.[37] It was a prime example of the complex and contradictory situations that John McCloy called the imponderables of public policy.[38]

On December 7, 1941, came the imponderable that changed everything. McCloy was among the first civilians at the War Department to hear the shocking news out of Pearl Harbor—the Japanese had bombed and inflicted heavy damage, with untold casualties, on the U.S. naval base in Hawaii. No one knew what further attacks might already be in motion, and protection of west coast military and civilian targets, in addition to securing the president, Congress, and sensitive sites in the nation's capital, became first in a chain of urgent actions. McCloy immediately called in Grenville Clark, while Stimson spent most of the afternoon at the White House conferring with the president. Later the secretary gathered his trusted crew at the War Department. McCloy's biographer recounts the tense meeting, the stunning attack, and its mixed blessing:

> At 4:00 pm, McCloy convened in his office a meeting of the chiefs of the various armed services. Stimson then came in and gave them all a little "pep talk." Afterward, he sat around with McCloy, Marshall, Grenville Clark, Lovett, [an army intelligence specialist, General Sherman] Miles, and Patterson, discussing what form the declaration of war should take. Only by the end of the day did the full dimensions of the disaster become clear. Even so, Stimson felt somehow relieved: "When the news first came that Japan had attacked us, my first feeling was relief that the indecision was over and that a crisis had come in a way that would unite all our people."[39]

Immediately after the meeting Clark helped Stimson draft the formal declaration of war.

With selective service enshrined in law, and America officially at war, Clark turned his attention to the vital domestic half of the war effort—raising adequate numbers of workers to run the factories, farms, and other businesses that would feed, fuel, and equip the soldiers. Patterson was in charge of the massive labor effort and quickly saw that, with respect to arms, equipment, and especially aircraft, "the cupboard was nearly bare." In most cases raw materials were not in short supply, and adequate facilities existed—they simply lacked sufficient workers to run them. Grenville Clark saw the solution in a familiar theme, a national service program. The United States was the only major nation at arms that had not enacted legislation to mobilize labor for the domestic war effort. This made no sense to Clark, who asked rhetorically, "Why should we alone . . . be so careless and arrogant as to suppose that we can wage war successfully without mobilizing our human resources with a thoroughness at least approaching that of our enemies and our principal Allies?"[40]

But the American public was not persuaded, and a compulsory labor program proved more unpopular than military conscription. In many ways it was an even harder sell, with a less vivid and compelling rationale. Urgent news reports from the front spoke of victories and losses on bloody battlefields, not of stilled or underproducing factories. Opponents of national service cried, "Totalitarian system!" "Slave labor!" and inaccurately argued that the voluntary labor system was working just fine.[41]

By 1943 stateside labor shortages were a deepening crisis, with such vital programs as aircraft, tank, and ordinance production substantially cut back for lack of workers. The situation was bad enough that Clark was finally able to find Republican sponsors for a national service bill in the Senate (Warren K. Austin of Vermont) and in the House (Wadsworth). The bill applied to all men currently eligible for the draft and added women aged nineteen to fifty. Citizens would be required to register and agree to provide war service in a "noncombatant capacity to industry, agriculture, or any other occupation, activity or employment which the President shall from time to time determine to be essential to the effective prosecution of the war."[42]

Despite the support of the president and Stimson, and the tireless efforts of one of Clark's classic civilian committees (the Citizens Committee for a National War Service Act), the public never got behind the bill and it ultimately failed. A bitterly disappointed Clark wrote to Felix Frankfurter, explaining his decision to fold his citizen's committee in November 1944:

> It's a real tragedy, I think, that we couldn't get National Service.
> I believe the German war has been prolonged somewhat by the
> lack of it and the Japanese war by at least a year—very likely
> much more. For with National Service we could have mobilized
> on a much greater scale, and faster, so that it would not have been

necessary to permit the Japanese to make still further inroads in China this year. . . . So the inevitable result is coming to pass. However it seems the milk has been spilt and it's now too late to remedy it. We'll just have to reconcile ourselves to a longer war and greater loss of life than there needed to be.[43]

While Clark's primary War Department focus was on manpower, he was also weighing in on virtually every major issue that crossed Stimson's desk. And those issues were endless. Clark's later summary of the period ("Five Years of Crisis") is a handwritten twenty-page (legal-size), month-by-month, rapid-fire statement of the facts—names, dates, places, actions. It has the feel of an auditor sifting through the wreckage after a natural disaster or plane crash, trying to piece together exactly what happened. The brimming activity report is interspersed with cable news–type war bulletins: "1939: September 1—Germany invades Poland"; "September 3—Britain declares war"; "1941: Pearl Harbor Day—at War department (got call from McCloy)," and so on for the duration of the war years.

Important family matters also commanded Clark's attention during the war years; domestic milestones lace his compendious summary. In 1939 daughter Mary D. married the future law professor Gray Thoron at the family home in Dublin. Louisa enrolled at the Winsor School in Boston, and Grenville Jr. returned to Harvard for his junior year. In 1941 Grenville Jr. graduated from Harvard, enlisted in the marines, and began training at Marine Corps Base Quantico in Virginia. Gray Thoron enlisted in the army, and Mary D. delivered the first Clark grandchild, Claire Thoron. The next year Louisa entered Radcliffe, and the Thoron family moved to Kentucky, where Gray trained with an inventory division at Fort Knox. Grenville Jr. met his future wife, Franny Kingsford, while on furlough at a Tucson resort in January; in August he shipped out for Samoa with the Third Marine Division. In 1943 he returned from Samoa in September with a difficult tropical illness and then married Franny in December. (Their first child, Grenville Clark III, would be born the following year.) Also in 1943 Gray Thoron deployed to France with the Fourteenth Armored Division.

On top of his War Department and family obligations, Clark was still writing, speaking, lobbying, lawyering, and managing his various public and private service committees (the Harvard Corporation, NEL, NEC, and more, all still actively meeting). It is exhausting merely to read the summary of those years. Not surprisingly the volume, intensity, and sheer logistics of his duties in New York, Washington, Boston, and Dublin were taking a toll on Clark's health and on his family. A private 1942 memo-to-self, titled simply "Family Policy," may reflect soul-searching in connection with Clark's sixtieth birthday that year. Whatever the impetus, it offers a rare glimpse of the personal considerations and professional obligations he constantly juggled.

In the memo the methodical lawyer begins by setting out the "elements of problem." At the top of the list was Fanny's "physical health and state of mind," and that his wife's main interests and responsibilities were in Boston and Dublin. Clark's own health and state of mind were also factors, and those were largely influenced by "(1) War work in New York and Washington. (2) Firm and personal business, finances, trusts. (3) Harvard. (4) Civil Rights—Bill of Rights Review (minor)." The Clarks' youngest child, at the transitional age of sixteen, was another important consideration: "Louisa's education and bringing-up—Radcliffe, Boston. Importance of this as factor in past and now." The family's resulting "personal problem," in a nutshell, was:

> By having headquarters in New York and trying to keep some contact with the firm and with national affairs in an active way in New York and Washington, we are attempting the impossible because: a) With the place in Dublin and Louisa in Boston, F.D.C. [Fanny] must be in Dublin and Boston at least 5 months each year it has proved impossible for me to be away from her since: (1) because of my health record I may get ill if absent alone and (2) anyhow F.D.C. thinks I will become ill and gets so worried it makes her ill. This situation necessitates my being in Dublin and Boston, say, 5 months per annum and makes it virtually impossible to carry on any steady or active work in New York and Washington.
>
> A further reason is F.D.C.'s health which, especially in winter, keeps her so under par that she can not travel or be left alone much. She should go or be able to go to warm climate for 2–3 months in winter. If I am in New England 5 months and South even 2 months it is impossible to carry on active relationships in New York and Washington in remaining 5 months.
>
> All the above leads to the conclusion we had better take a new line, viz: (1) Headquarters in Dublin and Boston; (2) cut off firm; (3) cut off *active* relations with New York and Washington but do Harvard, and write, with perhaps 1 month on Long Island or New York in December–January (or March–April). Spend year: June 1– October 15 = 4½ [months] in Dublin; October 15–December 15 = 2 [months] in Boston; December 15–April 1 = 3½ [months] in South; April 1–June 1 = 2 [months in Boston].[44]

It was a valiant try, but Clark's schedule would only intensify during the next two years, and his carefully planned balance of duties, rest, and other activities would remain ideas on paper.

Among the many responsibilities of the War Department, and therefore under Stimson's direct authority, were scientific research and development projects related to warfare. The most infamous of these was undoubtedly the top-secret development of the atomic bomb. Stimson's chilling diary entry of November 6, 1941, notes: "Dr. Vannevar Bush [initiator and administrator of the Manhattan Project] came in to convey to me an extremely secret statement from the Scientific Research and Development office—a most terrible thing."[45]

When Stimson shared the report with Clark, both men saw well beyond the new weapon's fearsome war potential. As unusually farsighted individuals, with long experience working with (and against) other countries, they immediately understood what the atomic scientists would later struggle to make the public understand: once the United States developed the bomb, it was only a matter of time before other nations had nuclear capability, too. Absent an unprecedented reordering of the anarchic international system, the rivalries that bred competition, mistrust, and self-protection would inevitably result in an escalating arms race with increasingly deadly potential. This sobering awareness affected Clark deeply and set the course for the remainder of his life's work.

Clark continued in his War Department role through July 1944, but after D-day brought the war to a foreseeable close, he was ready to once again get loose of Washington. Before Clark took leave of his unofficial boss of the last five years, the two old friends spoke frankly about the one thing so top secret that it was almost entirely absent from their written communication during the war years—atomic warfare and its catastrophic implications. Clark never forgot Stimson's parting instructions: "Grenny, go home and try to figure out a way to stop the next war and all future wars."[46] Clark took on that daunting assignment, and worked at it for the rest of his days.

CHAPTER 11

Retreat to Dublin
Organizing for Peace

Back home in Dublin, Grenville Clark spent the summer of 1944 regaining his strength and examining his options in the restorative New Hampshire hills. The tumultuous war years in Washington had been a strain, but the sixty-two-year-old characteristically looked on the bright side. As he and Fanny settled into the domestic rhythms of Outlet Farm, they had reason to feel hopeful. World War II was finally drawing to its ragged close, with the Allied victory at hand in Europe and in sight in Asia. Summer faded into a crisp New England fall, and on November 7, 1944, Franklin Delano Roosevelt was elected to an unprecedented fourth term. On December 31 Clark sent a personal greeting to his old friend, as he did each New Year's Eve, wishing FDR another year of "continued health and vigor."[1] Just four months later, on April 12, 1945, Roosevelt died unexpectedly of a cerebral hemorrhage while sitting for a portrait at his vacation cottage in Warm Springs, Georgia.

As news of the president's death spread through Washington, crowds of dazed citizens gathered in and around Lafayette Square in front of the White House. The veteran political reporter Arthur Krock described the surreal scene: "They made no demonstration. But the men's hats were off and the tears that were shed were not only to be seen on the cheeks of women." Assistant Secretary of State Dean Acheson looked out his State Department window and noted the visibly numbed masses: "They merely stood [there] in a lost sort of way."[2]

The whole nation was in shock. Perhaps it should not have been. The ailing president had looked pale and grown noticeably thinner in recent months. At times he had seemed confused, and rumors abounded about his ill health. But almost no one, by every account including FDR himself, expected him to die so soon, just eighty-three days into his fourth term. The author and legal scholar Noah Feldman describes Roosevelt as having "towered over American political life as no president had before

155

and no president ever will again."[3] The length of his tenure alone was remarkable. In office for more than twelve years, Franklin Roosevelt was the only president most young people could remember. His death also came at an extraordinary moment in history, summed up in his obituary in the *New York Times*:

> No President of the United States has died in circumstances so triumphant and yet so grave. . . . World War II, which the United States entered in Mr. Roosevelt's third term, still was being waged at the time of his death, and in the Far East the enemy's resistance was still formidable. The United States and its chief allies, as victory nears, were struggling to resolve differences of international policy on political and economic issues that have arisen and will arise. And the late President's great objective—a league of nations that will be formed and be able to keep the peace—was meeting obstacles on its way to attainment.[4]

As the nation struggled to absorb the shock of Roosevelt's death, the simple but dignified processes of democracy took over. The little-known Harry S. Truman from Missouri was sworn in as America's thirty-third president, his hand resting on a Bible borrowed from Roosevelt's office. If at this fraught moment Truman's future success at the world's toughest job was an open question, Roosevelt's place in history was not. Grenville Clark echoed the sentiments of presidential scholars and historians ever since when asked years after FDR's death which of the two Roosevelts was the greater president. "Oh, I guess FDR," answered Clark, even though he was in many ways closer to the Roosevelt he warmly called Ted. "[FDR] was a more flexible man than TR and more capable, I think, of grasping the big issues. . . . From early youth, later at Harvard, and all through his years as President [he] was constantly growing in breadth of view and understanding."[5]

Five months later came a much less traumatic transition in Washington. On September 21, 1945, the seventy-eight-year-old Henry Stimson officially stepped down as secretary of war, handing the responsibility to his capable undersecretary, Robert P. Patterson. Clark never lost his deep admiration and affection for his unofficial boss of the last five years and close friend of many more. On Stimson's official retirement Clark wrote:

Dear Henry:

I don't imagine that on June 19 or 20, 1940, when F.D.R. called you up, that you had any idea that your tour of duty would be as much as five years, two months, and eleven days, as I figure it was. But it was a great thing for the country and the world, and I never did as good a day's work in my life as when I went down to see Felix [Frankfurter] and we worked up the Stimson-Patterson ticket.

Clark also revealed he had been keeping a secret duty:

You may have forgotten it, but you once asked me (I think it was in the summer of '42) to give you a tip if I ever thought you were weakening at all and that it was time to get out. I took that perfectly seriously and thought about it at various times, but I certainly never saw any occasion to take you at your word. Quite the contrary, it seemed to me always that you were going strong and that no one else whatever could have done as well.

All this you must know comes from the heart,

Affectionately yours, GC[6]

As unswerving as Clark's personal devotion to Stimson was his dedication to the task the Colonel had assigned Clark as he left the War Department. When Stimson told Clark to find a way to stop the next war and all future wars, the secretary was deadly serious. Neither man saw world peace as an idealistic abstraction but rather as an urgent practical necessity after the battering the world had just taken in two world wars.

In the second war alone the raw numbers were staggering—worldwide more than 60 million dead. The toll in individual countries was unfathomable. The USSR lost more than 24 million people, China more than 20 million. Across Europe and parts of Asia an entire generation of men was decimated. Cities were in ruins, agriculture and industry crippled, and the survivors' misery escalated with severe and widespread shortages of food, housing, and medical care. (An ocean away the United States, with its own pain of 416,800 war dead, got off lightly in comparison.) Then came the surreal shock of eleven-mile-high mushroom clouds over Hiroshima and Nagasaki that cleared to reveal at least 210,000 dead Japanese, the overwhelming majority civilians.[7] This from a single bomb dropped by a single plane flying over each city. With World War I, the previous benchmark for mass human suffering, still a vivid memory for most adults, it was reasonable to predict that the world would likely not survive another global conflict.

Clark may have had an even deeper, more personal, motivation to prevent future wars. The author Gerald Dunne has suggested that, as a member of Stimson's inner sanctum, Clark could not avoid participating in the atomic bomb effort, "from shepherding the gargantuan but disguised appropriation through Congress, to riding herd on the production effort, and, finally, to prophesying what terrible holocaust the weapon would produce when it was used," which must have led to a "deep and abiding sense of personal involvement." As the atomic scientists who later formed an important part of the world peace movement found, the psychological steps from involvement to responsibility, responsibility to guilt, and guilt to shame are short. Clark readily acknowledged that his decades of dogged work for peace after the Second World War stemmed from "a sense of shame," although he framed it broadly rather than personally: "When I ask myself why I have spent many years of work and considerable money in the effort to prevent future wars, I feel that my dominant reason is the sense of shame at the incapacity of the human race to summon up enough intelligence and will to solve this problem, when the knowledge and means to solve it are at hand."[8]

From 1944 until his death in 1967 Grenville Clark devoted the bulk of his time and energy to what he called simply "the peace problem." On a resume prominently featuring preparedness efforts for both world wars, earning the Distinguished Service Medal in one and serving as private adviser to the secretary of war in the other, this looks like a radical change—former military hawk suddenly transformed into cooing dove. Most men in Clark's back-to-back-war generation had army backgrounds or some kind of military tie, as he did. But relatively few took the difficult next step from defense to prevention. To Clark it made perfect sense: What better defense than prevention? Many of his former associates, however, found this new project of their old friend to be a real departure. Although they still liked, admired, and respected the man they all called Grenny, they "just [could not] go along with him on this One World stuff."[9]

In truth Clark hadn't changed his position but rather had sharpened his focus on one he had long held. His interest in world order went at least as far back as the First World War. Despite sparring with the Wilson administration in the early Plattsburg days, Clark admired the president's statesmanship at the Paris Peace Conference and endorsed his Fourteen Points blueprint for an enduring postwar peace. Clark advocated strongly that the United States join Wilson's proposed League of Nations, and even joined the League of Nations Association himself, virtually alone among his peers. He was dismayed when the U.S. Senate blocked America's participation in the league and was saddened, if not surprised, when it eventually disintegrated. Clark took the league's failure as direct evidence that no mere association of sovereign states could prevent war; he decided a more comprehensive legal structure was needed to ensure the peace.

In the fall of 1939 James B. Conant had encouraged Clark to write up his ideas on world peace.[10] Conant was a complex man. President of Harvard from 1933 to 1953, he was a gifted scientist with a PhD in chemistry. He worked on developing poison gases and creating synthetic rubber during World War I and later led the top-secret Manhattan Project. Conant would remain a leader in the development of nuclear weapons and America's nuclear program through the Cold War. All the while, however, he advocated for a world body to control the spread and use of these weapons.[11] The Conants were regular weekend visitors at Outlet Farm, where creating such an organization was a constant theme.

During the winter of 1940 Clark produced the first formal statement of what would become his lifelong mantra—the foundation of world order must be based on world law. Mindful of the lawyer's adage "If you think you know something, put it in a statute," he drafted a complete constitution for a world government of strictly limited powers to show precisely how it could be done. He circulated the document privately, but Germany invaded Norway on April 9, 1940, before Clark's work could be published. Clark turned his attention to the war effort and put world law on temporary hold. But while his peace plan was deferred, it in no way lost importance for him. Clark had the too-rare ability to hold two or more large, seemingly contradictory, ideas in his mind at the same time without compromising either. In this case he rejected the false choice between national security and international law, just as he had rejected the similarly false choice between national security and civil liberties with his Bill of Rights Committee.

With the war drawing to a close, Clark published his first major article on peace in the *Indiana Law Review* in July 1944: "A New World Order— The American Lawyer's Role." The article was widely reprinted, with copies sent to President Roosevelt, Secretary of State Cordell Hull, Secretary of War Stimson, Soviet ambassador Andrei Gromyko, and others. It laid out Clark's four major principles for an effective global peace-keeping organization that never essentially changed: Include everyone— membership should be universal or at least not exclude any major power; make it fair—representation should be weighted and balanced, taking into account population, economic output, and other relevant factors, with no veto; limit its power—strictly limit the organization's powers to preventing war and providing for the common defense, with all other political, economic, and social powers retained by individual member states; do it now—make the transition to such an organization as rapidly as possible, while the evidence and memory of war's carnage are still fresh, lest people forget.[12]

A month later, on August 21, 1944, representatives of the United States, the Soviet Union, Great Britain, and China secretly gathered at Dumbarton Oaks, a stately Georgetown mansion just two and a half miles from the Capitol. (They met in two separate configurations: the United States, Great Britain, and the Soviet Union, and, separately, the United States, Britain, and China because the Soviet Union was still observing its 1941 nonaggression pact with Japan.) Their knotty task was to establish ground rules and a preliminary framework for the brand-new United Nations Organization. All the major nations fighting the Axis powers had agreed to the ground rules and framework in principle as early as January 1, 1942.[13]

The meetings were closed to the public so delegates could speak frankly and freely on highly sensitive matters of national sovereignty and defense. (Transcripts of the proceedings remained sealed until 1994.) Introductory speeches by Hull and others were released to the press the next day; the only other media coverage was an exclusive (and unauthorized) series of articles by the *New York Times*'s national correspondent, James Reston, which later netted him a Pulitzer Prize. Reston revealed decades later that his source for the major scoop was a member of the Chinese delegation whom Reston had met before the war.[14]

The delegates sequestered themselves for six weeks and emerged with a basic structure in place. The UN would have two chambers: a General Assembly, including all fifty initial members, with each nation having an equal vote in plenary sessions; and a five-member Security Council made up of the four Dumbarton Oaks participants plus France. Security Council decisions would require unanimity, effectively giving each Security Council member veto power. A larger conference the following spring would be held in San Francisco to formalize the new charter.

Public enthusiasm for the UN was high, and Congress even appeared willing to go along, in stark contrast to the doomed League of Nations effort two decades before. But to Clark the Dumbarton Oaks plan was fatally flawed. Even before the plan was formally announced, private conversations with State Department insiders had convinced him that, given the proposed Security Council structure, the new UN would be "nothing better than a new league of sovereign states hamstrung by the veto and the rule of one vote for every country in the Assembly." Clark had tried to persuade Secretary of State Hull of his concerns, but "was unsuccessful because . . . our policy became fixed long before, largely because of fear of Senate disapproval over anything that would impair U.S. sovereignty."[15]

Clark had put his finger on a prickly problem that would not soon be resolved. In 2012 Kofi Annan, the widely respected secretary general of the United Nations from 1996 to 2006, wrote: "The core problem at the top of the U.N.'s power structure is the composition of the Security Council. Today we have five permanent members with veto powers . . . based essentially on the geopolitical reality that existed at the end of World War II." Not surprisingly, among other member states, "[the] situation is intolerable to some and unjustifiable to most." Annan could be reading from Grenville Clark's diary when he concludes, "For the Security Council to enjoy legitimacy in the twenty-first century, it needs to be not only effective but also representative."[16]

Still, Clark may have been overly harsh with the secretary of state, given the time and situation. Hull was right to consider the Senate's concerns—in fact he had no choice: two-thirds of the senators had to ratify American participation in the UN. Likely because of the State Department's careful groundwork, the Senate ultimately ratified the UN Charter without reservations. And, contrary to an oft-repeated argument by world federalists, the historian Joseph Baratta points out that the drafters of the UN charter "did not simply revive the [failed] League of Nations . . . they rethought what sort of cooperative organization might solve the world political problems [and] made numerous changes."[17] The changes included binding clauses obligating states to cooperate, renunciation of both the threat and the actual use of force, and members pledging to use peaceful means of settlement for the resolution of international disputes.

To Clark all that was irrelevant if the organization was structurally unsound, as he was convinced it was. Just three days after the conference began, Clark approached a newly formed internationalist group to help him influence the cloistered delegates to build a stronger framework. Among the prominent members of Americans United for World Organization (AUWO) was Clark Eichelberger, who had close ties to FDR and the State Department. Clark wrote to Ulric Bell, AUWO's executive director, on August 24: "Feeling strongly as I do that the Dumbarton Oaks conference is on the wrong track and is likely to bring out a plan that is weak, inefficient, and hardly worth while, I urge that 'Americans United' ought not wait until an ineffective plan is produced and then begin to oppose or try to improve it. It might then be too late. I think that *now* is the time to tackle the problem."[18]

While Ulric shared many of Clark's concerns, more conservative members of the group, including Eichelberger, urged unconditional acceptance of the Dumbarton Oaks proposals and a gradual strengthening of the UN over time. In the end the group released a lukewarm endorsement that pleased no one. Clark later grumbled, "I got into the wrong pew."[19]

Still searching for the right pew, Clark headed west to the San Francisco convention the following spring. From April 25 to June 26, 1945, the Bay Area swarmed with diplomats, lawyers, journalists, and hopeful onlookers from around the world. Clark attended planning and policy sessions and met privately with delegates, leaders of peace groups, government representatives, and others. He listened, lobbied, and suggested. But as the weeks wore on, he grew increasingly disheartened. The new UN constitution would be approved virtually unchanged from what had been drafted at Dumbarton Oaks. However well intended, the United Nations "was not given by the framers of its Charter adequate powers to fulfill the main purpose for which it was organized, namely, the prevention of war."[20]

It was time once again for a citizen action campaign, but who would be Clark's troops? In the past he could have made a few phone calls and filled the Harvard Club with well-placed friends ready to rally to his cause. This time he found himself virtually alone among his former allies. Before long, however, Clark found a new collaborator in an old acquaintance: U.S. Supreme Court Justice Owen Roberts. Roberts, the famed "switch in time that saved nine" in the FDR court-packing case, was still serving on the court, although he planned to step down once its term ended in June. This was ostensibly to devote full-time efforts to the cause of peace, although Roberts's decision was more likely the direct result of his alienation from a bitterly fractious court in which he was increasingly in the minority, if not alone, on major decisions.[21] Regardless of motive, Roberts's retirement was timely for Clark. The two men began talking in May 1945 about their shared concerns about the deficiencies of the new United Nations. They agreed to hold a conference for prominent thinkers who were in favor of some form of limited world government. Clark offered to hold the event in Dublin.

In October 1945 the Dublin Conference drew forty-eight leading educators, attorneys, business leaders, journalists, and other influential citizens for five full days at the Dublin Inn in Clark's hometown hamlet. Their mission, "to consider how to best remedy the weaknesses" of the UN, was clearly spelled out in both their formal invitations and all printed literature.[22] The group's peace agenda got shocking emphasis when atomic bombs obliterated Hiroshima and Nagasaki on August 6 and 10, just two months before the opening gavel for the conference.

Grenville Clark and Owen Roberts served as conference hosts, along with the former New Hampshire governor Robert P. Bass and the attorney Thomas H. Mahoney. Another notable attendee was Norman Cousins, the gifted young editor of the influential *Saturday Review of Literature*. On the evening of the Hiroshima explosion Cousins had written a gripping editorial, "Modern Man Is Obsolete," with the premise that humankind had now learned the means for its own destruction but not yet the means for its survival. To Cousins dropping the bomb "marked the violent death of one stage in man's history and the beginning of another."[23] The Dublin group was keen to help shape that new beginning. Other conferees with big futures were the young journalist Alan Cranston, later a long-serving U.S. senator from California (1968–92), and Kingman Brewster, a bright and idealistic former student dissident at Yale who would be that same university's president from 1963 to 1977. Both men spoke of the Dublin Conference (and Grenville Clark) as a formative influence throughout their lives.

Also attending were several recent veterans fresh from the war, including Cord Meyer Jr. Meyer had already seen much in his twenty-four years: a generation younger than Clark but with similar east coast establishment credentials, Meyer came from a wealthy New York family and went to school at St. Paul's and Yale. His father was a diplomat and a real estate developer, his mother came from a wealthy coal family in Pennsylvania. Meyer was at Yale studying literature and philosophy as World War II closed in. When he heard the news of Pearl Harbor, he enlisted in the marines and saw early, awful battle as a machine-gun platoon leader in the South Pacific. By the war's end Meyer would lose his left eye, his twin brother, and too many friends. The horror and futility of combat left him deeply, permanently motivated to prevent future wars.[24]

Meyer had attended the San Francisco UN conference as an aide to the delegate Harold Stassen. With eloquence beyond his years Meyer channeled his grave concerns about its structure into a compelling article for the *Atlantic*, "A Serviceman Looks at the Peace." One especially moving passage undoubtedly spoke for many a young returning soldier: "When one's first battle is done, when the inexhaustibly patient wounded have been cared for and those past caring have been buried, one feels no exultation in victory. Rather, there is no one who does not ask himself what beneath the sun could possibly be worth it." Describing the new UN as "all we have won from the War," he urged that it be given adequate ammunition to be a real, and not just symbolic, force for lasting peace.[25]

On October 11, 1945, Clark delivered the keynote address. He quoted from memory passages of the doomed League of Nations charter and the failed Treaty of Versailles. Then he went back even further, to the Constitutional Convention of 1787, when the Founders labored in Philadelphia to create the document that would save their frail and already fraying new democracy. The Philadelphia convention was a recurring analogy, as in Clark's preconference letter to the *New York Times:* "I emphasize that we need above all imagination and a creative spirit, capable of a great leap forward in the organization of a world now truly made one by modern invention. The founders of 1787 not only had the vision of this nation but also the practical skill to find the formulae that made it possible. If we cannot fully equal their mature political wisdom, we can at least try to rival their capacity for original and adventurous thought."[26]

Clark passed the gavel to Owen Roberts, who read aloud a letter written for the occasion by James Conant. Speaking with unmatched authority as head of the government's highly classified nuclear development team, against the backdrop of the recent Hiroshima and Nagasaki bombings, Conant was blunt. He stressed the urgent need to control the production and use of atomic weapons and called for the creation of an international agency with a monopoly on the possession of all atomic weapons and the means of producing them. In closing Conant shocked many in the audience by predicting that despite official assurances to the contrary, "several nations, including Russia, could shortly have the atomic bomb."[27]

The Dublin Conference had its contentious moments. The participants all agreed that some kind of world federation was needed, but they differed sharply on who should be in it. Opinion fell roughly into two philosophical camps. Owen Roberts was closely aligned with Clarence Streit, whose 1939 book *Union Now* advocated a federation of Western democracies that would essentially be a new and improved League of Nations. (Clark had introduced Roberts to Streit.) Clark, as previously noted, favored a more comprehensive organization made up of all the world's nations, including those that were not democracies, most specifically the Soviet Union. It was a large and important distinction.

In the audience was Stringfellow Barr, president of St. John's College in Annapolis, Maryland (which he and Scott Buchanan, the dean, had recently reinvigorated with their innovative "great books" curriculum). Barr favored the *Union Now* approach and recalled being "shocked by the speed with which the anti-Streit forces took over." Convinced that Clark "was helping to get action without hearing [the other] side of the argument, [I] made some pretty biting remarks. Mr. Clark flushed and prepared for battle. Then he caught himself and made such a handsome apology that I felt thoroughly unjustified in my attack, and thoroughly won over to him as a person."[28]

Clark's handsome apology didn't budge his own position, of course. A majority of the group agreed with him, including Cord Meyer and the other young veterans. They argued that Streit's democracies-only plan would "alienate half the world, . . . heighten east-west tensions, [and] inevitably [lead] to a disastrous arms race which [could] in turn cause war." Alan Cranston agreed and countered the frequent charge that an all-inclusive world government was impossibly idealistic. He impressed his host by quoting one of Clark's favorite George Washington pearls from the Philadelphia Conference: "It is too probable that no plan we propose will be adopted. Perhaps another dreadful conflict is to be sustained. But if, to please the people, we offer that which we ourselves disapprove, how can we afterward defend our work? Let us raise a standard to which the wise and the honest can repair."[29]

The final sentence became the Dublin group's rallying cry and guiding philosophy.

Justice Roberts unwittingly aided the Clark camp with an ugly unscripted aside during the conference's penultimate night. Governor Bass, who lived nearby, had thrown a cocktail party at which Roberts became quite inebriated. The justice loudly confided within earshot of several guests that he "had no use for a world government with 'chinks' and 'niggers' and anyway we'd be fighting them and the Russians in a few years." As the highest-profile member of the group—a sitting member of the U.S. Supreme Court no less—any remark Roberts made carried extra weight or, in this case, created extra baggage. The veterans in particular "made much of the incident," and the Streit position rapidly lost ground.[30]

Emotions were high on the final day of the conference. With a powerful speech and a good idea Clark deftly averted a threatened walkout by the Streit supporters. He reminded the group that they had far more in common than that which divided them and suggested their impasse on the membership question be resolved by issuing a dissenting minority opinion. The suggestion was clearly directed at Roberts, as it is a technique often used in Supreme Court decisions. (Justice Roberts had in fact written a stunning dissent in the landmark *Korematsu v. United States* just a year before, arguing that Roosevelt's wartime internment camps for Japanese Americans were unconstitutional.) In the end Roberts acquiesced, the Streit group remained, and the declaration was completed and signed. Henry Cabot of Massachusetts called it "the most remarkable handling of a tense situation he had ever seen."[31]

The final Dublin Declaration was a set of eight resolutions:

1. That the implications of the atomic bomb are appalling; that upon the basis of evidence before this conference there is no presently known adequate defense against the bomb and that there is no time to lose in creating effective international institutions to prevent war by exclusive control of the bomb and other major weapons.
2. That the United Nations Charter, despite the hopes millions of peo-

ple placed in it, is inadequate and behind the times as a means to promote peace and world order.

3. That in place of the present United Nations Organization there must be substituted a World Federal Government with limited but definite and adequate powers to prevent war, including power to control the atomic bomb and other major weapons and to maintain world inspection and police force.

4. That a principal instrument of the World Federal Government must be a World Legislative Assembly, whose members shall be chosen on the principle of weighted representation, taking account of natural and industrial resources and other relevant factors as well as population.

5. That the World Federal Government should be responsible to the World Legislative Assembly.

6. That the Legislative Assembly should be empowered to enact laws within the scope of the limited powers conferred upon the World Federal Government, to establish adequate tribunals and to provide means to enforce the judgments of such tribunals.

7. That in order to make certain the constitutional capacity of the United States to join such a World Federal Government steps should be taken promptly to obtain a Constitutional Amendment definitively permitting such action.

8. That the American people should urge their Government to promote the formation of the World Federal Government, after consultation with the other members of the United Nations, either by proposing drastic amendments of the present United Nations Charter or by calling a new World Constitutional Convention.[32]

The dissenting minority opinion, signed by Roberts and other Streit supporters, endorsed all eight resolutions but also recommended exploring a democratic union simultaneously with efforts to establish a world federal government.

The Dublin Conference got a lot of press, most of it negative. The reaction of the *New York Times* was fairly typical: it described the group as able and sincere but essentially dismissed the plan as utopian: "A true world federation, such as they contemplate, is beyond attainment at this stage of history. . . . The actual choice is not between the UNO and an ideal world government. It is between the UNO and chaos."[33] A few individuals and groups already in favor of some form of world legal umbrella responded warmly, but the committee's proposals were largely rejected by the public, the press, and—not surprisingly—by the new United Nations itself. Hopeful internationalists accused the Dublin group of trying to sabotage the fledging organization before it ever had a chance, while the far right predictably decried the Dublin Declaration as a totalitarian manifesto for an all-powerful, all-encompassing world state.

If criticism from the right was virtually unavoidable, alienating the peace-seeking, mostly moderate, UN supporters surely was not. It was almost certainly a rare tactical mistake for Clark to publicly oppose the tremendously popular United Nations before it had even gotten started. Perhaps handled more diplomatically his ideas might have gained greater traction. Owen Roberts spoke to this point in a letter to Clark: "I perhaps ought to mention that our flatfooted declaration respecting the inadequacy of the United Nations charter seems to have started more resistance than anything else the Conference did. I got a good many repercussions to the general effect that the UNO [United Nations Organization] is all we have, that we worked very hard to get it, and that to start to condemn it before the Assembly and Council have even organized causes a good deal of disappointment and disillusionment."[34]

Alan Cranston thought Clark was also wrong in his insistence on the loaded term *world government* to describe what he sought:

And it was a deliberate decision of his to use the term "world government" to describe his prescription for the world's ills. This was an honest mistake, if there ever was one, for he wanted to describe precisely what he had in mind, and he concluded no other term would do so.

But those two words meant to many others, who never bothered to read [Clark's] detailed explanations, something quite different from what they meant to him. They aroused visions of a vast superstate interfering in national and community affairs and in the private lives of everyone—something Clark most assuredly wanted to prevent, not provoke.

He forever sought to make clear that what he was advocating in the world institutions he envisaged was—in the words of the Dublin Declaration—"closely defined and limited powers" restricted to those matters plainly and directly related to war prevention.[35]

Undeterred, Clark organized another conference to be held just three months later, this time on the lovely and historic Princeton campus. It was a fitting location: in 1777 George Washington had driven the British Army from Princeton's Nassau Hall, and from March to November 1783 Princeton served as the U.S. capital, with the Continental Congress holding its spring and fall sessions there.[36] Those early Americans could hardly have foreseen that in the middle of a tumultuous twentieth century, sixty modern-day patriots would gather in the very same spot to discuss and debate the next logical evolution of government.

A surprise visitor to the Princeton Conference was Albert Einstein, who was then in residence at the Princeton Institute for Advanced Studies. Clark learned of Einstein's interest by way of a folded note, handed to Clark as he presided over an early session. It surely created a stir when Clark, reading aloud from the note, announced that the great scientist wished to join their conference. The topic was a natural draw—Einstein had been advocating for world peace since the onset of World War I. In fact his outspoken pacifism and other "allegedly radical activities" had led the FBI to closely monitor the "dangerously peace-minded" scientist as early as 1932.[37]

Einstein arrived in his famously disheveled style. A fellow attendee described him as "a surprisingly small personage, arrestingly dressed in gray flannel trousers (of varying hue) . . . natty black suede shoes [and] above all that a tangled mop of Skye-terrier-style locks (hiding the eyes), strangely reproducing the brown-blue-yellow-gray shades of the voluminous gray [trousers]." Einstein participated with great enthusiasm, nodding vigorously, clapping loudly, and raising his hand to vote both aye and nay on the same proposals. (Asked about this later by a puzzled Alan Cranston, Einstein replied: "The people on both sides are so nice, I can't vote against any of them!") The eminent visitor signaled his departure as he had his arrival, by delivering a folded note to Clark. This one, again read aloud to the group, said: "I will be happy to vote for any conclusion at which your conference arrives."[38]

Despite the celebrity of Einstein, and collective prestige of the rest of the group, newspapers took little notice of the Princeton Conference, and it had virtually no impact on policy makers or the public. Clark pressed forward.

The Dublin and Princeton conferences were not held in a vacuum, of course—people have sought peace for as long as there has been war. In 1945–46 the worldwide peace movement was in a state of flux. Organized peace groups that had flourished after the First World War found themselves steamrolled by the seeming inevitability of the second war just twenty years later. Then came visions of the apocalypse, as the atomic bomb explosions at Hiroshima and Nagasaki raised public awareness as well as the stakes for achieving peace. "The good news of damnation" became an edgy, darkly optimistic catchphrase in the peace community— meaning the clear and present danger of total annihilation might finally bring people to their senses about the need for world peace. (Clark, in the same vein, sometimes said: "I'm an optimist, I think things will get worse.")[39]

In the United States, as elsewhere, peace groups fell roughly into three categories: pacifists, scientists, and internationalists. The venerable pacifists (religious and otherwise) had centuries of experience, organization, and noble inspiration to draw on. And while the terrible toll of two world wars reinforced the pacifists' antiwar, antimilitary, antiviolence message for a time, Pearl Harbor came along and essentially ended public debate about America's joining the war. As the peace historian Lawrence Wittner puts it, by the end of World War II "not only had the war badly mauled pacifist groups, but the movement's [own] inability to stop fascist aggression or to halt the war itself had shattered its confidence and left it, in many instances, discredited and isolated from broader public currents."[40]

It was quite a different story for the atomic scientists. The war had significantly raised their political profile, and they were suddenly a potent new force in the peace movement. After Hiroshima the scientists spoke with unmatched authority on the question that preoccupied the globe. They had both a unique grasp of atomic technology and the knowledge that scientific research rarely recognizes national boundaries. Nuclear fission was a prime example: the German physicists Otto Hahn and Fritz Strassman published the first report of a successful nuclear fission experiment in 1938; then in April 1939 a French team led by Frédéric Joliot-Curie published its own work on neutron emission in the widely read journal *Nature*. News of both experiments raced through the international scientific community, and soon official atomic bomb programs were under way in Germany, Great Britain, and perhaps the Soviet Union. Within a year came the supposedly top-secret Manhattan Project in the United States. But as Einstein and his colleagues well knew, there were no secrets in science, at least not for long.[41]

The scientists were also motivated by a sense of social responsibility, if not guilt, for the Frankenstein monster their research had spawned. They tried to educate the public about the real possibility of nuclear annihilation through war or nuclear accident, and they warned that, absent a strong international nuclear authority, a deadly international arms race was virtually inevitable. Einstein put it most poetically: "The unleashed power of the atom has changed everything save our modes of thinking, and thus we drift toward unparalleled catastrophe." One peace leader said the scientists were "part of the conspiracy to preserve our civilization by scaring men into rationality." The scientists were brilliant and sincere but lacked organization and cohesion. By 1947 they had been sidelined as a major force in the global nuclear discussion by "[disillusionment], fatigue, the attractions of pure research, loyalty slurs, and lack of international opportunity—all [of which] conspired to wear down the remnants of the movement."[42]

The third major peace camp, into which Grenville Clark fell, was the internationalist, or world federalist, group. They represented an array of positions from Clarence Streit's initially popular *Union Now* federation of democracies movement to the more comprehensive world government the Dublin group had proposed. In April 1947 a half-dozen of the largest groups of the world federalist persuasion gathered in Asheville, North Carolina, to create an umbrella organization: the United World Federalists for World Government with Limited Powers Adequate to Prevent War, usually shortened to United World Federalists, or UWF.[43]

Grenville Clark was by this time considered a "background eminence" in world federalist circles. He offered support and guidance to the Asheville conference organizers but did not attend the actual meetings and declined to be the group's front man. Instead Clark and two well-connected friends, T. K. Finletter, a prominent banker and future secretary of the air force, and W. T. Holiday, president of Standard Oil of Ohio, persuaded their fellow Dublin conferee Cord Meyer to serve as the UWF's first president. The older men assured Meyer that they would serve as vice presidents and help with any necessary fund-raising. Meyer accepted and later remembered having been impressed that these "older men of stature and wide practical experience shared my concerns and my belief that something could be done to avert a worldwide arms race [which] persuaded me to take an active part in the growing national debate."[44] It was an unusual move for the establishment-born and -bred Meyer, who had been groomed for a dignified postwar career in the diplomatic service. But as he later explained:

> My reason for making such an abrupt change in my career was a conviction that the United States, through its atomic monopoly, had for a brief period the opportunity to lead the world toward effective international control of the bomb. I was not optimistic, but it seemed to me that if there was one chance in a hundred it was worth taking in view of the consequences of an unrestricted competition between national states for more and bigger nuclear weapons. . . . We acknowledged that Marxist ideology and the totalitarian structure of the Soviet state would make it enormously difficult for the Soviet leaders to accept international inspection and control, but we argued that, faced with the alternative of a nuclear arms race and mutually destructive war, they might accept.[45]

Meyer was an inspired choice and an impressive early leader for the UWF. But Clark had another reason for demurring from a more active role in 1947: he was not completely convinced that combining so many individual groups into one entity was a good idea. The inevitable compromises necessary to create one big tent risked diluting the organization's platform into irrelevance. And he knew from experience that smaller independent groups could far more easily take vigorous action than big bureaucratic ones.

From a more personal standpoint he was also coming to realize, as one historian put it, "This business of moving the [U.S.] government . . . toward a policy of world government was much harder than moving it toward a policy of traditional defense, as in his old Plattsburg and Selective Service Act Days." This was going to be a long slog, and pacing would be important, as Clark wrote to his Dublin follow-up group: "I am impressed with how slowly the thing develops. . . . The moral is, I think, that the advocates of world government ought to be prepared to go through with their efforts over quite a long period and not strike so fast a pace that they get tired and can't put on a spurt at the critical moment."[46]

Adjusting his own pace, as well as his tactics, Clark stepped back from the larger movement and went back to doing what he did best—quietly, doggedly influencing national and world events from behind the scenes.

CHAPTER 12

Resisting Cold Warriors
Writing for Peace
Defending Academic Freedom

While recalibrating his peace strategy, Clark had a health scare that kept him close to home, at least for a while. In February 1947 he was turned down for a health insurance policy after a routine physical turned up an intermittent heart murmur. The news led to a thorough cardiac review, which also revealed some irregular heartbeats, mild to moderate hypertension, and other symptoms now commonly associated with Clark's hard-driving type-A personality. Clark didn't panic but, ever precise, queried his doctor and friend Paul Dudley White, the renowned cardiologist at Massachusetts General Hospital, about finding just the right activity level: "My general philosophy is that on the one hand, I don't want to wrap myself up in cotton wool, avoid all activity, etc., to an extreme extent, just for the sake of breathing a few years longer than otherwise. But, on the other hand, I am desirous of not smashing up and going out prematurely and unnecessarily, so to speak, because of failure to take every reasonable precaution."

As always, Clark's motives involved duty: "The reasons are (a) that my life is happy and satisfactory; (b) that I can be of some use to my wife and children; and (c) that I have work to do in the shape of some systematic writing that I would like to complete and which, at a slow pace, would require several years."

Moving on to specifics, he proposed a plan: "How about mild exercise in the country—short walks, mild canoe paddling, a little swimming, and riding an old pony. Is this OK or is it better to confine activity to the minimum?"[1]

Between Dr. White's good advice and Fanny's hawk-like care, Clark would walk the line between cotton-wool and smashing up for nearly two more decades. He temporarily moderated his peace efforts and dutifully severed most of his professional obligations, except for the Harvard Corporation. The pull of citizen action did at times prove irresistible, as when Clark organized his neighbors to protest the planned installation of an ungainly FM radio tower on his beloved Mount Monadnock. The communications officials were surely given a lesson in the power of an activated citizenry, and the tower was never built.[2] But at least he was beginning to find some balance.

The "systematic writing" Clark mentioned to Paul White of course meant formalizing his ideas about world peace through world law. That would eventually happen, and it would take much longer than several years. But for the time being, Dr. White and Fanny encouraged their patient to take a break from that all-consuming topic and consider writing a memoir. Why not tell the remarkable story of his recent Washington years? Clark was intrigued and updated Charles Burlingham on the new plan in September 1947:

Dear C.C.:

We have settled down to live [in Dublin] nearly eight months of the year. It suits Fanny and she is occupied every minute with the little farm. And it suits me very well with my office and work, and [Harvard Corporation duties] on the side . It is quite convenient to go to meetings from here—only a two-hour trip.

I still work away on [the] subject of world peace, but simultaneously for the last few months, I have been working up notes for a Memoir of my own to really cover the nine years 1939–'47. I want to give a really correct and documented account of the initiation and passage of the Selective Service Act and of the appointment of Stimson and Patterson (both 1940); various things of interest in the War Department and outside it that I worked on, etc. . . . I have an office here with my books and papers and have had an excellent young assistant from the Harvard Graduate School for the summer months.[3]

The excellent young assistant Clark mentioned was Samuel R. Spencer Jr., who would serve for many years as president of Davidson College in North Carolina. In 1947 Spencer was a doctoral student in Harvard's History Department, after having served in World War II. When Clark inquired for a student to help him write his memoirs, Spencer's name came up. The young man did not know "Mr. Clark" but agreed to meet him at the Hotel Vendome in Boston to discuss the project. There he learned that Clark's doctors had advised him that he could not keep up his hard-driving life, that he had heart trouble, and that he needed to take it easy. Perhaps it was a good time to write his memoirs.[4]

Clark may have been taking a page from Henry Stimson, who had recently entered into a similar arrangement with McGeorge Bundy to write his own memoir: *On Active Service in Peace and War*. Stimson was enthusiastic about Clark's following suit: "You certainly should record your work. At almost every critical period in our history, which I can remember, it was your sagacity which diagnosed and pushed forward the best remedy, and you have not had a quarter of the recognition for it which you should have." (Stimson's letter was one of very few that Clark deliberately saved, saying he'd "rather have [it] than a half-dozen medals.")[5]

Clark proposed that they begin with the recent Selective Service Act campaign and the ensuing War Department years. It was a meaty and interesting story—Spencer agreed and got right to work. He spent the next two summers in Dublin, where Clark had turned his barn into a quasi-office-cum-storehouse, with office furniture and equipment shipped up from New York along with towering stacks of boxes, files, records, books, and the like. But despite Stimson's urgings, Clark's good intentions, and Sam Spencer's able assistance, the memoir project was doomed from the start.

It quickly became clear to Spencer that Clark's involvement would be limited at best. Every time the young man arrived at Outlet Farm, Clark was busy meeting with individuals or groups about world peace, the UN, Harvard, or some other major project. Spencer soon realized he was really serving as the older man's cover for his wife and doctors— Clark could truthfully say he was "working on his memoirs" without actually disrupting his other activities. This was no deliberate plan of deception, which would not have been in Clark's character. Rather it was that Grenville Clark, then sixty-five, was incapable of living largely in the past while there was important work to be done in the present.

At the end of the second summer Spencer approached his boss directly. "Mr. Clark, you know you're not going to finish this [memoir] project; in fact, you're not even going to finish this [selective service campaign] part of it. Would you mind if I take the research I've done so far and use it for my doctoral dissertation?"[6] Clark happily agreed, undoubtedly much relieved. Spencer went back to Cambridge, finished his dissertation, got his PhD, married his longtime sweetheart, Ava—the engagement ring came from a Boston jeweler recommended by a twinkling Clark—and struck out on his own impressive career. The two men remained in warm contact throughout Clark's life. Later Spencer served as a founding member of the board of the Grenville Clark Fund, established at Dartmouth College after Clark died.

With the memoir alibi removed, Clark tried again to be semiretired. He spent extra time with Fanny and did some directed puttering around Outlet Farm. In fact the Wall Street lawyer and Washington agitator sounds every bit the gentleman farmer, if no less meticulous, in a delightfully domesticated letter to his younger daughter:

Dear Louisa: It has quit raining and is lovely weather. The garden is behind and we shall be late starting haying because of the wet but the hay is amazingly high and thick. We are having a big time with the milk to get the bacteria count down. It is too high, apparently due to "slow cooling" in the refrigerator. Even though it gets very cold in there, it apparently does it too slowly, being put in a 20-quart can, and needs to be put soon after being milked into cold water. So we are embarked on having a four jug cooler in the barn cellar. We are negotiating for a secondhand one owned by a man in [nearby] Antrim. We are learning quite a lot. . . . [In other news] Mr. Maier got a big fish (probably three pounds) out of the water but it broke the hook and got away.[7]

While Clark was sending his daughter local farm and fishing reports, he was also paying close attention to national and world events. Throughout 1947 Clark had been filling "notebooks with observations of the perplexing course of American foreign policy."[8] There was much to observe that year, with the architecture of the Cold War rapidly changing the U.S. foreign policy landscape.

The Truman Doctrine was announced in March, specifically to provide aid to Greece and Turkey during the Greek civil war, although the underlying purpose of the doctrine clearly was to counter Stalin's increasing subordination of Eastern Europe and fears of the spread of communism around the globe. In June came the Marshall Plan, the massive rebuilding and relief effort to aid war-ravaged Europe. Clark was alarmed that both major international initiatives were conceived completely outside the UN despite their enormous implications for member nations. Also in March came Truman's Loyalty Order, which instituted mandatory loyalty oaths for federal employees and limited freedoms of the press and of assembly. In September the National Security Act created the modern Departments of Defense, Army, Navy, and Air Force, along with the brand-new Central Intelligence Agency. To many observers, including Clark, it all added up to the U.S. government's putting "itself on a new institutional footing for renewed total war."[9]

Clark never stopped pressing for amendments to the UN Charter, working through friends both inside and outside the UN. He drafted two resolutions calling for charter review that were introduced in the UN's General Assembly by the Cuban delegation; Argentina later introduced another resolution Clark wrote on a related topic. Clark also worked behind the scenes through the Washington columnist and foreign policy commentator Edgar Ansel Mowrer to try to bring the regulation of atomic energy under UN control.[10] While none of these initiatives passed, each provoked vigorous debate, and for Clark the public conversation-education component was nearly as important as the final outcome. All the while Clark's circle of reform-minded men and women continued to expand.

In February 1948 Clark made a major address on UN reform to the New York City Bar Association. He was on his old home turf and speaking to a friendly audience, even if most of the attorneys were much more conservative than he on the topic of world law. Clark argued eloquently and persuasively that the root cause of war was anarchy among nations, absent an official international structure, and that the American containment policy outlined in the Truman Doctrine only made things worse—reinforcing the age-old "us versus them" mentality that could only provoke a similar or worse reaction from the Russians. He proposed a series of UN Charter amendments with concessions by both the Americans and the Soviets. Clark received a warm reception, but any hope of influencing policy was extinguished three weeks later with the communist takeover of Czechoslovakia.[11] The Cold War loomed ever larger, and containing communism was foremost on the minds, lips, and policy pens of elected officials in both parties.

Nevertheless Clark sent out printed copies of his New York speech, along with a cover letter, to friends, colleagues, and high-ranking UN and U.S. government officials. He included President Truman on his distribution list and quickly hit a brick wall. Despite having enjoyed cordial personal relationships with U.S. presidents from Theodore Roosevelt to Franklin Roosevelt and most in between, Clark never managed to establish a rapport with FDR's immediate successor—the chasm between the two men's upbringing, influences, and outlook was bigger than either man's apparent need or willingness to bridge it. Clark's major premise in the speech—that the United States should negotiate more closely and in better faith with the Soviet Union—was underscored in his cover letter: "The truth is that in 'containing' Russia, we have gone a long way in imitating Russian ideas in respect to coerced conformity. We had better look this straight in the eye and realize that this result is just as adverse a consequence . . . as deficits and trade restrictions."[12]

Truman, who considered himself a historian, responded testily: "I don't know what people expect from governments represented by Molotov, Vishinky, and Gromyko. They have fixed ideas and these ideas were set out by Peter the Great in his will." The president was referring to a document, supposedly the infamous czar's will that expressly states the Russian goal of world domination. But Clark himself was no slouch when it came to history. He knew, and had top Russia experts at Harvard reconfirm, that the sensational "Will of Peter the Great" was in fact an inauthentic propaganda piece well on its way to becoming urban legend. Clark fired off a distinctly imperial telegram to the White House, effectively ending the conversation: YOU WERE GREATLY IMPOSED UPON IN BEING LED TO BELIEVE THE AUTHENTICITY OF THE SO-CALLED WILL OF PETER THE GREAT. . . . IT WAS PUBLICIZED FOR PROPAGANDA PURPOSES SHORTLY BEFORE NAPOLEON'S INVASION OF RUSSIA AND IS APPARENTLY BEING USED FOR SIMILAR PURPOSES NOW. [13]

Even without the testy exchange about Peter the Great's will, a close association between Clark and Truman would have been unlikely. The vast differences between them in many ways mirrored those between Truman and his predecessor, Franklin Roosevelt—elite New England upbringing versus Missouri hill farmer, Ivy League education versus no formal college degree, Wall Street lawyer versus Kansas City haberdasher—, and so many more. The plain-spoken president from the "Show-Me State" would surely have received coolly any advice from the Harvard Brahmin about negotiating with the Russians or about virtually any other topic.

More puzzling was the dearth of communication between Clark and Truman's successor, Dwight D. "Ike" Eisenhower. Eisenhower was a similarly liberal-minded conservative with a military background who later became a vocal advocate for peace. At a glance he and Clark would seem natural allies. Some of Eisenhower's public statements on world peace, disarmament, and international law sound as if ghostwritten by Clark: "Since the advent of nuclear weapons, it seems clear that there is no longer any alternative to peace, if there is to be a happy and well world"; "There can be no true disarmament without peace, and there can be no real peace without very material disarmament"; "The peace we seek and need means much more than mere absence of war. It means the acceptance of law, and the fostering of justice, in all the world"; and many more.[14]

Yet all that exists on record between the two men is one stilted exchange in which Eisenhower offers a somewhat garbled reply as to whether he has read Clark's 1950 book, *A Plan for Peace,* Clark's slim cogent summary of the underlying world problem as he saw it—international anarchy in a nuclear age. The president does address his and Clark's shared concern about the difficulties inherent in sacrosanct notions of national sovereignty, but beyond that a clear message is hard to decipher:

Secretary Dulles and I and others, have discussed this matter frequently, and, by coincidence, only within the last few days. Now, I have not read this particular book, although I have read much of what Grenville Clark has written, and I have no doubt that it is on the same vein really a world of peace through world law.

I, myself, quoting my favorite author, wrote a short chapter to conclude a book that I wrote back in 1947 or '48 and in it I pointed out there was going to be no peace, there was going to be no real strength among the free world countries unless each was willing to examine its—simple sole sovereign position and to see whether it could make some concessions, each to the others, that it could make a legal or law basis for settling disputes.

Now I still think—I think that that is the gist of Mr. Clark's and, as a matter of fact, Justice Roberts was of the same group—it is the kernel of his thinking.

Ike Eisenhower[15]

Not a particularly illuminating response, let alone an eloquent endorsement. There is no record the two men attempted to communicate again.

It is hard to guess how the president on whom Clark arguably had the most influence, Franklin Roosevelt, would have felt about Clark's peace proposals. Clark was convinced FDR would have been a strong supporter had he lived to see the Cold War and nuclear arms race develop. A reporter asked Clark near the end of his life whether Roosevelt have supported world peace through world law, belatedly making good on his own "great objective" to keep the peace. "Yes, I believe he would have," Clark answered. "Although he was not ready in 1944 to sponsor the truly revolutionary changes that [were] required to constitute an effective United Nations, I firmly believe that today [1966] he would have perceived the absolute necessity for total disarmament under effective world law. He would have gone for it in a bold and determined way."[16] Clark wanted to think every head of state could be persuaded to the logic of world peace through world law, once they fully understood it.

In 1949 the instigation of repressive Cold War–era policies and tactics was bold, determined, and had academic freedom in its crosshairs. Harold Dodds, the president of Princeton, described academic freedom as "at best a unique sort of freedom difficult for many laymen to comprehend" and noted that it was undergoing its "periodic hostile scrutiny."[17] These tactics were reminiscent of the teacher loyalty oath campaign Clark had battled in the 1930s, except this time scrutiny came from a different source. The teacher oaths had been largely the work of state legislatures, but now wealthy conservative alumni were protesting against professors at their alma maters who were seen as in any way red, or sympathetic to communism.

Against this backdrop Grenville Clark became a considerable celebrity in academic circles for his resounding response to one such protester—an angry right-wing Harvard Law School alumnus named Frank Ober. Ober was a rabid anticommunist and the author of a Maryland antisubversion statute that bore his name. He threatened to withhold a large pledged contribution to the university unless Harvard disciplined certain faculty or fired for them for their left-leaning political views. Harvard President James B. Conant immediately turned to Grenville Clark for assistance. He wrote to Clark, "Ordinarily, I do not trouble the members of the Corporation with my fan mail. In this case, however, I was wondering if you would not care to take Mr. Ober on." In an essay published in 1975, Conant recounted: "I turned to Grenville Clark for assistance. I knew no one could write a better defense of Harvard's position."[18]

Clark agreed, relishing the opportunity to defend both his alma mater and academic freedom as a foundational American liberty. He later called the Ober incident "by far the most significant matter in which I had a part . . . the re-affirmation in 1949 of the University's adherence to its traditional refusal to police or discipline its faculty for unpopular views."[19] Clark's response to Ober was a twelve-page, single-spaced tour de force—part legal brief, part history lesson on Harvard, part ringing treatise on civil liberties. His epic communiqué began:

Dear Mr. Ober:

Mr. Conant [asked me to] write you regarding the "history and significance of the traditional Harvard policy" on freedom of expression for the faculties and students. I am willing to do this because I think your letter raises questions that go to the very life of Harvard and all other colleges and are, therefore, of vital consequence to the country at large. . . .

Let me say at once that your proposals—apparently to dismiss or censure two professors, and certainly to impose drastic controls on the activities as citizens of all professors—cannot and will not be adopted at Harvard, so long as Harvard remains true to her principles.

To clarify those principles Clark quoted from the 1869 inaugural address of his esteemed mentor, former Harvard president Charles W.

Eliot: "A University must be indigenous; it must be rich; but, above all, it must be free. The winnowing breeze of freedom must blow through all its chambers. . . . This University aspires to serve the nation by training men to intellectual honesty and independence of mind. The Corporation demands of all its teachers that they be grave, reverent, and high-minded; but it leaves them, like their pupils, free."

Clark then summarized Ober's specific complaints, namely, that the Harvard professor John Ciardi had spoken at a Progressive Party meeting in Maryland held to protest Ober's anticommunist bill, and that another professor, Harlow Shapely, had taken part in a recent world peace conference in New York that Ober considered subversive. Clark pointed out that "both the Maryland and New York meetings were on public issues and were open to the press" and continued:

> You do not question the complete legality of either meeting. And yet you seem to say that the two professors committed some sort of grave offense. . . . I do not see how you can expect reasonable men to think of participation in open and legal meetings on public subjects as the equivalent of secret plotting to commit crime, merely because Communists or "fellow travelers" take part in such meetings. On this line of reasoning, literally thousands of reputable citizens would have offended. By no possibility could Harvard adopt a view which, to put it mildly, is so extreme.
>
> I believe . . . that [academic freedom] is an especially vital segment [of all the constitutional freedoms] because it concerns the students as much as the professors. If the professors are censured, constrained or harassed, it affects not only themselves; it affects also those whom they teach—the future voters and leaders upon whose integrity and independence of mind will depend the institutions by which we live and breathe a free air. For if the professors have always to conform and avoid unpopular views whether in class or not, what kind of men will they be? And where will our young men and women go to hear and weigh new ideas, to consider both sides and acquire balance and integrity?

Clark wrapped up his arguments by acknowledging that Ober would probably not find them convincing, at least not yet:

> I am under no illusion that this letter, or any similar argument, is likely to affect your attitude in this matter, at least for some time. For my observation in the corresponding period after the First World War was that in a period of alarm, proposals to restrict

free expression rest on strong feelings which for the time override sound judgment. . . . I hope, though, that I may have convinced you that there is another side, and that there is a deep-rooted tradition at Harvard utterly opposed to your view—a tradition that must and will be upheld as long as Harvard remains true to herself.

Grenville Clark[20]

While Ober likely was not persuaded, Clark had hit a home run for academic freedom. He had also won from all practical standpoints. Professors Ciardi and Shapely were not censured, Harvard's integrity was not compromised, and Clark's letter may stand as the classic defense of the rights of professors everywhere to freely express their views, even— and perhaps especially—when those views are outside the prevailing political mainstream.

CHAPTER 13

Uneasy Peace—The 1950s

Grenville Clark's penultimate decade opened with a jittery and divided world on the brink of a third world war. On June 25, 1950, four short years after Hiroshima and Nagasaki, communist North Korea invaded quasi-democratic South Korea. Predictably the United States and the UN came to the aid of the South, while the Soviet Union and China variously backed the North. It was the first dramatic instance of what the historian Stephen Ambrose describes as "the Cold War flaring hot."[1] Many observers feared it could be the last, with the nuclear arms race now officially under way. (The Soviets had shocked the West the year before by successfully exploding their first atomic bomb; the United States responded by fast-tracking development of the thousand times more lethal hydrogen bomb, and what the nuclear physicist Herbert York later called "the race to oblivion" was on.)[2]

Meanwhile the fragile new United Nations organization was being sorely tested. In 1949 Mao's communist army had emerged victorious in China's long and torturous civil war, but the UN refused to acknowledge the new government or to oust the former Chinese nationalist government (which had fled to Taiwan) from the Security Council. The Soviet Union boycotted its own Security Council seat in protest, a move that backfired when, in the Soviets' absence, the other members approved a resolution backing South Korea. Alan Cranston sought Clark's counsel in making sense of the turbulent international scene. Noting that World War II had begun in remote places like Manchuria and Ethiopia, Cranston wrote to Clark: "There are those in Washington and elsewhere who believe that World War III has now started in Korea." Clark was of course deeply concerned about the events unfolding on the Korean peninsula. But for someone who had worked so strenuously to prevent precisely what seemed to be happening, his immediate reaction was surprisingly calm. As always he took the long view, as summarized in a reassuring letter to Cranston: "The crisis may well further deepen, but this should not much discourage us because it is often the case that formidable and proud opponents will only settle at the last moment, and must actually look down into the abyss before they turn away. Now we are coming somewhere near to doing just that and probably, if we now avoid a general war (as I think we will), we will continue near the abyss for quite a long time. If this be so, people will continue more and more to be looking for a constructive way out."[3]

Clark was already at work on the blueprint for at least one way out. In 1950 he published *A Plan for Peace.* In eighty-three concise pages it steps through the likely progression of a third world war, whether triggered deliberately or accidentally, and the specific (and horrific) consequences that each country, continent, and region would likely suffer as a result. It is a shockingly eyes-wide-open discussion with none of the usual euphemistic language—"collateral damage," "blow back," "friendly fire"— commonly used to deflect attention from the deadly consequences of military action. In his foreword Clark acknowledges the Korean crisis, saying: "The Korean War will, I believe, once more enforce the lesson that it is an illusion to expect peace in an armed and ungoverned world."[4]

The book came to be published in an unusual way. In the early anxious days following the invasion of South Korea, Clark received "a very pressing invitation" from friends on the Senate Foreign Relations Committee to appear before it and "go deeply into my ideas on world peace through world law." Ever protective of her husband's health, Fanny discouraged a Washington trip on the ground that "to testify at length under pressure was the last thing in the world [I should] do." So Clark instead wrote up a thorough summary of those ideas for his "Senatorial friends." He tells the story from there: "Somebody sent a copy of the statement I prepared to Cass Canfield, of Harper's, who put it in a book. . . . Senator Ralph Flanders, a friend of mine, read it and phoned me. 'I've written a letter to every member of the United States Senate about this book,' he said. 'I want ninety five copies of it and I want them tomorrow morning. Can you get them here tomorrow morning?'"[5]

In the days before Fedex that was no small request, but Clark found a (rare) air freight messenger, and the books were in Washington the next morning to be distributed along with Flanders's letter to all the other senators. Clark did eventually appear before both the Senate and House Subcommittees on Foreign Affairs to expand on his plan and answer questions.

A copy of *A Plan for Peace* was also sent to the Ford Foundation, where Paul Hoffman and Robert Maynard Hutchins were looking to fund peace research with Ford Motor Company's abundant surplus profits. This was partly to reduce scrutiny by the Internal Revenue Service but also to honor the late Henry Ford's well-known enthusiasm for peace.

Hutchins spent a full day at Dublin discussing Clark's vision of a world education program on international law and world government, starting with about a dozen centers around the globe. Hutchins was enthusiastic and didn't balk at the tens of millions of dollars Clark suggested would likely be required. In fact Hutchins suggested "that it might be *too little* money for the declared purpose and that it ought perhaps to be done on a greater scale."[6]

Clark got right to work on the project, and his files from 1951 and 1952 bulge with the voluminous related correspondence, including detailed drafts of the program, budgets, and so on. Then communication from the foundation suddenly stopped. It took some digging, but Clark eventually learned that his program was another Cold War casualty: "Joseph McCarthy came along, and . . . some friends on the corporation's board tipped me off that it was being said that my proposal was contrary to the policy of our government." Clark got a consolation prize of "$25,000 a year for research and a secretary for five years," and the chapter ended. He was naturally disappointed but not entirely surprised. He maintained then and later that no "Foundation to this day [1967] has done anything on an adequate scale for the cause of world order under law."[7]

Clark followed *A Plan for Peace* with the encyclopedic *World Peace Through World Law*, cowritten with Louis Sohn, a Harvard professor and Dublin Conference alum. The book was published by Harvard University Press in 1958, with second, third, and fourth editions through 1973 (the final version is a posthumous tribute to Clark by Sohn). In the book Clark and Sohn systematically rewrite the entire United Nations Charter— article by article—to address what they saw as its crucial deficiencies. It was an astounding effort, translated into more than a dozen languages, including Russian and Arabic. (The Arabic version was introduced by the then-professor Boutrous Boutrous Ghali of Egypt, who would become UN secretary general.) Clark's private distribution list for the book was impressive; one early mailing list was broken down into orderly subcategories, each recipient a personal friend: "Governors (18); Senate (28); House (53); Cabinet (7); University Presidents (7)," plus uncounted "Lawyers, Ministers, Organizations, Heads of State, U.N. Delegates," and more.[8]

Clark knew this audience well, and they knew him. The book carried added weight for not coming from an armchair theorist or political zealot. Each idea and prescription was firmly rooted in a lifetime of experience and observation of the U.S. government and the international system. As Sohn put it, "Mr. Clark's unique experience as advisor to the secretaries of state and war, his leading role in preparing the United States for two World Wars, gave him an insight into many problems, which could not be easily matched." Sohn also appreciated Clark's extreme care with the text: "He was forever trying to improve a text. He hated deadlines and resented the need to stop changing a draft in order to get a copy to the printer. He would sometimes revise a galley or even a page proof completely and the poor printer would have to start all over again. . . . But the result of this tinkering . . . was usually beneficial; the text would gain clarity and the thought would come through not only for an expert but even for an untutored layman."[9]

One such untutored layman was a head waiter at a Minneapolis hotel. The man became so intrigued by Clark's speech during a peace conference dinner that he brought home a copy of the 540-page *World Peace Through World Law.* Unsure whether he'd even begin to understand it, he "took the plunge and began at the beginning. I read it through the night and I did not find anything too difficult for me. Everything clearly explained, step by step, and everything fitted perfectly."[10] For Clark each person educated, whether head waiter or head of state, counted as a victory.

On top of his major writing projects, Clark continued to lecture widely on world peace through world law, disarmament, and related topics. Simeon Adebo, Nigeria's ambassador to the UN, once said: "Wherever two or three people were gathered to hold serious discussions on this subject, [Grenville Clark] was almost sure to be with them."[11] Clark's speeches did not take place under particularly auspicious circumstances in the early 1950s. "The good news of damnation's" powerful appeal immediately after Hiroshima and Nagasaki had lost much of its traction as fear of communism overtook fear of the bomb. "Better Dead than Red" was the slogan of the day, used even by normally measured individuals, including President Eisenhower.

The Cold War was also having a predictably chilling effect on civil liberties in the United States. In 1950 Senator Joseph McCarthy made his sensational charge that more than 200 known communists were working in the State Department. McCarthyism in its full virulence would define the decade, as anticommunist committees, panels, and loyalty review boards sprang up in federal, state, and local governments, as well as many private enterprises, bent on rooting out suspected communists in their midst.

In response to the perceived security needs of the Cold War, Congress passed antisedition and immigration-control bills, and the Supreme Court approved imprisonment of (legal) Communist Party leaders. Republicans and Democrats alike fought to be perceived as more anticommunist than anyone else. One peace historian said, "After the early 1950s only the lonely professed to doubt the need for a vigilant security state and the danger of subversives within and enemies without."[12] If he was lonely, Grenville Clark didn't show it. He crisscrossed the country and the globe for peace-related conferences, perhaps all the more vigorously because of the hostile climate: London in 1951 and 1952; Copenhagen and Princeton in 1953; New York and Minneapolis in 1954; St. Louis in 1957.

Many of these conferences were held under the auspices of the United World Federalists, to which Clark continued to offer advice and support. The UWF was near its 1949 height, with 47,000 members in 720 chapters across the United States. (More than 150,000 people worldwide belonged to various federalist groups.) This was not a fringe liberal crowd by any means; nearly fifty national associations, including the American Veterans Committee, National Grange, the Young Republicans, and many religious groups, formally supported the UWF. In early 1949 the governors of nine states and the mayors of fifty American cities had proclaimed an official World Government Week. By mid-1950 twenty-nine state legislatures had passed resolutions endorsing world government. That June a bipartisan group of ninety-one members of the U.S. House of Representatives introduced a resolution supporting world federation as the "fundamental objective" of U.S. foreign policy; the resolution shortly had 111 cosponsors in the House and Senate.

The peace historian Lawrence Wittner acknowledges this "unprecedented challenge to nationalism" ironically resulted in part from one version of nationalism itself—extrapolating the American federal government system to cover the entire world. But it also owed much to the widespread public feeling succinctly expressed by Cord Meyer, that "federation [was] the alternative to atomic war." Joseph Baratta, the scholar of record for the world federalist movement, notes that "long study of great power politics may incline us to forget the hope and willingness that characterized the last year of World War II and at least a year thereafter." On this point Baratta quotes William C. Bullitt, the former ambassador to the Soviet Union: "After a great war like this there comes a brief moment when world affairs are in a period of flux . . . or as Tom Paine would have put it, when 'we have it in our power to begin the world over again.'"[13] Clark and the world federalists strove to seize that brief moment.

Beyond Clark's official and unofficial affiliations with organized peace groups, he found in his personal associations seemingly limitless opportunities to spread the word. (Had Clark been a religious man, he would have made a superb missionary.) He traveled the world to personally persuade heads of state on almost every continent of the logic of his ideas. In England Clark became close to former prime minister Clement Atlee, an enthusiastic collaborator in the cause of peace. Even vacations were not exempt from peace work. In 1956 Grenville and Fanny took an around-the-world cruise on the Swedish ocean liner *Kungsholm*, and on a shore stop in India the Clarks shared a memorable hour with Prime Minister Jawaharlal Nehru. Always learning as well as teaching, Clark observed the wretched conditions in the southern hemisphere and put world economic development and "radical steps to deal with world poverty" on his agenda and into his peace prescription from then on.[14] That same cruise included another private detour, a visit with President Gamal Abdel Nasser in Egypt. Both Nehru and Nasser received copies of *World Peace Through World Law* in their native language.

Clark had official or unofficial meetings with leaders in virtually every country of world prominence, including the Soviet Union. The one exception was China. Clark tried hard and sometimes ingeniously to get into communist China, but he never succeeded. In 1949 the bamboo curtain era began as the freshly victorious Mao government and the wary U.S. government became ever more mistrustful of each other. (See Chapter 14 for details of Clark's efforts to break through that curtain, often through the journalist Edgar Snow.)

An important aspect of Clark's ongoing campaign to create a more effective United Nations is that he worked closely with people inside that organization as well as those on the outside. He formed strong collaborative associations with UN officials and administrators at all levels. Many became personal friends, including Carlos Romulo of the Philippines, who was president of the General Assembly; Undersecretary Adebo; and Muhammad Zafrullah Khan of Pakistan, head of the International Court of Justice of the United Nations. Clark invited these leaders and forward thinkers and their wives to spend weekends in Dublin in addition to meeting at conferences around the world. Clark undoubtedly complicated their lives with his relentless pursuit of a more perfect UN , yet they greatly respected his extraordinary legal and historical grasp of their organization.

When Carlos Romulo mentioned Clark's work to the early and influential UN Secretary General Dag Hammarskjöld of Sweden ("not an easy man to impress," according to Romulo), Hammarskjöld said, "I have great respect for Grenville Clark. I think he knows the United Nations better than most of us do." Romulo agreed, recalling "the spontaneous flow of [Clark's] knowledge of the United Nations and wisdom in the changes he wanted made and his sound proposals to correct them. . . . His mind was a reservoir of great ideas on how to establish and maintain world peace."[15] The enduring friendships established with Romulo, Khan, Adebbo, and so many others were a hallmark of Clark's uniquely collaborative brand of agitation.

In part to accommodate his nonstop work for peace, Clark resigned from the Harvard Corporation in 1950 after twenty years of continuous duty. The university acknowledged his long service with an honorary doctoral degree in law. Clark accepted the gesture graciously but not without gentle humor. His reply to Henry Friendly's congratulatory letter is typical:

Dear Henry:

It was awfully good of you to bother to write me about those honorary degrees. [Clark had also recently received one from Princeton.] I never had such a thing before so it was quite an experience to have two within ten days.

The Harvard degree wasn't so surprising because I did retire from the Corporation last November after twenty years and it is more or less customary there to give a degree to a former member who has served quite a while and hasn't done anything disgraceful. The one at Princeton, though, was a complete surprise.   GC[16]

(Clark received a third honorary degree in 1953, this time from Dartmouth. Clark's Plattsburg and War Department ally, John J. McCloy, was honored at the same ceremony, and President Eisenhower gave the keynote address, but the real pleasure was accepting the award from John Dickey, a close, longtime friend of Clark's.)[17]

Although Clark had deeply enjoyed his years on the Corporation board, his tenure on it ended uncomfortably for all involved. Clark and the Harvard president he helped appoint, James B. Conant, had become close friends and allies on world peace activities, among other things. Clark summarized his Harvard association in a brief biographical sketch for the fiftieth reunion of his 1903 Class: "Apart from invaluable friendships, I look back on my seven years at Cambridge and twenty years on the Corporation as worth-while and a privilege."[18] The relationship should have glided peacefully into the New England sunset, but that was not to be.

A disagreement involving Harvard's Arnold Arboretum began while Clark was still on the Corporation but was not resolved until after he left. The arboretum is located in Boston, across the Charles River from Harvard's Cambridge campus, but is administered by Harvard under a trust set up by the arboretum's original donors. At issue was whether Harvard's Botany Department would be permitted to dip into the arboretum's endowment to fund some of its own projects in Cambridge. Clark and other passionate friends of the arboretum insisted that the trust instrument defined the purpose of the arboretum as horticulture, which meant its resources could be used only to directly maintain and improve the arboretum's extensive collection of trees, plants, flowers, and other flora. The funds could not be diverted to the Botany Department, or any other department, for any other purpose. The disagreement escalated and ended up in court. Expert witnesses testified about the differences between horticulture and botany.[19]

If the issue seems esoteric, and differences between the two sides like hairsplitting, the emotions the arboretum controversy aroused were real and intense. The Arnold Arboretum was given to Harvard in the 1800s and soon became a cherished historic landmark in Boston, a city that takes historic landmarks seriously. It was beloved by Bostonians, none more so than Fanny Dwight Clark, who had been visiting it since she was a little girl. Perhaps Fanny, with her deep affection for the place, combined with her professional-level interest and skill in horticulture, rallied her husband. Whatever the impetus, Grenville Clark made clear he was horrified that Harvard was not honoring the terms of the Arnolds' gift (even though he had initially approved the diversion to botany while he was on the Corporation board and even though the donor was long dead and the reason for the diversion of resources potentially valid).

The disagreement escalated, and when Clark threatened to drag his famously private university into court over the matter, Conant became enraged, publicly accusing Clark of "dirty pool." For its part Harvard did not exactly behave nobly, apparently treating certain of the arboretum people quite shabbily. According to one historian, "It got personal. [Harvard] wouldn't go see [the other side] without having a lawyer with them."[20]

Harvard prevailed after a nasty fight, and Clark and Conant never really forgave each other. Lasting effects on Harvard seem to have been minimal—both its Arnold Arboretum and Botany Department thrive to this day. But the controversy effectively ended the two men's friendship—or at least reduced to occasional forced pleasantries what had been a close, personal, collaborative association. (Conant did contribute an eloquent essay for the book of memoirs Clark's older daughter collected upon her father's death.)[21]

The controversy had one happy, if unintended, consequence. It brought Grenville Clark into contact with George Avery of the Brooklyn Botanic Garden. Avery was both a botanist and a horticulturist and therefore the perfect expert witness for the highly nuanced arboretum case. During the lengthy legal contest the two men became good friends. The Averys visited Dublin, and the Clarks toured the Brooklyn Botanic Garden. The Clarks' admiration for Avery's impressive operation inspired them to donate their family home on Long Island and its twelve acres to the Brooklyn Botanic Garden after Fanny's death.[22]

Clark had formally retired from Root, Clark in 1946. If he did not exactly follow the related strategy of relaxing into the life of gentleman farmer and armchair memoirist, he did at least give up the active practice of law. Old ties beckoned, however, and on October 1, 1954, Grenville Clark and his former partner and lifelong friend Elihu Root Jr. became of-counsel to the Wall Street firm of Cleary, Gottlieb, Friendly, and Ball (or "Cleargolaw," as the name was usually shortened). The designation was a mark of prestige and respect, much as when the young Root, Clark partners had similarly appointed Elihu Root Sr. as counsel to their own fledgling firm at the outbreak of World War I. The two law firms were directly linked, as four of the original five Cleargolaw partners, including the future federal judge Henry Friendly, had early Root, Clark pedigrees. It was a happy reunion for all parties, and the normally restrained senior partner Leo Gottlieb practically gushed:

> It is almost impossible to express adequately the importance to our firm of the event. . . . It is not too much to say that it placed our firm in a brand new class. It transformed the firm from one of any number of small firms of good reputation for character and competence . . . to a firm which would have to be regarded as an important Wall Street firm plainly destined to become one of the big league. . . . There is no accolade, no citation, no honor of any kind that could have meant more to us than the willingness of Elihu Root, Jr. and Grenville Clark to become identified with our relatively small off-shoot of Root, Clark and to lend their names and prestige to the image we present to the world.[23]

In 1954 Root, who initiated the of-counsel role for the two former partners, was still in active law practice, in addition to serving on the boards of large corporations and civic organizations. He by design became an active partner at Cleargolaw. For Clark the of-counsel designation was mainly symbolic. Although he was "very keen" on the proposed arrangement and looked forward to renewing contact with many old Root, Clark friends now at Cleargolaw, it was understood that Clark would spend virtually all his time at Dublin working on his own public service projects. At his insistence he received no pay, did not take an office at the firm, and was not assigned a secretary. He was available mainly for consultation by telephone, and by mail, and made occasional trips to New York for meetings and conferences. The affiliation pleased Clark greatly, perhaps more than he anticipated. Both he and Root continued in their advisory roles until their deaths within a few months of each other in 1967.[24]

All was not pure harmony in Clark's relationship with the legal establishment, however. He was dismayed to see the resurgence of loyalty oaths, which he had battled decades before on behalf of teachers, now cropping up with alarming frequency across a range of professions. The final insult came when the oaths arrived at his own American Bar Association. The association president opened the annual ABA convention in 1950 with an insidious warning, echoing similar calls being sounded across the country: "We are faced with an attack from within on our form of government and our American way of life by foreign ideologies."[25]

The ABA membership responded with a reactionary solution to what Clark saw as a hysterically inflated problem, recommending mandatory loyalty oaths for all new and existing members of the bar. The idea, which should have been instantly repugnant to trained guardians of the Constitution, was instead approved with "less discussion than would have been devoted to the menu at the next annual banquet." This grim account was reported to Clark by Zechariah Chaffee, coauthor of the amicus brief for the *Minersville v. Gobitis* flag-saluting case back in the Bill of Rights Committee days. Another veteran of that committee, Ross Malone, said of the oaths: "I must confess that having had some small part in the glorious past of the Bill of Rights Committee I was perhaps [more] disturbed than the average person to see its [the ABA's] perverted efforts on that occasion."

After agreeing to self-imposed loyalty oaths, the ABA established the Special Committee to Study Communist Tactics, Strategy, and Objectives, the antithesis in motive and operation of the Bill of Rights Committee organized by the same body just nine years earlier. Clark fumed. He allowed Chaffee to fight the fight but offered his customary behind-the-scenes counsel and support. Clark wrote to Malone that the "supineness" of the ABA appalled him, just as had the effective death of their cherished Bill of Rights Committee after Clark left it.[26]

In 1959 the supineness of the U.S. Supreme Court drew Clark's ire. In December of that year Dr. Willard Uphaus, an elderly and eccentric New Hampshire pacifist and Methodist minister, was imprisoned because of his continued refusal to provide New Hampshire authorities with the names of hundreds of people who had visited his World Fellowship summer camps. Uphaus had been the target of a 1953 investigation led by a firebrand state attorney general, Louis Wyman, to root out "subversive persons" under the 1951 New Hampshire State Subversive Activities Act. Uphaus had cooperated fully with Wyman in discussing and disclosing his own activities. But Uphaus steadfastly refused to name his visitors, convinced that Wyman's sole purpose in seeking their names was to harass Uphaus's guests, as Uphaus himself was being harassed, for their lawful but allegedly unpatriotic pacifist views.

Wyman then prosecuted Uphaus, whose defense was three pronged. First he cited the biblical command not to bear false witness against his brother. Next he cited the teachings of the Methodist Church to uphold civil and religious rights and to condemn guilt by association. Finally Uphaus held up a copy of the Bill of Rights and said: "I love this document, and I propose to uphold it with the full strength and power of my spirit and intelligence." Uphaus was convicted, appealed, and the New Hampshire Supreme Court sided with Wyman. In 1959 Uphaus appealed to the U.S. Supreme Court. The high court ultimately upheld the New Hampshire ruling in a 5–4 decision, with Clark's increasingly conservative friend Felix Frankfurter in the majority.[27]

The verdict left Uphaus to be imprisoned, potentially indefinitely, unless and until he abandoned his conscientious objections and disclosed the names of his guests to state authorities. Uphaus, a theologian of strong conviction, remained firm and so did the State of New Hampshire. Enter Grenville Clark.

In December 1959, three days after Uphaus was incarcerated at the Merrimack County Jail, "there to remain for one year . . . or until he purges himself of contempt or until further orders of this court," Clark had written to the governor of New Hampshire, Wesley Powell, urging Uphaus's immediate release.[28] Powell did not respond. Grenville Clark made it his mission to have the *Uphaus* case reargued before the U.S. Supreme Court at his own expense.

The seventy-seven-year-old Clark tapped a pair of talented younger lawyers to help with the enormous work of preparing and presenting a Supreme Court case. They were Robert Reno, a respected New Hampshire lawyer and world peace advocate, and Louis Lusky, a former Root, Clark associate and Bill of Rights Committee member now practicing down in Louisville, Kentucky. Clark would personally cover all costs. The veteran lawyer stayed in the background but daily advised the younger men by telephone, wire, and/or letter. Reno recalled Clark's expert guidance: "His analysis of the legal niceties of the case was superb, and his direction of both strategy and tactics indicated why he was one of the great lawyers of the twentieth century."[29]

Clark understood the power of public opinion and worked the press with an open letter in local newspapers summarizing his case:

> I regard the jailing of Dr. Uphaus as a glaring injustice, which is a disgrace to New Hampshire and a discredit to our country. I also

believe that his continued detention in jail because, for reasons of conscience, he will not disclose certain names is unconstitutional under our Federal Constitution; and I believe that the legal issues, some of them new, should be reconsidered by the Supreme Court of the United States. These are the reasons why I have assumed the legal expenses of the new proceedings. It is a privilege to help in the effort to remedy this shocking injustice.[30]

Clark's team worked through the summer of 1960, but when the U.S. Supreme Court opened its session that fall the *Uphaus* appeal came up one vote short of the four needed to grant the hearing (aka "granting certiorari," or to "grant cert" in legal lingo). Only Associate Justices Hugo Black and William O. Douglas, and Chief Justice Earl Warren voted to rehear the *Uphaus* case. In an unusual move two of the three justices in the minority wrote formal dissenting opinions.[31] Black's dissent was a particularly eloquent affirmation of free speech and free assembly. In it he addresses squarely an issue long close to Clark's heart and career— defending the protections in the Bill of Rights: "I think the summary dismissal of this appeal without even so much as the benefit of oral argument, when the abridgment of the rights of free speech and assembly is so obvious, is a sad indication of just how far this Court has already departed from the protections of the Bill of Rights and an omen of things yet to come."[32]

Clark, who had vehemently opposed Black's appointment by FDR in 1937, in part because Black, a southerner, had once been a member of the Ku Klux Klan, sent a congratulatory letter on the justice's seventy-fifth birthday the following February:

> Mr. Justice Black: On your 75th birthday, please accept my respect and admiration for your inspiring example on the court. And my best wishes for a further period of fruitful work. . . . You struck a strong blow for the rights of conscience with your superb opinion. I wish you many years of health and vigor.
>
> Grenville Clark

Black quickly replied:

> I cannot tell you how much I appreciated the message you sent me on February 27th, my 75th birthday. While I have never had an intimate acquaintance with you, I have known through the years about the public service you have given so unselfishly.
>
> Hugo Black[33]

But what of Uphaus? New Hampshire authorities quietly released him on December 12, 1960, two days before his original one-year, but potentially renewable, jail term ended. He left the state and the matter officially ended. Clark was of course disappointed by the Supreme Court ruling but assured his young associates that "the effort we have made has been well worth it from my point of view." He was buoyed by the strong dissents of justices Black and Douglas, and in any case Clark cared most for results, and Uphaus was free. Clark also understood there was more than one way to solve a problem. The intense pressure he and his team brought to bear in the case had mattered, whether it led directly to Uphaus's release or not. Had the elderly theologian been rearrested as threatened, Clark, the complete lawyer, had detailed plans already drawn up for three different potential prosecution strategies.[34]

Despite his differences with the American Bar Association over loyalty oaths and other issues, the ABA in 1959 awarded Grenville Clark its highest honor—the American Bar Association Medal for "conspicuous service to the cause of American Jurisprudence," placing him in the company of legal legends like Elihu Root Sr., Oliver Wendell Holmes Jr., and Charles Evans Hughes Jr. Clark accepted the medal, gave a gracious acceptance speech, and then undoubtedly filed both with his growing collection of such things. His greatest enjoyment surely came from the calls and letters from friends and associates. Felix Frankfurter, still a close friend despite their widening philosophical divide, summed the situation up nicely:

Dear Grenny: The American Bar Association couldn't honor you, but it honored itself by formal recognition of your intrinsic worth and the high uses to which you put it. In crowning you, the ABA has done a valuable thing in advertising you as a symbol of what is honorable and distinguished in the eyes of our profession.
Affectionately and fondly yours, Felix[35]

Honors and awards aside, Clark tried to keep his customary low profile and avoid the glare and tentacles of an official public role. This required vigilance. He continued to be sought out for both private and government consulting positions, as in this 1951 offer from the Truman administration: "Last evening, Averell Harriman phoned me from the White House about the Commission announced on the radio yesterday p.m. and in the press this a.m. of which Admiral Nimitz is to be Chairman. Harriman, for the President, asked me to serve. . . . I declined (because of other commitments and not for lack of interest)."[36]

The commission had been created to investigate and report on the balancing of national security and civil rights concerns, which would have been right up Clark's alley. As with virtually every such offer he declined, it is tantalizing to speculate how he might have shaken things up had he accepted. Clark and Harriman's close ties spanned more than fifty years. In a poignant memorial essay Harriman was clearly touched that Clark "gave me the feeling he was interested in matters that concerned me" and offered "considerate encouragement whenever I sought his advice."[37] In this case that encouragement resulted in the referral of several other potential candidates for the post, in lieu of acceptance.

While Clark continued to deflect official appointments, he took seriously his role as a community member. He joined Dublin's Unitarian Church, finding a natural fit with the Unitarians' emphasis on freedom of thought and relative lack of dogma. In 1952 the church struggled to find a new pastor for its tiny congregation (then eighteen members). Funding was as scant as the membership, offering little financial security for the pastor. Clark was not a member of the official search committee, but when he learned of a promising applicant he stepped in to privately scrutinize the new man.

Determining that Lyman Rutledge passed muster, Clark took him aside for a private conversation. To mitigate any personal financial risk, Clark told Rutledge, if he agreed to stay, Clark would personally guarantee the pastor's salary and all expenses for a full six months, including a proviso in his will should he die in the meantime. Rutledge accepted and was continually astonished by Clark's quiet subsidies, including paying in full the considerable medical bills when the pastor underwent a major surgery in 1953. Clark's only stipulation was that no one should know. Envelopes with encouraging notes, and even more encouraging checks or wads of cash that arrived out of the blue, were routine. When Rutledge presided at Clark's memorial service at the Dublin Unitarian Church fifteen years after their original six-month agreement, the sadness, affection, and admiration in his eulogy were real.[38]

Clark's civic engagement expanded well beyond his community church. Grenville and Fanny were both vigorous participants in town improvement and preservation projects. They deeded land and access rights for a public landing and parking area on Dublin Lake, helped plan and put on Dublin's bicentennial celebration in 1952, and spearheaded a large and successful citizen campaign to save Mount Monadnock from an unsightly proposed radio tower. They contributed to the Dublin Garden Club, Dublin School, Society for Protection of New Hampshire Forests, and other local improvement groups. And demonstrating that civic and community improvement begins at home, the Clarks meticulously managed Outlet Farm, tended Fanny's exquisite garden, and kept an open door for their circle of family, friends, and neighbors. As the 1950s came to a close Grenville Clark looked forward to the next decade, which would be his last.

CHAPTER 14

Sprint to the Finish: The 1960s

Grenville Clark's final decade was marked by turbulence in America and around the world. Protests against the war in Vietnam intensified in the 1960s as that morass deepened. Clark, who had engineered military training and recruitment efforts for two world wars, was a Cold War dove. He deplored the Vietnam War as unnecessary and deeply mistaken. He found the official U.S. containment policy toward the Soviets misguided and dangerous, convinced that real progress could come only from human interaction, intelligent discussion, and good-faith negotiation. Of course this may not have been possible given the Soviet regime, but Clark staked his hopes on the people. Convinced that "the citizenry is almost always ahead of the professional politician," Clark bucked Cold War trends by actively encouraging and facilitating direct citizen engagement with Russians.[1]

In 1960 Clark organized the first Dartmouth Conference, bringing together prominent American and Russian citizens—primarily scientists, educators, and other nonpoliticians—to discuss disarmament and other difficult issues. Despite the cooperative intent of the conference, the topic was so contentious and positions so hardened that the tension level soon approached a saturation point. Norman Cousins, Clark's good friend and ally for peace since the Dublin Conference, recalled how Clark stepped in to restore harmony and a sense of common cause:

> The Americans were steadfast in their advocacy of a plan of disarmament with full inspection and control. The Russians reacted sharply to what some of them described as a plan for violating the sovereignty and security of their country. The tone of the meeting was becoming harsh and strident. Grenville Clark, who until that moment had been silent, began to speak.
>
> He began by saying he accepted fully the sincerity of the Soviet delegates to reduce and eliminate the dangers of war. He spoke of the enormous numbers of casualties suffered by the Russian people

in the Second World War, some twenty million dead. He referred to the siege of Leningrad and the heroism of its people. He paid tribute to the Russian contribution to victory during the war. He spoke movingly and with great dignity. Then he told of the need to avert even greater wars in an age of nuclear weapons. He defined the basic principles that had to go into the making of a workable peace. He described the opportunity before leaders of public opinion in gaining acceptance for these principles. He called on both Americans and the Russians to see the problem of disarmament in a larger and more historic setting than weapons alone. When he sat down both sides gave him sustained applause.

And from that moment, Grenville Clark's name was magic with all the Russians who heard him and many who did not. He had demonstrated not just the power of logic but the prodigious force that is represented by an empathetic understanding of the next man's experience and problems. Even more, he had demonstrated that even the most hardened positions tend to dissolve in the presence of honest good will and friendliness.[2]

That same year the seventy-eight-year-old Clark realized it was time to pass to the next generation the leadership of some of his more strenuous peace efforts, particularly those involving travel. He deputized two younger recruits, Harry and Betsy Hollins, who were well qualified to be Clark's foot soldiers. Betsy Jay Hollins was the daughter of Clark's lifelong friend Delancey K. "Lanny" Jay, and Betsy grew up with the Clark family in her life and living room. (As a small child, seated next to "Mr. Clark" at lunch, she decided the distinctive purple birthmark on his left temple "must be heel marks made by the trampling of some German officer's boot when he lay almost dead in the mud!" The little girl couldn't have known that Clark's World War I service was performed in Washington, D.C., but the man did inspire dramatic thoughts.)[3]

By 1960 the Hollinses had already traveled to several continents with and for Clark to help spread the word and distribute copies of *World Peace Through World Law*. That fall they were summoned to Dublin "on a matter of some importance." Soon after they settled into the Clarks' comfortable living room, "G.C. went right to the point. . . . He told us he had contracted a form of cancer and that while he might live a number of years, he had insisted that the doctors give him a reasonable estimate," Harry Hollins recalled. "As he put it, he had a 50–50 chance of living better than a year." The sobering news had quickened Clark's resolve to implement a global education campaign for world peace, which had never left his mind since the aborted Ford Foundation project.

Always seeking the lessons of history, Clark had been carefully studying the twenty years leading up to the U.S. Constitutional Convention of 1787. His reading uncovered "throughout this period a continuing discussion about theories of government that were absorbed to a marked degree not only by the leading public figures of the time but, most important, also by the people." As Clark emphasized to the Hollinses, until citizens of all nations clearly understood that world anarchy was the root cause of war, "the best brains would be wasted in attempting to cope with the symptoms." (Harry Hollins later mused, "G.C's views were most radical [in that] he was interested in root causes rather than symptoms.")[4]

Clark was determined to duplicate the Founders' high-level public discussion on a global scale. He called his new project the World Law Fund (WLF); its mission was international education about the root causes of war and systems of international dispute resolution that eschew violence. Harry Hollins took the lead role in setting up the new organization. Clark outlived his grim one-year prognosis and was able to provide inspiration and guidance as the WLF took shape. In 1965 he endowed the fund with $750,000.[5]

With his global education project in good hands, Clark continued his personal lobbying for peace closer to home. In early 1961, as John F. Kennedy embarked on his brief but impactful presidency, Clark sent a letter of congratulations and advice. He urged the young president to steer a fresh bold course toward "universal and complete disarmament"—coupled with UN revisions and legal institutions that would make possible careful inspection and verification. Kennedy already knew of Clark's work. He called *World Peace Through World Law* a landmark and noted Clark's past and present influence on national events: "Grenville Clark was an effective force in securing our readiness for war when war was imminent—and most recently he has been a force in making disarmament a concrete issue." (Kennedy's Russian counterpart, Nikita Khrushchev, had actually been given a Russian translation of *World Peace Through World Law* in 1958. The emissary was Adlai Stevenson, the forward-looking governor of Illinois, two-time Democratic presidential nominee, future U.S. representative to the United Nations, and Clark's friend since the 1930s through the ABA Bill of Rights Committee.)[6]

Kennedy was a committed internationalist. He had attended the 1945 United Nations conference in San Francisco as a naval officer just returned from his now widely known heroics as a PT boat commander in the Pacific. He talked with world federalists at the conference and agreed in principle that "world organization with common obedience to the law would be the solution." But the prescient young man was not convinced the public had "been horrified . . . by war to a sufficient extent" that they would demand action from their political leaders. The pressure would have to come from the people, not an organization, and "it would have to be so strong that elected officials would be turned out of office if they failed to do it." In short, Kennedy feared, "war will exist until that distant day when the conscientious objector enjoys the same reputation and prestige that the warrior does today."[7]

As president, Kennedy was nonetheless serious about exploring disarmament and appointed a dedicated lieutenant to handle the highly charged issue. The president's special adviser on disarmament was none other than John J. McCloy, whose warm and respectful friendship with Clark dated to the Plattsburg days. A consummate negotiator who had handled numerous high-level negotiations with the Russians since the war, McCloy was a natural choice for the sensitive assignment. He said of his new mission: "We must be ready to consider the most far-reaching proposals. Grenville Clark's ideas, while idealistic, are the only light I can see at the end of the tunnel."[8]

While obviously just one of many influences, Clark offered steady guidance and support to McCloy during the complicated negotiations leading to the McCloy-Zorin Accords of 1961 and the Limited Nuclear Test Ban Treaty in 1963. McCloy also turned to his old mentor during national emergencies such as the Cuban missile crisis.[9] Clark, naturally, was urging negotiation rather than retaliation to effect the removal of Soviet missiles from the island.[10]

But while Clark generally approved of Kennedy's international agenda and felt hopeful about his willingness to pursue disarmament, Clark grew increasingly unimpressed with the administration's civil rights efforts at home. In the early 1960s a journalist showed Clark the draft of an article containing this sentence: "Among those in high places who have admired Grenville Clark is President Kennedy. Praising him as a man alert, in both war and peace, to vital needs, the President has well said that 'his example is one for which we can all be grateful.'" The quote was accurate, but Clark urged the journalist to omit it, saying, "I really don't know him at all and am about to criticize him quite sharply about his lack of zeal in the racial problem."[11]

"The racial problem" was a vast understatement of conditions in the early 1960s. Civil rights protests escalated, with demonstrations, lunch counter sit-ins, and brave and dramatic acts of civil disobedience such the Freedom Riders' campaign to bring about de facto desegregation of interstate travel. Perhaps surprisingly, given his age and social class, Clark approved of the protesters—they were taking a page from his own playbook in applying direct citizen action in the face of inadequate government response to an intolerable situation.

In Clark's 1959 speech accepting the ABA's medal, he had challenged its members to take a vigorous stand on racial justice, saying: "Until we wipe out the stain of racism, we will not only not have a good society in the United States, we will not have a tolerable one."[12] Like other Americans Clark was deeply disturbed as television brought graphic images of discrimination and brutality against black citizens into his living room. As a lawyer his moral outrage was compounded by the wholesale complicity of the legal and judicial system in the South. And as the grandson of LeGrand Bouton Cannon—abolitionist, Civil War colonel, friend of Abraham Lincoln—the deplorable situation called for a direct and forceful citizen response. Clark was particularly stimulated by the Freedom Riders, the young civil rights activists, black and white, men and women, who in May 1961 boarded buses bound for the segregated South, the routes well publicized in advance. The press in the South stoked Confederate flames by describing the Freedom Riders as outside agitators backed by liberal Yankees bent on dismantling the southern way of life. The young people who headed into this cauldron risked not just arrest but their very lives. With grim predictability the Freedom Riders were cruelly harassed—detained, arrested, subjected to vicious mob attacks and beatings, and all manner of insult and intimidation.[13]

In Montgomery, Alabama, federal troops had to be called in during a rally in support of the Freedom Riders at Martin Luther King's First Baptist Church. As King spoke into the evening, a menacing mob gathered and surrounded the church. Armed with torches, tear gas, and firebombs, the angry crowd shouted epithets and vowed violence. Local police were conspicuously absent. As the mob grew in size and aggression, King called U.S. Attorney General Robert Kennedy and implored him to send help before massive bloodshed occurred. Urgent negotiations involving Kennedy in Washington, Alabama authorities, and King inside the church continued until dawn. The next morning National Guard troops finally rescued the trapped Freedom Riders and King's parishioners after a night of unremitting terror.[14]

The situation became a national and international embarrassment for the Kennedy administration. Communist governments seized on the opportunity to show what hypocrites Americans were for pushing freedom and democracy on other countries while denying it to citizens in their own. Propaganda purposes aside, it was a good point and resonated with many noncommunists at home and abroad.[15]

Clark was unequivocally behind the Freedom Riders. Without denying the administration's preoccupation with international concerns—the missile crisis, Vietnam, and planning for the Bay of Pigs—these were beside the point. The nation would always face competing demands for its attention and resources. But there was never an excuse to tolerate injustice or flagrant disregard for the nation's laws as the South was currently flouting the Supreme Court's desegregation rulings. Clark wrote to his friend and physician, Paul Dudley White, about the situation:

> With regard to the Freedom Riders, my inquiries show, as I write you, that there is really no foundation at all for the allegations that they included riffraff. On the contrary, I think it can be demonstrated that with hardly any exceptions these young men and women, both whites and Negroes, represent about the best we have in this country, by which I mean the most idealistic and disinterested of the younger generation.
>
> They have nothing to expect from this effort except hardship and ill treatment with a considerable risk of serious bodily injury which, however, they have been willing to undergo as a matter of principle. Really, I believe that the volunteering of these many hundreds of young people of both races has been one of the most encouraging signs in our American life for many years.[16]

Typically Clark supported the young activists without vilifying all southerners. With an unusually charitable reading of the other side on such a polarizing issue, Clark told White about a racially charged letter he had recently received from a mutual southern friend:

> I must say it is discouraging and even saddening because I feel sure that he is a humane and reasonably intelligent man and yet . . . is compelled to adopt some of the stereotyped views that have long prevented much of any progress in the Deep South towards equal rights for Negroes.
>
> I have repeatedly seen the same thing with various other really fine people from the Deep South who really know that racial discrimination is not only immoral but also contrary to our American pretensions of equal opportunity for all yet are so conditioned and constrained by their inheritance and environment that they simply have to find reasons for not doing more about it.[17]

For Grenville Clark a reasoned and sympathetic understanding of the other side did not preclude taking immediate and strong action to defeat it. He went well beyond moral support, recognizing that the civil rights demonstrators would need money and legal assistance to assert their rights. Working with the National Association for the Advancement of Colored People, Clark personally raised more than $80,000 to meet the extortionate bail requests and other defense costs for Freedom Riders who had been arrested. He also worked to ensure long-term funding for the NAACP's Legal Defense Fund, establishing the Committee of 100, which later was called the Grenville Clark Plan. The plan secured large annual commitments ($1,000 or more) for a ten-year period from a core of one hundred serious donors. Clark kicked it off with a $5,000 check of his own. He and Fanny later gave the Legal Defense Fund $500,000, the largest donation ever received by a civil rights organization at that time. The Legal Defense Fund's president, Jack Greenburg, said later that "Grenville Clark gave early impetus to the transformation of the NAACP Legal Defense and Education Fund from a tiny organization to the substantial public interest law firm it now is. . . . Not often is there a family or are there individuals [like the Clarks] who have both the means and inclination to regularly devote themselves to public service over the years."[18] Clark also joined the advisory board of the Congress of Racial Equality, which had organized the Freedom Rides.[19]

Clark also applied his trademark personal pressure at the highest levels. In 1965 he fired off a scorching letter to Attorney General Nicholas Katzenbach after reading a rousing opinion piece in the *New York Times* by Martin Luther King, who had eloquently excoriated the administration for its inadequate measures to enforce the Voting Rights Act in the South.

Dear Mr. Attorney General:

You have doubtless seen the devastating charges made by Martin Luther King, Jr. in his public statement of July 26 in the *New York Times* to the effect that the present Administration defaulted on its duty with reference to the enforcement of the 1965 voting rights law. If it be correct what he says, that "fewer than forty registrars are appointed and not a single Federal law officer capable of making an arrest was sent into the south," so that the "old way of life—economic coercion, terrorism, murder and inhuman contempt—continued unabated," this is indeed a shocking indictment of the Department of Justice and yourself.

All the evidence which has come to my attention verifies the truth of his statements and if there can be any reply thereto, I should much like to hear it. Anyone with the slightest knowledge of conditions in the Deep South could surely have predicted that in the absence of vigorous enforcement action, the resistance to the registration and voting of Negroes [there] would continue, and since your Department and yourself must have had *some* knowledge of these conditions, it would seem to be totally inexcusable if the facts, as stated by Dr. King, are correct.

Have you any answer?

Very truly yours, Grenville Clark[20]

Clark sent a copy of the Katzenbach letter to King, along with a personal note and a check:

Dear Dr. King:

I agree with every word of your admirable statement in the *Times* of July 26 and am sending a small contribution as a token of my appreciation for it.

I am a member of the Advisory Committee of CORE having been an admirer of [founder] James Farmer. . . . I have also been much interested in the NAACP Legal Defense Fund, to which my first wife and I in 1964 gave $500,000, to be paid in installments of $50,000 per annum over the ten year period. . . . My opinion is that the Legal Defense Fund is doing fundamentally important work but that it has an indefinitely long and hard task ahead. I believe, however, that the kind of work it is doing must be constantly supplemented by the "mass non-violence direct action" which you have so effectively used; and I hope that you will continue to work in the closest possible cooperation with the Legal Defense Fund.

I enclose a copy of a letter which I have just written to Attorney General Katzenbach with reference to your devastating and doubtless correct charge that the present Administration grossly neglected its duty in connection with the enforcement of the 1965 voting rights law. I was glad to see stress put by you in your statement upon this shocking default.

Sincerely yours, Grenville Clark[21]

Clark's concern about the racial problem was real and intense. John Dickey, the president of Dartmouth, remembered many conversations in a cramped duck blind on Clark's marshland on Lake Champlain, during which the unsatisfactory state of racial affairs "unleashed [Clark's] capacity for outrage as was rarely the case with the other things he talked about." Dickey appreciated Clark's "lively sustained interest in the A.B.C. (A Better Chance) program we pioneered at Dartmouth to help educationally disadvantaged youngsters, mainly Negroes, prepare for attendance at first-rate secondary schools and eventually colleges."[22]

Clark went to Hanover one summer to work on the problem of increasing minority admission to highly competitive professional schools, especially law schools. Dickey remembered, "He finished off the visit by taking dinner that evening with the A.B.C. boys, an experience he liked to recall as one of unusual pleasure for him."[23] For an elderly white male, born in the 1800s and raised in homogeneous elite New York society, to have found this dinner an unusual pleasure might seem strange. Yet, given Clark's family history, all the way back to Grandfather Cannon in the Civil War, these experiences with promising African American youth were without question deeply fulfilling.

Was Clark's taking up this cause in his twilight years a rather belated awakening, if not the deathbed conversion of an establishment man born to wealth and privilege? Clark's early military preparedness projects did not always afford equal rights to black recruits. The African American attorney Francis Rivers points out in a largely complimentary essay about Clark that his Plattsburg and Selective Service programs both retained discriminatory elements of that day's military, resulting in subordinate status and some humiliating conditions for Rivers and other African American soldiers who participated. In Clark's defense, however, Rivers notes that not challenging racial discrimination in those early military programs was the result of Clark's unbending focus on the most urgent matter at hand, which in both cases was preparing for and then winning a world war.[24]

Consciously or not, Clark may also have shared his friend Henry Stimson's hesitation about using the military as a vehicle for social change (although Truman later did just that with his landmark military desegregation order). Appropriately the secretary of war who pushed for desegregation was Robert P. Patterson (1945–47), former Plattsburger and Root, Clark associate who had bonded with his ethnic soldiers in World War I.

Clark traced his concerns about racial inequality to his boyhood and, beyond that, to his DNA. His revered Grandfather Cannon had created the first Union army regiment of freed slaves during the Civil War. Clark also never forgot trips to the South in his youth and the appalling treatment of African Americans that he witnessed there. In another letter to Paul Dudley White, Clark encourages his friend's civil rights efforts:

I think you were a little surprised when I said I had been following this racial problem very closely for sixty years, but that is a literal fact, since I first came in close contact with it at the age of eighteen in Jasper County, South Carolina in the winter of 1901. I was then so profoundly impressed that I have never ceased studying and discussing the problem. . . . As I needn't tell you, this is really a tremendous problem and I think that with all your experience and good will and talent for human relations, you can do a lot of good in it.[25]

Completely aside from politics, Clark would have been deeply pleased to know that on November 4, 2008, the day before what would have been his 126th birthday, America elected its first African American president. Barack Obama's reelection four years later, and his inauguration on Martin Luther King Day 2013, would have doubled Clark's satisfaction.

Clark's support of civil rights and civil liberties was not limited to racial or domestic issues. In 1962 the journalist William Worthy was the surprised beneficiary of Clark's assistance. Worthy had established solid dissident credentials while reporting from China in the 1950s and Cuba in the 1960s in defiance of State Department travel bans. He later recalled: "Rarely does a person facing a possible five years in a federal penitentiary in an unpopular political case open the morning mail to find an unsolicited defense fund contribution from a prestigious Wall Street lawyer with impeccable Establishment credentials. . . . That was my personal introduction to Grenville Clark."[26]

Worthy had been reporting from Cuba and was indicted upon his return by a federal grand jury in Miami on "the novel and startling charge of returning to my native land without a valid passport." The charges were "a transparent attempt to discourage any reporting from Cuba that deviated from the official line ('chaos' on the island, the 'imminent collapse' of Fidel Castro, a population yearning to rebel against a 'brutal tyranny' of Hitlerian proportions)." The heavy-handed charges were not to be taken lightly in those highly charged times. Young people today "are largely unaware of the hysteria that gripped this country early in the 1960s in the wake of the Cuban revolution," Worthy writes. "It was a forgone conclusion that I would be convicted and sentenced to prison in the U.S. District Court in Miami—and I was."[27]

Clark had read about Worthy's case in a civil rights newsletter put out by the NECLC (National Emergency Civil Liberties Committee—a name that surely made Clark feel at home). The journalist's struggle resonated, and Clark immediately sent Worthy a supportive letter and a check toward the costs of his appeal, which Worthy ultimately won. Worthy was impressed: "That so distinguished a partner in what my mother would call 'a princely law firm' even read an NECLC publication—in a period when that organization was being attacked as a 'Communist front' and worse—also surprised me initially. At the time I was unaware of Mr. Clark's regal indifference to what others might think of his determination to uphold civil liberty."[28]

All Clark's activities in the 1960s were shadowed by his and Fanny's deteriorating health. As he learned to live with lymphoma (the cancer Clark told the Hollinses about in 1960), Fanny was enduring the cruel and fatal progressive paralysis of ALS (amyotrophic lateral sclerosis, aka Lou Gehrig's disease). On May 3, 1964, Fanny Dwight Clark died in the couple's Long Island home after a lengthy and difficult struggle. It was undoubtedly the greatest loss in Grenville Clark's life. His grief must have been staggering, given his adoration of his wife throughout their fifty-four-year marriage. Typical is this handwritten letter from 1937 while they were apart on their twenty-eighth anniversary. They were nearly three decades into their marriage, but it could have been written by a starry-eyed newlywed:

Dearest Fanny:—Twenty-eight years ago was the best day of my life for me and I wish we were together. Every day and week and year has been better than the last and indeed it's true that I love you and love you "more than ever."

Weren't we happy on "Kungsholm?" It's wonderful that the more hours we are close together the more we need each other. Now although it's only four days I think it's a dreadful deprivation that I can't see your sweet face and eyes and hear your dear voice. But after this we won't be apart very much.

The most wonderful part of all is that I really know you feel the same way.

I love you.

Your loving adoring husband.[29]

Twenty-seven years later Clark expressed his devotion in an even more poignant way, by doing everything he could to make Fanny's final days as bearable as possible. He chartered an ambulance to take her back to her beloved Dublin one last time, but she died four days before the trip. Clark wrote to his old friend Felix Frankfurter, who was contending with his own long list of health problems, about Fanny's final days: "We were on Long Island and she had hoped to get back [to Dublin] by ambulance on May 7, but her strength didn't quite hold out. Her mind was perfectly clear and alert right to the end although she hadn't been able to speak for months because of the paralysis of her throat. She would write briefly and did write many short very cute and humorous things, no matter how sick she was."[30]

One of the sharply humorous things Fanny wrote near the end of her life spoke to the awfulness of being entombed inside an unresponsive body by ALS: "I want to get back to Dublin if it kills me which it probably will, thank God."[31]

On news of Fanny's death, cards, letters, and telegrams of condolence arrived from around the world. The Clarks were such an indivisible unit that Grenville's global army of friends were virtually all also Fanny's, in addition to her own family and friends. As the couple had previously agreed, Clark made a gift of their Long Island home to the Brooklyn Botanic Garden in 1967, a fitting memorial to Fanny Dwight Clark, who had created the twelve-acre oasis from a scrubby sandlot next to the railroad tracks so many years before.

Later that same year, on a trip that must have been bittersweet but also therapeutic, Clark organized a private peace junket to Moscow. No one was more surprised to be invited than Einar Rørstad, a young Norwegian who had been working on Scandinavian-language translations of *World Peace Through World Law*. Rørstad received one of Clark's trademark out-of-the-blue phone calls, this one transatlantic. Just two weeks before the scheduled trip Clark invited Rørstad and his wife to join him in Moscow for a week on one condition: "I'll not permit you to spend one penny of your own money." Of course the couple was "regularly knocked out." Rørstad describes the trip:

Moscow, December 1964, with Grenville Clark, a week never to be forgotten. Our personal talks, our whole group having vodka and caviar together overlooking the Manege Square and the floodlit Kremlin, with Grenville Clark as the natural group leader. His talks with outstanding Russian scientists, the meeting in the Institute of State and Law when he discussed *World Peace through World Law* with a big group of Russian lawyers, and when you really had the feeling that he was only fifty-five or sixty years again, sparkling, brilliant, to the point, witty if necessary—the eminent, piercing advocate of world law. Everyone present, regardless of nationality, had reason to be impressed.[32]

Back at home, however, with the realities of age and illness encroaching, Clark acutely felt the absence of his wife and constant companion. After Fanny died, Grenville Clark had confided to his distant cousin, Senator Joseph Clark of Pennsylvania, that he was considering remarrying. He told Joseph Clark that one of Fanny's last instructions before she died was that Grenville must marry again. After more than fifty years together, she understood better than anyone, perhaps including Grenville himself, that he would need companionship, as well as someone to look after his own health problems.[33]

The senator concurred, as did Clark's children, and in 1965 Grenville Clark married Mary Brush James. Mary was an artist, a widow, and a

Dublin neighbor. She had a solid Dublin arts pedigree as the daughter of the painter George de Forest Brush, and she had been married to the accomplished portrait and landscape artist Alexander James. (Alexander was the son of William James, the well-known psychologist and philosopher, and nephew of the prolific novelist Henry James.) Mary could hardly have been more different from Fanny, but she was a devoted and attentive second wife, and the couple had a brief but apparently happy twilight marriage until Clark's death in 1967.

Mary Clark was quickly drafted into her husband's global peace efforts. Using her spacious art studio as the venue, Grenville Clark in 1965 gathered another group of influential educators, journalists, and public servants for a Second Dublin Conference. If the twenty years since the original Dublin Conference had not brought another world war, neither had they been especially promising for lasting peace. The wartime alliance between the Soviets and the West had been replaced by the iron curtain. Both sides had the bomb. The Cold War was real, the United Nations was not a powerful forum, and the World Federalists had not become a major force. Clark's keynote address varied little from that for the original Dublin Conference: he advocated a strengthened and expanded United Nations with weighted representation and no Security Council veto, mandatory disarmament with enforced inspections and controls, and the like.

With relations between the East and West more hardened than ever, Clark's essentially unchanged prescription did not seem to be based on reality. But he never wavered and continued to make his lawyerly case for what he still considered the only real solution to an intolerable problem. At eighty-two and several years into terminal lymphoma, Grenville Clark was still a commanding presence. First-time attendee E. Grey Dimond, who later married Clark's daugher Mary D., described the event years later: "[Clark] pulled forth such strength and skill that none of us felt we were seeing a dying man, struggling to stay on stage. Instead, he was not of any age but of all time. He was seeking to show us how the questions were unchanged, and reasoning people could only conclude the answer rested in moving on to another level of government."[34]

Dimond continued, remembering the stark setting:

We met in an artist's large studio. It was very cold and the vast, barn-like room was heated by a single wood stove. Mr. Clark, as did most of us, wore his topcoat at all times. He stood at the left front of the room, and a clear north light gave a soft glow to his face. The dark wood paneling behind framed him in a portrait. He was bareheaded, tall, and erect, speaking with all the skills of a thousand public appearances. If there is perfection in this thing called civilization and a man rising up to its ultimate expectation— it was there in Grenville Clark.[35]

Dimond fundamentally disagreed with Clark's prescription for all the world's weapons and military power to be collected into one world body. Sharing the prime concern of many, he feared the likelihood—at some future point, if not immediately—of a dictator's taking advantage of such a concentration of power. But Dimond couldn't help being profoundly impressed with the dignity, intelligence, and sheer presence of the consummate elder statesman who was persuasively lecturing his assembled guests in the freezing Dublin studio.[36]

Another new attendee at the second Dublin Conference was the Kansas City–born journalist Edgar Snow. He had become famous with his 1937 book, *Red Star over China*. The book, dubbed "the scoop of the century," details Snow's four months holed up in the caves at Pao'an (now Bao'an, deep in the loess hills of northwestern China) with Mao Tse-tung and other young leaders of the Chinese Revolution. Snow presented a unique and dramatic account of China's distant struggle, told from the point of view of the revolutionaries. It was a radical departure from the Asia reporting of the time. What little news from the Far East made it into the Western press was heavily weighted toward the Nationalist, or Guomindang, Party led by the pro-West Chiang Kai-shek, whom the U.S. government strongly supported. In *Red Star* Snow made the shocking (and correct) prediction that the young rebel leader Mao and his band of communist followers would win their war and become China's next leaders.

Snow brought the unexpected to the Dublin gathering, as he was the one person there who was not from a traditional background of academic or legislative or corporate elitism. Almost everyone else in the room knew, or at least knew of, each other's careers and contributions. They were essentially sympatico on the basic goal of world peace, important differences about how to get there notwithstanding. Snow was different. He startled the group, not least his host, by drawing on his fourteen years in China, his years abroad as a foreign correspondent, his harassment by the hypervigilant U.S. intelligence agencies and Congress of those years (who labeled him a communist sympathizer for his China reporting, effectively ending his career in America), his subsequent years living in Europe, and the awareness he had gained of another world beyond traditional conceptions of the United States versus the Soviets.

Snow spoke to the worldly yet insulated group about a third world before that term was in common usage. This third world existed completely apart from the communist East or democratic West, and the millions of people in it did not want world government or even world peace to preserve the status quo; they wanted revolution. For them the existing governments were but an extension of the imperialism of the nineteenth century. The rebelling world was not ready for some rich comfortable nation, or group of nations, to declare that all could remain unchanged under international law.[37]

Clark appreciated Snow's message. Without deviating from his core belief in the necessity of a world governed by law, Clark became good friends with Snow. Clark liked to "pick his brains" (a favorite expression) about the conditions and hopes of this little studied and poorly understood third world, with its massive population that would be an essential part of any functional world body. He also hoped to use Snow's China contacts. Clark first sought the journalist's help in 1963 on behalf of his doctor and good friend, Paul Dudley White. White had received an invitation to visit a Chinese physician but was not granted a visa because of the "unsatisfactory state of Chinese American affairs."[38] Snow was sympathetic and tried to help but was unsuccessful. The results were the same the following year when Snow tried to facilitate Clark's going to China to talk to Chinese leaders about world peace through world law. This request probably had an even slimmer chance of impressing Mao, who, speaking to Snow, dismissed Clark's peace premise as "Utopian, because the imperialists would never agree to it."[39]

Although Snow could not get Clark into China, the two men stayed in touch. Snow grew gradually more sympathetic to Clark's ideas about world law, with one important exception—how to reconcile an effective world organization to prevent international wars with the right of oppressed peoples to change intolerable regimes. How would world federalism "make the world safe for revolutions"?[40] But that major point did not stand in the way of their friendship, and each man had more influence on the other than he would likely have guessed. Clark largely funded Snow's documentary film about China, *One Quarter of Humanity*, and also helped finance the last edition of *Red Star over China*. That edition was published just after Clark's death in 1967; its dedication reads: "To Grenville Clark, who was taller than his time."

Clark tried without success to get into mainland China for the rest of his life. One particularly plucky attempt involved traveling to Moscow with a briefcase full of cash and copies of *World Peace Through World Law*, hoping he might somehow book passage from one communist country to the other. It didn't work, but as Winston Churchill once said, "We must not let ourselves be accused of lack of imagination." On another foiled attempt Clark was summarily educated on the unique position Edgar

Snow held in China. Hoping to advance his own case through diplomatic channels, Clark pointed out to the Chinese ambassador to Switzerland that the American Edgar Snow had been invited twice to China in recent years. The diplomat succinctly replied that Snow "was the exception."[41]

In September 1971 Clark's older daughter, Mary, in no small part represented her father when she accompanied her husband, Dr. E. Grey Dimond, and Helen and Paul Dudley White, on the first trip by an American medical delegation into mainland China since the communist takeover in 1949. Richard Nixon did not make his famous visit until the following February. Fittingly the Dimond-White trip was arranged by Edgar Snow.[42] It is impossible to know what changes might have been made to Clark's world peace plan, which was based on the tenets of Western law, had he been able to visit China and exchange ideas with the Chinese leaders. But he certainly would have given his special brand of citizen diplomacy a try.

Badly weakened from worsening lymphoma and blood poisoning acquired on a recent Caribbean trip, Grenville Clark lay in a Boston hospital in late 1966. A much-needed bright spot came from a major effort by a dedicated cadre of friends to nominate him for the 1967 Nobel Peace Prize. Clark had been nominated for a Nobel several times before, beginning with a 1959 attempt by Judge Henry Friendly, with repeat attempts in 1961 and 1963. Those efforts were unsuccessful, perhaps because Clark had insisted that he be nominated in tandem with his coauthor of *World Peace Through World Law*, Louis Sohn. (At that time it was unusual for the Peace Prize to be awarded to a pair or group, although shared prizes were common in science and other specialized research fields.) This time, perhaps because of his weakened and depressed condition, the man who shunned the limelight assented to being nominated solo.[43]

The writer and editor Mary Kersey Harvey of the *Saturday Review* and *McCall's* spearheaded Clark's nomination for the 1967 Nobel Peace Prize. She later wrote, "Ever since I met the man in 1960 at the first Dartmouth Conference . . . my conviction that the Nobel Peace Prize should go to Grenville Clark had grown to almost obsessional proportions."[44] Under Kersey Harvey's orchestration Team Clark competed—despite its pacific title, the prize engenders fierce competition—enlisting officials from the UN, educators, authors, World Federalists, British and other parliamentarians, even certain cardinals at the Vatican with whom the Unitarian Clark had worked closely on peace. A torrent of nominating letters and endorsements of Grenville Clark rained on Oslo. But it was too late— twelve days after the January 1 nominating deadline, Grenville Clark died at eighty-four. The prize is bestowed only on a living person. No Nobel Peace Prize was awarded in 1967.[45]

Grenville Clark's final hospitalization was at Massachusetts General Hospital's comfortable hotel-like Phillips House. There he received the best of care, but ultimately there was nothing more to be done. He told his loyal secretary, Ruth Wight, "They are sending me home to die."[46]

Clark died at home in Dublin just before midnight on January 12, 1967. Paul Dudley White attributed his patient's "considerable longevity" to "the frequent periods of rest at critical times imposed by doctors and [mainly] his wife and grudgingly accepted by the patient." White further noted that this longevity in turn "made possible accomplishments of all sorts, in particular, political measures to aid the government in both World Wars and, finally, internationally, the promotion of world peace."[47]

As news of Clark's death spread, tributes and laudatory obituaries appeared in newspapers across the country and around the world. They were printed in a rainbow of languages, usually accompanied by a stock press photo of Clark's strong patrician face, with the caption invariably featuring some translation of *friend* and/or *peace*. The *New York Times*'s obituary included a line that surely had Clark's many friends (and some of his enemies) nodding their heads: "Publicly inconspicuous, Grenville Clark was privately a man of uncommon powers of persuasion."[48] Thousands of personal expressions of sympathy poured into Dublin. Edgar Snow's poetic pen captured the man and the moment for many: "Some of the warmth and light of humanity at its best went out with Grenville Clark's departure." Snow closed with a line that would have meant everything to the statesman incognito: "His work will continue."[49]

CHAPTER 15

Legacy, Lessons, Relevance

So Much to Do . . . , Clark's proposed title for his never-completed autobiography, would have been a good one.[1] Throughout his long life each of his major achievements seemed to lead to a new challenge with even higher stakes. From championing military preparedness before two world wars to protecting Americans' civil liberties, including academic freedom, and civil rights for African Americans, to the eternal struggle for world peace—what he achieved and, as important, what he attempted adds up to one remarkable life. Of course taking on such enormous problems virtually guarantees there will be no total victories, and Clark would have been the first to point out that his successes were not unqualified.

Within Clark's most impressive accomplishments were some of his most disheartening failures. The Plattsburg camp movement was an extraordinary success, yet he still could not sell his ultimate goal of universal military training. Twenty-five years later his winning passage of the 1940 Selective Service Act was leavened with bitter disappointment that Congress never approved the more comprehensive national service program he hoped would follow. Service was a constant theme. Although he backed away from the draft during the Cold War and deeply disapproved of U.S. intervention in Vietnam, Clark never wavered in his belief in duty and a citizen's obligation to serve in some capacity. Had his attention not been diverted by the compelling issue of preventing a third world war, it is easy to imagine that he would have continued to call for some kind of national service, along the lines of the expanded Civilian Conservation Corps that Clark and Franklin Roosevelt collaborated on without success in the 1930s.

Clark's principled (and effective) opposition to FDR's court-packing plan almost certainly cost Clark a seat on the Supreme Court—an unknowable but probably great loss to him and to the country. Some of Clark's successes were fleeting, such as his celebrated ABA Bill of Rights Committee, which was a force under his leadership but withered as soon as he left it. Does that make it a failure? The Gobitis family wouldn't think so, nor would the many Americans whose civil liberties were upheld in *West Virginia Board of Education v. Barnette* (the case in which the court reversed its ruling in *Minersville v. Gobitis*). The same would hold for the CIO or countless other organizations whose right to use public spaces to gather and hold public conversations was affirmed in *Hague v. CIO* (1939).

Did Clark's efforts significantly advance civil rights for African Americans? It depends how you measure. Clark's legal, financial, and advisory support to the NAACP's Legal Defense Fund deeply strengthened and sustained that important organization in its critical early years, yet huge racial disparities remain within the American legal and judicial system. Clark recognized the markedly uneven application of the death penalty between races as just one sliver of that vast problem. He would likely point out how far the country has come in a relatively short time but would also urge Americans to continue the fight and never let up. Vast problems take time to resolve, but they also take resolve over time.

And what to say about world peace through world law? Despite Clark's unflagging efforts, especially in his last three decades, the world seems further from anything resembling world peace than ever. Or is it? Americans who lived through the Cold War have perhaps forgotten (and increasing numbers of young people did not experience) the quiet daily dread of those years—backyard fallout shelters, air-raid drills in grade schools, annihilation-themed movies like *On the Beach,* and Top 40 songs like "Eve of Destruction," not to mention the awful phrase and nihilistic logic of "mutually assured destruction," which chillingly became a part of the national vocabulary. At least now, in these still plenty-troubled years of the early twenty-first century, the Harvard professor Lawrence Lessig can suggest that "we are on the cusp of this time where I can say, 'I speak as a citizen of the world' without others saying, 'God, what a nut.'"[2]

There is evidence to back up Lessig's claim. While Clark's specific solution, world peace through world law, never came to fruition, slow but notable progress in international justice has occurred. An early United Nations colleague, Sir Muhammad Zafarullah Khan, a Pakistani jurist who served on the first UN International Court of Justice and was later the court's president, remembered Clark's deep interest in the International Court: "He understood well that without a wider acceptance of international adjudication as the normal way to settle legal aspects of disputes between states, the rule of law cannot be established in the world community."[3] Khan and Clark would both have been pleased to know that the very same UN International Court of Justice in 2008 conducted high-profile trials of Serbian military leaders for genocide and other war crimes in the brutal Bosnian War of the early 1990s. While some protested the ultimately mixed verdict, the very fact of the trials, and their international legitimacy, was a landmark achievement.

An international trial with a more decisive outcome was concluded in 2012, when a UN- backed international tribunal convicted and sentenced former president Charles Taylor of Liberia to fifty years in prison for his role in atrocities committed during Sierra Leone's civil war in the 1990s. It was a watershed case for modern human rights law. Taylor is the first head of state convicted by an international tribunal since the Nuremburg trials after World War II. His trial lasted four years and was conducted in an international criminal court near The Hague's Peace Palace, which houses the UN International Court of Justice.[4]

Separately the long-envisioned International Criminal Court (ICC), which exists outside the United Nations, was formally chartered when the Rome Statute took effect in 2002. A decade later the ICC is finally a reality, with headquarters also just outside The Hague. In accordance with its charter, the ICC "is the first permanent, treaty based, international criminal court established to help end impunity for the perpetrators of the most serious crimes of concern to the international community." Its jurisdiction includes genocide, crimes against humanity, and war crimes. Active cases on the ICC docket as 2013 ended involved the Democratic Republic of Congo, the Central African Republic, Darfur, Sudan, Kenya, Cote d'Ivoire, and Mali.[5] Perhaps too slowly and perhaps too spottily, but international justice is beginning to be realized; Grenville Clark's decades of effort and influence were steps toward that still elusive and evolving goal.

How best to explain the apparent contradiction between Clark's efforts toward world peace and his earlier military preparedness campaigns? If it seems paradoxical, the simple truth is that Clark was an unusually complete and complex human being with every paradox that implies: a capitalist who defended socialists; a lawyer who enjoyed breaking the occasional rule, as when he brought nonmembers into the Porcellians' hallowed halls; a crusader for public causes who represented the ultra-elite homeowners in the Long Island parkway case; a defender of civil liberties who was silent about the internments of Japanese Americans during World War II, and during that same war sought to indict isolationists under the Espionage Act—the list goes on.

This paradox extended to individuals. Adversaries became allies and vice versa throughout Clark's life. Franklin Roosevelt, Felix Frankfurter, Burton Wheeler, and James Conant are but a few of Clark's friends and sometime close associates who at one point or another found themselves on the wrong side of one of his public or private crusades. Nobody got a pass. It was all about actions, not the person or his relationship with

Clark. Conversely disagreements, no matter how contentious, rarely killed a friendship.

In some ways this reflects Clark's legal prowess. Competent lawyers must be prepared to argue their opponent's case as well as their own. But while many successful lawyers grasp that tenet tactically, Clark took it to the much deeper and more essential level of basic human understanding and genuine empathy. An associate described Clark as the consummate legal professional: "He never forgot that part of being a lawyer is being a professional man in the best sense of the word. He never forgot his obligations to the public. He utilized the opportunities that the freedom of being a professional man afforded him to embark on his many great endeavors. There are many pedestrian, brilliant, money-saving, successful craftsmen in the law. There are rich lawyers. There are famous lawyers. But even some of the attributes that Grenville Clark exemplified can make of a lawyer a mighty person."[6]

Clark also understood that paradox is part and parcel of the democratic tradition. He wrote and gave lectures on the rich and complicated traditions of English-American liberty, with characteristic emphasis on the lessons of history. In one particularly eloquent passage, he drives home a subtle but crucial point: "English-American liberty is the opposite of doctrinaire. Rather it has developed out of the experience of self-government of the English speaking peoples over a period of centuries. It is pragmatic, plastic, and adaptable. Consequently it is non-logical, non-symmetrical, and full of inconsistencies. On the other hand, by reason of these very characteristics, it has proved eminently *workable* under varying conditions."[7]

Princeton president Harold Dodds encouraged Clark's daughter Mary D. to purse a biography of her father, saying, "A life [story] of him would be an inspiration to college students. (I could have used it in the course I taught at Princeton). He never sought personal fame or popular credit yet the range of his contributions was so broad; higher education, federal affairs in war and peace, civil rights, etc. They add up to an impressive example of what one able and honest man can achieve."[8] The recollections of Clark's friends around the world offer insights into the major imperatives of that life:

Educate. John Dickey, the long-time president of Dartmouth, remembered: "Grenny's talk on all subjects revealed an abiding faith in the power of education. . . . Needless to say, his concept of education reached far beyond the classroom. He had a fastidious taste for good thinking, but he was not afraid of considered conviction as part of the educational process. . . . Above all else, he kept saying, education will ultimately bring the people of the world to understand their stake in lawful community.

And if they understand it, he would say with closing-curtain finality, they'll get it."[9]

Act. The lawyer, banker, and presidential adviser John J. McCloy said: "In terms of his range of mind and effectiveness in achieving what he set out to accomplish, I am not certain I ever knew his equal. He was one of the most liberal-minded men I ever knew, and yet his singleness of purpose when he set out to marshal the forces needed to accomplish his objectives was about as liberal as a railroad train plunging through a tunnel."[10] A particularly apt benediction at Clark's memorial service was "Blessed are the peacemakers, but the accent is on the verb." Clark's accent was always on the verb.

Collaborate. Lloyd Garrison, a Root, Clark associate, said: "By letting the other fellows talk [Clark] never seemed to be running the show but he always managed to steer it in the direction he wished. He had clear and simple objectives—nothing fancy or erudite, but practical and down to earth. He was patient, humorous, and always gave his committee members the feeling he was enjoying each of them as human beings even more than the work of the committee. They responded in kind and would have done anything he asked."[11] Collaboration can include good-spirited coercion. Kingman Brewster Jr., president of Yale and two-time Dublin conferee, called Clark the "operator extraordinary," noting that "more people found themselves doing and saying and endorsing things they would never have dreamed of . . . as a result of being goaded, cajoled, wheedled, kidded, and sometimes duped into it by Grenny. I was such a willing victim."[12] Another (presumably) willing victim was Pope John XXIII (1958–63), on whom Clark operated in the cause of world peace. When a dinner guest suggested in 1965 that Clark had influenced Pope John's just released *Pacem in Terris* (Peace on Earth, John's final major papal treatise), Clark "responded with a twinkle: 'He was a Pope and I am a Unitarian, but we are thick as thieves.'"[13]

Remain independent. Clark prized his independence perhaps above all else. Asked in later years about his famous resistance to holding public office, Clark responded: "My late wife, half in fun, [said], 'You've never taken public office because you've never been willing to take an order from anybody.' The nice way of putting it is that I want to preserve my independence."[14] Fanny Dwight Clark knew her husband well. And it is important to recognize that Clark's cherished independence was totally different from the antigovernment, modern-day "tea party" perspective. He applied pressure from outside government to improve the system, not to destroy it. *Government* was not a dirty word to Clark, whether it referred to local, national, or international authority. He supported the League of Nations and sought to improve, not destroy, the United Nations. No vigilante, Clark worked within the existing legal structure. When that structure was found lacking, he attempted to change, improve, modify, and often expand it through appropriate legal and political means. A perceptive journalist once wrote: "[Clark] is deeply conscious of the danger of a community splitting into isolated or opposing elements—the words 'Abolition' and 'Union' mean far more to him than forgotten phrases of a forgotten war."[15] Finally, and especially:

Think big. The NAACP director Jack Greenberg said: "[Clark] had the faith and vision and capacity to make large commitments and think in terms of the future of the nation and even the world."[16] Senator Alan Cranston of California said: "I've never, ever known anyone else who combined as deep a concern for and grasp of infinite detail with a seeming ability to cast his mind out beyond the horizons to the edge of infinity."[17] Clark might have added one of his favorite Abraham Lincoln quotes: "As our case is new, so must we think anew and act anew." As Clark himself told the American Bar Association when he accepted its medal, "I wish that our thinking shall not be crippled by timidity or undue regard for tradition, but shall be as imaginative and creative as the problem is vast and new. I further wish that we may resist any temptation to avoid the hardest problems."[18]

Thinking big, and acting on it, can of course be greatly aided by wealth. Grenville Clark did enjoy the undeniable advantage of wealth, with the freedom it can bring to serve, pursue public causes, and take on entrenched powers. Yet many have had far more and done far less. And inherited wealth can be a handicap. (W. K. Vanderbilt famously called it "as certain a death to ambition as cocaine is to morality.")[19] When I. F. Stone joked about Clark's having overcome a handicap worse than poverty—being born into the highest circles of wealth and social position —the journalist may not have been too far off the mark. The iconic American self-made person is not lessened by acknowledging that striving to improve one's lot is a logical human impulse. Less heralded but deserving of note is the person born to ease and comfort who chooses to work hard and give of him- or herself to public causes. Noblesse oblige is perhaps taken for granted at times.

While Clark was generous with people and causes he believed in, he didn't pretend to be a philanthropist. (And he would know, having had Andrew Carnegie and the Ford Foundation as clients.) This was a man who cofounded the Fiduciary Trust Company and wrote the three-generation-skipping trust to shelter wealth for future members of his family. He was a careful investor, and his annual financial review weekends were serious business. The family financial adviser would come to Dublin, where Clark and the head of each household, once the family became multigenerational, would be gathered. They would review each of the complicated investments in the family's portfolio line by line, and make "buy, sell, or hold" decisions made for each stock. ("Buy when blood is running in the gutter" was a memorable Clark battle cry.)[20] But Clark's contributions were bigger than money alone—intelligence, farsightedness, organizational skills, leadership, and determination to achieve worthy, well-defined goals. A friend noted that Clark "was fortunate in having the conveniences and assets of inherited wealth, but I doubt that its absence would have substantially affected his approach to life."[21]

So how best to remember Grenville Clark? It is remarkable that even so deliberately private a man could accomplish so much for so long yet leave so light a historical footprint. Which is not to say that Clark's legacy has been completely relegated to the ash heap of history. The *Congressional Record* on the day of his death contains a formal statement noting his achievements as a great American.[22] His portrait hangs at Harvard, among other luminaries of the Corporation. He appears briefly in the biographies of many of his more famous friends and in the annals of the many organizations to which he gave so much of himself. He was the subject of dozens of articles, interviews, and profiles in the popular press and scholarly journals during his lifetime. Literally tons of his papers are collected, catalogued, and available for research at Dartmouth College. Physical monuments exist in the form of the Clark Botanic Garden on Long Island and the Clarks' beloved Dublin farm on Dublin Lake at the base of Mount Monadnock, which is still in the family. Many Clarks, including Grenville and Fanny, rest peacefully in the quaint Dublin cemetery at the edge of town. And if one way of having arrived in America is to have your picture on a U.S. postage stamp, Grenville Clark qualifies—daughter Mary D. led a successful campaign to bestow that honor on her father in 1983.

Mary and others also formed the Grenville Clark Fund at Dartmouth to recognize and reward individuals who exemplify Clark's ideals of furthering world peace, good government, academic freedom, civil rights, and personal liberty. The fund is no longer in operation but its awardees were impressive: Archbishop Desmond Tutu of South Africa, for his work against apartheid; George Kennan, noted Cold War diplomat; Jean Monnet, founder of the European Common Market; Theodore Hesburgh, president of Notre Dame; Jack Greenberg, director of the NAACP Legal Defense Fund; Sydney Kentridge, civil rights activist; and Marian Wright Edelman, founder of the Children's Defense Fund.

But there should be more. We could use the lessons of this life—its purpose, its substance. Although Clark's circumstances were too rare for him to serve as a literal role model for most Americans, he nonetheless stands as a defined example of an informed, active citizen—the kind on which our democracy was modeled and that it needs to thrive. Cicero said, "In a democracy the most important office is that of Citizen." The line was quoted most appropriately at a memorial dinner for Clark in New York City by his friend Paul Freund, a professor at Harvard. Freund added, "Alas, it's all too infrequent that office is adequately filled. But surely if there ever was an exemplar of that truth, it was our friend, Grenville Clark."[23]

Final Words from the Source

Clark penned his own conclusions about his life and the future during an around-the-world cruise on the Swedish ocean liner *Kungsholm* in 1956. In a ruled university notebook he carefully handwrote his general observations and thoughts about what was likely to happen in "the next fifty years, which is about as far as one can look ahead with any profit in this fast-changing era." Fifty years from Clark's cruise brings us to 2006—the fairly recent past. Observe Clark's thorough analysis and his basic, if carefully qualified, optimism. His unguarded remarks sound much sunnier than many of his official statements about international anarchy from the same period, and he refrains from warning of armageddon, nuclear or otherwise.

It is also delightful to imagine the seventy-four-year-old statesman incognito stretched out on a fancy teak steamer chair on the deck of a luxurious ocean liner, with uniformed servants poised nearby to offer a cool beverage or a fresh towel. When GC's previously careful handwriting starts to trail off the page, perhaps they are pulling into port in India where the Clarks will visit with Prime Minister Nehru. Or, as a sentence suddenly ends in midthought, maybe they are cruising past old Canton (now Guangzhou), looking for the warehouses Fanny's ancestors built for their China trading enterprises in the 1800s. Is that little smear at the corner of the worn notebook page from a warm tropical raindrop or maybe it's condensation from a fresh pineapple daiquiri? It seems fitting that as the multifaceted Grenville Clark was enjoying a round-the-world luxury cruise, discussing world peace through world law with the presidents of Egypt and India, he was jotting down notes to his children for posterity.

Notes on My Life for My Children

Conclusion: I will conclude with some observations and reflections as to what the next few generations may look forward to and as to the basic values of life; not that I pretend to any superior wisdom but because having necessarily lived longer than you I should know a little more by experience on some subjects.

On the material side, I feel confident as [to] the future economic prosperity of the United States and of the security of property for the foreseeable future, say, for the next fifty years which is about as far as one can look ahead with any profit in this fast-changing era. I base this confidence on a combination of several fundamental factors: (a) the still remaining great natural resources of the nation (soil, forests, minerals, water) together with climate and our advantageous position for trade between the two oceans; (b) a still vigorous people and growing population; (c) very stable political institutions which are nevertheless sufficiently flexible to be adaptable to changing conditions. In particular, the independence of the courts has been preserved in my generation and promises to continue—a vital factor safeguarding the liberties and property of the people. Another stabilizing factor is the widespread diffusion of property and the existence of a strong middle class, with the absence of any very shocking gap between the extremes of economic status, the existence of which seems throughout history to have been a principal cause of instability and insecurity for property. (The French and Russian revolutions and King Farouk are classic examples.)

Subject to the risks of new World Wars and of great deterioration in our people, the above factors give good ground for confidence in the continued and increasing prosperity of the U.S. On this assumption it follows that well chosen common stocks in industries likely to grow at least as fast as the population will continue to be the best form of investment; and an incidental advantage is that they would form the best practicable hedge against inflation in case the assumption of stability proves to be wrong.

An important risk for property is certainly the possibility of a new world war on a scale which, while perhaps not directly damaging the U.S., would bring unprecedented destruction to the world as a whole. Unless disarmament and world law are accomplished this risk is a great one, since a world armed to the teeth with modern weapons might become so tense and nervous that war might occur as if by spontaneous combustion even against the strongest wish of all the peoples. I am, however, hopeful, that disarmament and world law will be achieved within a generation and therefore, while not dismissing world war as a threat to property, I do not consider it an imminent or serious threat. Moreover even if a world war should occur it might be that it would be so short that even if the destruction were great in absolute terms it would be relatively slight in terms of world population and capacity, so that the damage could be repaired within a decade or so. On this point the recovery of Germany within ten years after World War II is significant.

The other major risk seems to be a possible deterioration of our people in moral and physical qualities. Is it possible that our success and wealth have brought us to a climax from which we will now decline? Have we reached the point where in Oliver Goldsmith's words "wealth accumulates and men decay"? I am somewhat disturbed over this possibility. Too much liquor is drunk; too much tobacco is consumed; too many crude and dirty books are read; too little healthy exercise is taken. And one could pile on the indictment. On the other hand, there are counter influences: an apparent revival in religious life, at least on the surface; increased medical knowledge; a more widespread, if superficial, interest in nature and outdoor life; a movement to the suburbs, etc. It is hard to say which set of contending influences will tend to prevail in the next 50 years. But they seem quite evenly matched and certainly I do not think it is clear that we are on the down grade either morally or physically, even if there are no signs of marked improvement. As applied to property, which would decline in value and stability during a period of moral and physical deterioration, I cannot see that any such probability exists in the next 50 years, although the *possibility* is there.

On the moral side, what I have just said covers my view. There is the possibility that our people will rapidly decline in moral standards, but in my judgment no reason to anticipate this any more than a slight but steady improvement in the next half century. Needless to say it is far more important that we should improve morally than materially. But it is probably not a case of one or the other. It is more likely that a United States steadily declining in morality would soon decline materially; and correspondingly that a United States that is improving its moral behavior would also increase its material prosperity.

GC—January–February 1956,
aboard the *Kungsholm*[1]

Notes

Introduction

1. Grenville Clark, autobiographical notes made in Antigua in 1966 and taped from Dictaphone belts in 1967 (hereafter Antigua tape), Clark Papers. Clark's papers are at Dartmouth College, in Hanover, New Hampshire, despite his many ties to Harvard. This likely reflects both his primary residence, from the 1940s on, at the family's Outlet Farm in Dublin, New Hampshire, and even more so his long and close friendship with Dartmouth's president, John Dickey.

2. Grenville Clark to Irving Dilliard, July 16, 1963; Theodore Roosevelt to Grenville Clark, July 3, 1901, both in Clark Papers. Clark's next encounter with Roosevelt came less than three months later in Burlington, Vermont, when President William McKinley was shot and critically wounded in Buffalo, New York. Roosevelt was on a friend's yacht on Lake Champlain when the news came. Clark, in Burlington for the summer, was chosen to hand-deliver to the vice president's boat an urgent batch of telegrams updating the president's condition. As he stood by Roosevelt's side, Clark witnessed what he later described as "TR's remarkable and almost instinctive capacity for rapport with the people." Roosevelt opened the telegrams one by one and read them aloud to the anxious assembled crowd at the Burlington dock. He began: "Fellow Citizens: the news in these telegrams belongs to you as much as to me." Within eight days McKinley was dead, and Roosevelt was president. Clark to Dilliard.

3. Grenville Clark obituary, *Cleargolaw News*, January 20, 1967, Clark Papers. *Cleargolaw News* was the newsletter of the firm Cleary, Gottlieb, Friendly, and Ball, which Clark and Elihu Root Jr. served as "of counsel" from 1954 to 1967.

4. Maurer, "Grenville Clark: Statesman Incognito."

5. Samuel R. Spencer Jr., "Grenville Clark," in Dimond, Cousins, and Clifford, *Memoirs of a Man*, 53.

6. Ibid.

7. Grenville Clark, "Notes about Myself from Grenville Clark for Messrs. Ogilvy & Mahony," December 28, 1948, Clark Papers.

8. Dunne, *Grenville Clark: Public Citizen*, 78.

9. Norman Cousins, "A Man for All Seasons," in Dimond, Cousins, and Clifford, *Memoirs of a Man*, 3.

10. Spencer, "Grenville Clark," 56. What Lincoln actually said was, "The people will save their government, if the government itself will do its part only indifferently well." Abraham Lincoln, "Message to Congress in Special Session," July 4, 1861, *Collected Works of Abraham Lincoln*, 4:432, http://quod.lib.umich.edu/lib/colllist/.

11. E. Grey Dimond, interview by author, December 8, 2008, Kansas City, MO.

12. Grenville Clark, fiftieth anniversary report to Harvard College Class of 1903, 47, Clark Papers.

13. Louisa Spencer speech, n.d. (ca. 1966), Clark Botanic Garden Archives, Albertson, NY.

14. Grenville Clark, "An Informal Memoir," January 1951, Clark Papers.

15. J. Garry Clifford, "Grenville Clark and His Friends," in Dimond, Cousins, and Clifford, *Memoirs of a Man,* 9.

16. Maurer, "Grenville Clark: Statesman Incognito," 113.

17. Ibid.

18. The six wise men were George Kennan, Dean Acheson, Charles Bohlen, Robert Lovett, Averell Harriman, and John McCloy. All were friends of Clark's. Isaacson and Thomas, *Wise Men,* 19.

19. John J. McCloy, "A Tribute to Grenville Clark," in Dimond, Cousins, and Clifford, *Memoirs of a Man,* 63.

20. Dunne, *Grenville Clark: Public Citizen,* 122.

1. Ninth-Generation Manhattanite

1. Grenville Clark, autobiographical notes made in Antigua in 1966 and taped from Dictaphone belts in 1967, Clark Papers.

2. Ibid.

3. Ibid. The venerable Players Club still stands at Gramercy Park today.

4. Clark, Antigua tape. Clark had an unfortunate affinity for odd punctuation, which has been silently corrected.

5. LeGrand Bouton Cannon, *Reminiscences of the Rebellion* (self-published, 1895), Clark Papers. (See especially Chapters 5 and 7 on the first use of freedmen in the Union army, and Chapter 12, which tells of Cannon's experiences with Lincoln.)

6. Clark, Antigua tape.

7. Hiram Carleton, *Genealogical and Family History of the State of Vermont: A Record of the Achievements of Her People in the Making of a Commonwealth* (Baltimore: Genealogical Publishing, 1998), 464. Sadly the Cannon estate was subdivided and the main home destroyed in 1925, long after Cannon's death. Only two outbuildings remain.

8. Grenville Clark to Irving Dilliard, July 13, 1962, Clark Papers.

9. Carleton, *Genealogical and Family History,* 464. Also, Grenville Clark, "Notes on My Life for My Children," 1956, retold in Clark to Dilliard, October 4, 1962; Cannon, *Reminiscences of the Rebellion,* 201–2, all in Clark Papers.

10. Clark, "Notes on My Life for My Children"; Clark to Dilliard, October 4, 1962.

11. Clark, "Notes on My Life for My Children."

12. Carleton, *Genealogical and Family History,* 464.

13. Clark, "Notes on My Life for My Children."

14. Clark, Antigua tape. Clark's godfather was another colorful figure in his life. Walter Webb's father had been a journalist and ambassador to Brazil. While still in college at Columbia, Webb had cruised up the Amazon, crossed the Andes, exited South America through Peru, then sailed back to the States around 1875. A lawyer, Wall Street banker, securities broker, and sometime chair of the Westminster Kennel Club, Walter Webb worked for Cornelius Vanderbilt at the New York Central Railroad. Webb's railroad ran the then-fastest train in the world, averaging nearly 60 mph. In 1893 he made the shocking but true prediction that within one hundred years a traveler would be able to have breakfast in New York City and dinner in Chicago. Webb would surely thrill to know that it is now possible to have dinner in New York City and breakfast in Paris. Walter Webb obituary, *New York Times,* June 19, 1900.

15. Clark, Antigua tape.

16. Ibid.

17. Mary Clark Dimond, "A Daughter's Viewpoint: Lighter Moments—and Many Exposures," in Dimond, Cousins, and Clifford, *Memoirs of a Man*, 172. Clark's tunelessness is confirmed in a separate account by Elizabeth Jay, "My Father's Friend," 187, in the same collection.

18. Clark, Antigua tape.

19. Ibid.

20. Colonel Cannon to Louis Clark, August 21, 1879, Clark Papers.

21. Clark, Antigua tape.

22. Grenville Clark, "An Informal Memoir," January 1951, Clark Papers.

23. Clark, Antigua tape.

24. Ibid.

25. Information about Harvard comes from its website, http://www .harvard.edu. The university's charter is posted at http://library.harvard.edu/ university-archives/using-the-collections/online-resources/charter-of-1650.

26. Joint instruction between Harvard and Radcliffe began in 1943, although full formal integration of the two schools did not occur until 1999.

27. Clark, Antigua tape.

28. Dunne, *Grenville Clark: Public Citizen*, 12–13.

29. Grenville Clark, "Notes on Activities of G. Clark," October 25, 1960, Dublin, New Hampshire, Clark Papers; Clark, Antigua tape.

30. Clark, Antigua tape.

31. Keller, *Fictions of U.S. History*, 116; Hart, "What Is American?"

32. Spencer, "Grenville Clark," in Dimond, Cousins, and Clifford, *Memoirs of a Man*, 57–58. In another version of the classic story, Clark's friend Cleveland Amory said the sniffy reprimand was prompted by General Pershing after World War I and General Eisenhower after World War II. J. Garry Clifford to author, March 2, 2012.

33. For biographical information about Felix Frankfurter, see the Supreme Court website at http://www.supremecourtus.gov/about. See also Martin, *Life and Century of Charles C. Burlingham*, 251.

34. Felix Frankfurter on Grenville Clark, n.d., Clark Papers. See also Samuel Spencer Jr., "File: GC and FF," diss. research notes [July 21, 1947], Clark Papers.

35. Francis E. Rivers, "One Man's Conception of Grenville Clark," in Dimond, Cousins, and Clifford, *Memoirs of a Man*, 118.

36. Feldman, *Scorpions*, 11.

37. For more on the case see Frankfurter, "Case of Sacco and Vanzetti"; Feldman, *Scorpions*, 13–25.

38. Grenville Clark to Irving Dilliard, October 8, 1962, Clark Papers.

39. J. Garry Clifford, "Grenville Clark and His Friends," in Dimond, Cousins, and Clifford, *Memoirs of a Man*, 19.

40. Clark to Dilliard.

41. Ibid.

42. Deresiewicz, "Disadvantages of an Elite Education."

43. John Schwartz, "An Ivy Covered Path to the Supreme Court," *New York Times*, June 8, 2009.

2. Wall Street

1. Grenville Clark, memoir, 1951, Clark Papers.

2. Ibid.; Spencer, "Clarks of Clark Botanic Garden," 58.

3. Grenville Clark, "Sketch for Class of 1903 at Harvard," 1953, Clark Papers; Dunne, *Grenville Clark: Public Citizen*, 21.

4. Grenville Clark, autobiographical notes made in Antigua in 1966 and taped from Dictaphone belts in 1967, Clark Papers. The 1901 Swastika Lunch Club had no relation to Adolph Hitler's Nazi Party, which co-opted the ancient good luck symbol decades later.

5. Grenville Clark, Root, Clark newsletter the *Bull,* silver anniversary edition, January 27, 1945, Clark Papers (hereafter silver anniversary program).

6. Ibid.; Leo Gottlieb, "Excerpts from proposed History of the firm of Cleary, Gottlieb, Steen & Hamilton for information of Professor Gerald Dunne," n.d. (ca. 1978), Mary Clark Dimond Papers.

7. Hoffman, *Lions in the Street,* 4.

8. Ibid., 61–62; *Cleargolaw News,* April 25, 1968, Clark Papers.

9. Leo Gottlieb to Mary Clark Dimond, December 17, 1981, Mary Clark Dimond Papers. "Club Boy Clark" lyrics are from Root, Clark annual "Dough Day" dinner program, January 24, 1936, Clark Papers.

10. Mary Clark Dimond, "A Daughter's Viewpoint: Lighter Moments—and Many Exposures," in Dimond, Cousins, and Clifford, *Memoirs of a Man,* 178.

11. "Dewey Ballantine LLP History," excerpted from *International Directory of Company Histories,* vol. 48 (Chicago: St. James Press, 2003) and posted at http://www.fundinguniverse.com/company-histories/Dewey-Ballantine-LLP-Company-history.html.

12. Mayer, *Emory Buckner,* 282–83.

13. Ackerman, "In Memoriam: Henry J. Friendly," 1715. Also see Gordon, "Friendly Fire," among many others.

14. Hoffman, *Lions in the Street,* 83.

15. Henry J. Friendly, "Grenville Clark: Legal Preceptor," in Dimond, Cousins, and Clifford, *Memoirs of a Man,* 89.

16. Cloyd Laporte, "G. C.," in Dimond, Cousins, and Clifford, *Memoirs of a Man,* 79.

17. Henry Friendly to E. Grey Dimond, June 30, 1983, Mary Clark Dimond Papers.

18. Robert H. Reno, "Grenville Clark and the Uphaus Case," Dimond, Cousins, and Clifford, *Memoirs of a Man,* 127; *Cleargolaw News,* April 25, 1968, Clark Papers.

19. Henry Mayer, "Grenville Clark," in Dimond, Cousins, and Clifford, *Memoirs of a Man,* 75–76.

20. John M. Korner, "A Lifelong Friend," in Dimond, Cousins, and Clifford, *Memoirs of a Man,* 73.

21. Silver anniversary program.

22. Joseph S. Clark, "Memories of Grenville Clark," in Dimond, Cousins, and Clifford, *Memoirs of a Man,* 37.

23. Caro, *Power Broker,* 299; Spencer, "Clarks of Clark Botanic Garden," 17.

24. Caro, *Power Broker,* 12, 14. See pp. 299–303 for the full parkway story and a map of the proposed versus the actual route, with labels denoting the estates of the baronial landowners involved.

25. Mary Clark Dimond, "A Daughter's Viewpoint: Lighter Moments and Many Exposures," in Dimond, Cousins, and Clifford, *Memoirs of a Man,* 177.

26. Dunne, *Grenville Clark: Public Citizen,* 53.

27. Caro, *Power Broker,* 303.

28. Ibid., 54.

29. See, for example, Clark to Franklin Delano Roosevelt, December 22 and 30, 1930, July 3, 1936; Clark to Herbert H. Lehman, August 10, 1934, and January 4, 1935; Clark to CCB (Charles C. Burlingham), September 14, 1935; CCB to Clark, September 28 and August 3, 1934; CCB to Roosevelt, September 20, 1934; Charles

Evans Hughes Jr. to Clark, October 23, 1934; Clark to Hughes, January 24, 1935, all in Clark Papers.

30. Dunne, *Grenville Clark: Public Citizen*, 200.

31. Silver anniversary program.

32. "Grenville Clark, of New York, Receives Highest Association Award," *ABA Journal* 45 (October 1959): 1059.

3. Domestication

1. Dunne, *Grenville Clark: Public Citizen*, 29.

2. Grenville Clark, "Memo for Irving Dilliard as to Heritage and Background of Fanny Dwight Clark (wife of Grenville Clark)," Clark Papers; Mary Clark Dimond, "Fanny Dwight Clark," memo for the biographer Gerald Dunne, Mary Clark Dimond Papers.

3. M. Dimond, "Fanny Dwight Clark"; Grenville Clark, "Memo for Irving Dilliard." The younger Holmes rarely discussed his Civil War experience afterward. During his last year on the Supreme Court, Fanny contacted the justice, identifying herself as Wilder Dwight's niece. She and Grenville were invited to visit Holmes at his Washington home on the condition that nothing would be said about the Civil War. Grenville Clark later recalled they spent "about an hour [with Holmes] during which he immediately brought up the Civil War days and his friendship with Wilder Dwight and not a single word was said, as I remember it, about anything except the Civil War." Grenville Clark to Irving Dilliard, November 1, 1962, Clark Papers.

4. M. Dimond, "Fanny Dwight Clark." The mothers of Fanny and Louisa were sisters. Fanny's uncle Walter Hunnewell was the grandson of an early and influential citizen of Wellesley. The family home is now officially the Hunnewell Arboretum, said to rival or even top the Arnold Arboretum, and still owned and actively maintained by the family.

5. Ibid.

6. Dunne, *Grenville Clark: Public Citizen*, 30.

7. Spencer, "Clarks of Clark Botanic Garden."

8. "Agenda 1928," Clark Papers.

9. Harold W. Dodds, "My Friend Grenville Clark," in Dimond, Cousins, and Clifford, *Memoirs of a Man*, 144.

10. M. Dimond, "Fanny Dwight Clark."

11. Elihu Root Jr., "The Showing Up of Grenny Clark," *Weekly Bulletin*, March 12, 1921, Clark Papers. The *Weekly Bulletin* was the Root, Clark newsletter.

12. Maurer, "Grenville Clark: Statesman Incognito," 115.

13. Ibid., 173. Grenville Clark, autobiographical notes made in Antigua in 1966 and taped from Dictaphone belts in 1967 (hereafter Antigua tape), Clark Papers.

14. John Dickey, "Conservation by Conversation," in Dimond, Cousins, and Clifford, *Memoirs of a Man*, 46.

15. Ibid., 146.

16. Grenville Clark to Charles C. Burlingham, May 8, 1935; Clark to CCB, March 24, 1941, both in Clark Papers. See also J. Garry Clifford, "Grenville Clark and His Friends," in Dimond, Cousins, and Clifford, *Memoirs of a Man*, 11.

17. Lyman M. Tondale Jr., "Grenville Clark: Some Stories and Personal Recollections," in Dimond, Cousins, and Clifford, *Memoirs of a Man*, 93–94.

4. Public Service Provocateur

1. Plattsburgh, New York, is now spelled with a final *h*. I have chosen to use the spelling from Clark's day.

234 • Notes

2. Genetics may also have been involved—in the spring of 1861 Clark's grandfather and idol, LeGrand Bouton Cannon, famously led an impromptu citizens' march up Broadway "to rally Copperhead Manhattan almost single-handedly for the Union cause." Following Cannon's rousing speech to a crowd he had gathered in Union Square, the boisterous group hit the streets, stopping off at "various newspaper offices and [demanding] that the Stars and Stripes be hoisted." Dunne, *Grenville Clark: Public Citizen,* 4; LeGrande Bouton Cannon obituary, *New York Times,* November 4, 1906.

3. Stevenson, *Cataclysm.*

4. NPR Staff, "WWI: The Battle That Split Europe, and Families," *All Things Considered,* April 30, 2011, http://www.npr.org/2011/04/30/135803783/wwi-the-battle-that-split-europe-and-families; Charles River Editors, *Kaiser Wilhelm II: The Life and Legacy of Germany's Emperor during World War I* (Cambridge, MA: Charles River Editors, 2013), Kindle edition, 1.

5. Clifford, *Citizen Soldiers,* 45.

6. As one of countless examples of how recent was the Civil War, in 1916 Oliver Wendell Holmes Jr., then a Supreme Court justice, was a Civil War veteran who had been badly wounded at Antietam. Oliver Wendell Holmes Sr., "My Hunt after the Captain," *Atlantic Monthly,* December 1862. The younger Holmes was apparently not pleased that his father was exploiting his son's war ordeal for literary gain. Their relationship reportedly suffered much animosity. C. D. Merriman, "Oliver Wendell Holmes (1809–1894)," *Literature Network,* 2006, http://www.online-literature.com/oliver-holmes/.

7. Why the instinctive sympathy for the Allies? Like a majority of Americans, Clark and his friends traced their origins to British (and in Clark's case French Huguenot) ancestors. His classic New England education and upbringing was Anglocentric, beginning with the very name New England.

8. "Major General Leonard Wood Has a Defense Plan," *Greater New York: Bulletin of the Merchants Association of New York,* December 21, 1914, 5–6; Clifford, *Citizen Soldiers,* 49.

9. Grenville Clark to Theodore Roosevelt, November 19, 1914, Clark Papers, reprinted in "Important Letters of Grenville Clark," in Dimond, Cousins, and Clifford, *Memoirs of a Man,* 267–69.

10. Chambers, *To Raise an Army,* 28, 66.

11. Ibid., 79. Proponents of universal military training frequently cited the Swiss and Australian systems of compulsory military service as evidence that such service is compatible with a democracy and a nonaggressive foreign policy. The problem with the argument, of course, is the much larger size of the United States and its significant involvement in international affairs.

12. Elihu Root Jr., "The Showing Up of Grenny Clark," *Weekly Bulletin,* March 12, 1921, 13.

13. Grenville Clark to Joseph Clark, November 9, 1908, Clark Papers; Clifford, *Citizen Soldiers,* 54–55.

14. Clifford, *Citizen Soldiers,* 55.

15. The reader of John Irving novels is reminded of Wilbur Larch, the unforgettable orphanage director and abortionist in *Cider House Rules* who nightly encouraged his orphans that they were "Princes of Maine, Kings of New England!" The original Plattsburg men were almost literally that.

16. Pearlman, *To Make Democracy Safe for America,* 28.

17. Carroll was a direct descendant of Charles Carroll of Carrollton, Maryland, the only Catholic to sign the Declaration of Independence and the last signer to die.

Delmonico's was the perfect location for launching a grand scheme: the New York City institution opened in 1837, and "meet me at Delmonico's" has been dropping from the lips of high-rollers ever since.

18. Hobbs, *Leonard Wood*; Pearlman, *To Make Democracy Safe for America*, 35.

19. Another of Wood's little-known contributions to public health was ordering the army's first mandatory typhoid immunization program as army chief of staff in 1911. While not as dramatic as charging San Juan Hill, the order saved untold thousands of lives and was decades ahead of civilian public health policy. That story is well told in Cirillo, *Bullets and Bacilli*.

20. Twain, *Weapons of Satire*. See also Bacevich, "What Happened at Bud Dajo."

21. Clifford, *Citizen Soldiers*, 2–5; also see unsigned, undated article, "Major General Leonard Wood, 1860–1927," Fort Leonard Wood, http://www.wood.army.mil/MGLeonardwood.htm.

22. Clifford, *Citizen Soldiers*, 57.

23. Ibid., 238.

24. The Plattsburg site was surely a happy and nostalgic one for Clark, as it was just across beautiful Lake Champlain from Burlington, Vermont, where he had spent summers of his youth at his grandfather Cannon's Overlake estate.

25. W. Averell Harriman, "Tribute to Grenville Clark," in Dimond, Cousins, and Clifford, *Memoirs of a Man*, 59–62.

26. Clifford, *Citizen Soldiers*, 65, 63, 66.

27. Ibid., 71–73.

28. Ibid., 80, 68.

29. Cirillo, *Bullets and Bacilli*, 57.

30. Dorey, "Plattsburgh Contribution to Military Training."

31. Clifford, *Citizen Soldiers*, 89.

32. Ibid., 74–75; Pearlman, *To Make Democracy Safe for America*, 59.

33. Clifford, *Citizen Soldiers*, 75; Pearlman, *To Make Democracy Safe for America*, 36.

34. Pearlman, *To Make Democracy Safe for America*, 59.

35. On the *Arabic* sinking see, for example, "Pledge Put to Test in *Arabia* Sinking," *New York Times*, December 8, 1916, http://query.nytimes.com/mem/archive-free/pdf?res=F30C14F63E5D16738DDDA90A94D0405B858DF1D3; Office of the Historian, U.S. Department of State, "Milestones: 1914–1920: American Entry into World War I, 1917," n.d., http://history.state.gov/milestones/1914–1920.

36. Clifford, *Citizen Soldiers*, 85.

37. Ibid., 86–87.

38. Ibid., 89, 90, 92.

39. Ibid., 93, 94–101, 108.

5. Wartime: Building on Plattsburg

1. Clifford, *Citizen Soldiers*, 92, 102.

2. Chambers, *To Raise an Army*, 24.

3. Clifford, *Citizen Soldiers*, 5, 7.

4. Ibid., 33, 117.

5. Ibid., 145, 147, 156, 110.

6. Ibid., 167, 171, 191.

7. Dorey, "Plattsburgh Contribution to Military Training," 233.

8. J. Garry Clifford, introduction to Patterson, *World War I Memoirs of Robert P. Patterson*; Slotkin, *Lost Battalions*, 34.

9. Clifford, *Citizen Soldiers*, 200. In 1946 Clark's close associate Robert P. Pat-

terson, then secretary of war, would appoint the Gillem Board, which studied and recommended the postwar use of "Negro Manpower," laying the foundation for President Harry Truman's executive order to desegregate the armed forces two years later. As undersecretary Patterson had been instrumental in creating the African American fighter group known as the Tuskegee Airmen during World War II. Dalfiume, *Desegregation of the Armed Forces*, 150–52; Eiler, *Mobilizing America*.

10. Clifford, *Citizen Soldiers*, 169, 181–90, 197.
11. Ibid., 194, 185, 209.
12. Ibid., 202, 203.
13. Ibid., 221, 222, 194.
14. Slotkin, *Lost Battalions*, 33.
15. Clifford, *Citizen Soldiers*, 223, 224.
16. Ibid., 225, 218, 217.
17. Ibid., 239, 236, 234; Grenville Clark, "Notes on Activities of G. Clark," October 25, 1960, Dublin, New Hampshire, Clark Papers.
18. Clifford, *Citizen Soldiers*, 241, 248.
19. Theodore Roosevelt Jr. to Grenville Clark, June 19, 1917, Clark Papers.
20. Colonel Walter Scott (for Newton Baker) to Clark, February 28, 1919; Franklin D. Roosevelt to Langdon P. Marvin, February 8, 1918, both in Clark Papers.
21. Grenville Clark, "Sketch for Class of 1903 at Harvard," 1953, Clark Papers; Patterson, *World War I Memoirs of Robert P. Patterson*, xiv.
22. Pearlman, *To Make Democracy Safe for America*, 71.
23. Clifford, *Citizen Soldiers*, 182–83; W. Averell Harriman, "Tribute to Grenville Clark," in Dimond, Cousins, and Clifford, *Memoirs of a Man*, 59–60.
24. Grenville Clark, autobiographical notes made in Antigua in 1966 and taped from Dictaphone belts in 1967, Clark Papers.

6. Suburbia, Breakdown, and Recovery

1. Spencer, "Clarks of Clark Botanic Garden," 58.
2. Weidman and Martin, *Nassau County Long Island*, 41.
3. Spencer, "Clarks of Clark Botanic Garden."
4. Paine, *Boys' Life of Mark Twain*; Rojo, "Mark Twain in New Hampshire" (blog).
5. Kenny, "An Interview with Grenville Clark." One guest described "the old hunched down Mount Monadnock" as "not a towering nor an inspiring mass, but a great stone uprising that seems to express persistence and durability [creating] an awareness that a major uprising of nature is before you, a physical presence anchored completely down into the earth. So it was when you were with Mr. Clark." E. Dimond, *Take Wing*, 303.
6. Grenville Clark to his daughter Louisa Clark Spencer, undated postcard circa 1960, Clark Papers.
7. See, for example, Miss Maloney office diaries for 1937 and 1938, Clark Papers.
8. Mary Dimond, "A Daughter's Viewpoint—and Many Exposures," in Dimond, Cousins, and Clifford, *Memoirs of a Man*, 173.
9. E. Grey Dimond, interview by author, September 4, 2009, Kansas City, MO. The story is from a rural Missouri trip with medical students in the early 1980s.
10. M. Dimond, "A Daughter's Viewpoint," 174–76, 177.
11. Benjamin Cardozo to Grenville Clark, March 21, 1934, Clark Papers.

12. M. Dimond, "A Daughter's Viewpoint," 179, 181–82.

13. Ibid., 177; Louisa Clark, Christmas epics, Clark Papers.

14. M. Dimond, "A Daughter's Viewpoint," 173; E. Dimond, interview by author, September 4, 2009, Kansas City, MO.

15. Theodore Roosevelt obituary, *New York Times*, January 6, 1919; Clifford, *Citizen Soldiers*, 262.

16. One author dubbed the Paris conference and its resulting treaty "the Peace to End All Peace." Fromkin, *A Peace to End All Peace*. See also MacMillan, *Paris 1919*.

17. Clifford, *Citizen Soldiers*, 270, 289.

18. Paul Dudley White, "Memories of Grenville Clark as Patient and Friend," in Dimond, Cousins, and Clifford, *Memoirs of a Man*, 190.

19. J. Clifford, "Grenville Clark and His Friends," in Dimond, Cousins, and Clifford, *Memoirs of a Man*, 11; Grenville Clark, "Sketch for Class of 1903 at Harvard," 1953, Clark Papers. Clark's close friend the New York legal lion Charles "CCB" Burlingham, who was a generation older and took an almost paternal interest in Clark, had a similar psychic break at roughly the same point in his working life in 1892. CCB's official diagnosis was nervous prostration. His treatment was the then-new rest cure, not unlike what Clark would undergo a quarter century later. Like Clark, CCB found the incident consumed a full year of life but did not reoccur. The main reaction of both men, neither of whom much discussed it afterward, was relief and an understandable increased wariness about their health. Martin, *CCB*, 380.

20. Grenville Clark to Tompkins McIlvaine, November 14, 1930, Clark Papers.

21. Grenville Clark to George Wickersham, October 7, 1929, Clark Papers.

22. Herbert Hoover to Grenville Clark, October 25, 1929, Clark Papers.

23. Grenville Clark to Grenville Clark Jr., February 16, 1943, Clark Papers.

24. J. Garry Clifford, e-mail to author, July 12, 2011.

7. Full Speed Ahead

1. Grenville Clark, "Sketch for Class of 1903 at Harvard," 1953, Clark Papers.

2. In 2013, under the leadership of Harvard's first female president, Drew Faust, the university undertook the first major structural reforms of the Corporation since 1650. Elias J. Groll, Zoe A. Y. Weinberg, and William N. White, "Harvard Corporation Announces Historic Overhaul to Governance Structure," *Harvard Crimson*, December 6, 2010, http://www.thecrimson.com/article/2010/12/6/corporation-members-university-governance/.

3. Erwin Griswold, "Grenville Clark: Notes," in Dimond, Cousins, and Clifford, *Memoirs of a Man*, 155.

4. Clark, "Sketch for Class of 1903."

5. Grenville Clark, "Freedom in Education: An Address by Grenville Clark at the Annual Meeting of the New Hampshire State Bar Association, January 1936," Clark Papers.

6. Lyman M. Tondale Jr., "Grenville Clark: Some Stories and Personal Recollections," in Dimond, Cousins, and Clifford, *Memoirs of a Man*, 94. In "Five Years of Crisis" (September 19, 1944, Clark Papers), Clark describes Conant's urging him to write up his thoughts on world peace.

7. See, for example, National Economy League, "A Petition to the President and the Congress of the United States Calling for the Maintenance of the National Credit through a Balanced Budget," December 18, 1933, copy in the Mary Clark Dimond Papers.

8. Dunne, *Grenville Clark: Public Citizen*, 64.

9. Oritz, *Beyond the Bonus March and GI Bill,* 64, 70, 71.

10. Ibid., 75; Maurer, "Grenville Clark: Statesman Incognito," 188.

11. Grenville Clark, "Notes on Activities of G. Clark," October 25, 1960, Dublin, New Hampshire, Clark Papers.

12. Hefner, "Legacy of a Great American," 165.

13. Ibid.

14. Ibid.; Clark, "Notes on Activities of G. Clark." Clark remained largely supportive of the president on economic matters until 1935–36, when Roosevelt began to shift away from conservative financial policies in favor of so-called Keynesian, or debt-fueled, policies.

15. Pearlman, *To Make Democracy Safe for America,* 231–37.

16. Ibid.

17. Ibid.

18. Mayer, *Emory Buckner,* 287; Emory Buckner obituary, *New York Times,* March 12, 1942; tribute to Emory Buckner issue of *Cleargolaw News,* April 25, 1968, Clark Papers.

19. Henry J. Friendly, "Grenville Clark: Legal Preceptor," in Dimond, Cousins, and Clifford, *Memoirs of a Man,* 90.

20. According to the *H Book of Harvard Athletics,* Littauer was the first collegiate coach in the country: "Until the fall of 1881 there were no coaches and no coaching by anyone except the [team] captain . . . [until we] got Lucius N. Littauer of New York, '78 [year graduated Harvard], to coach our team." Harvard finished the season 5–2–1 in Littauer's only season as coach. John Blanchard, *H Book of Harvard Athletics, 1852–1922* (Boston: Harvard Varsity Club, 1923). See also Bernard Postal, Jesse Silver, and Roy Silver, "Lucius Nathan Littauer," in *Encyclopedia of Jews in Sports* (New York: Bloch, 1965), available online at http://www.jewsinsports.org.

21. See, for example, Lucius Littauer to Clark, July 5, 1938; Clark to Littauer, July 14, 1938; Littauer to Clark, December 11, 1935; Littauer to Clark, June 16, 1937; Clark to Littauer, October 1937, all in Clark Papers.

22. Grenville Clark to Felix Frankfurter, June 21, 1938, Clark Papers.

23. See, for example, Grenville Clark, "Suggested Plan of Settlement," prepared for the Lucius N. Littauer Foundation, September 10, 1937; and Grenville Clark, "Estate of Flora Littauer," April 20, 1938, both in Clark Papers. The graduate school Littauer envisioned thrives today as Harvard's John F. Kennedy School of Government, a top-flight institution for public policy study and social science research. Its major building bears Littauer's name.

24. Grenville Clark to Frances Perkins, June 28, 1934, Clark Papers. For more information see "FDR and the Wagner Act: 'A Better Relationship Between Management and Labor,'" Franklin D. Roosevelt Presidential Library and Museum, http://www.fdrlibrary.marist.edu/aboutfdr/wagneract.html.

8. Taking on the President

1. Maurer, "Grenville Clark: Statesman Incognito," 113; Grenville Clark, "Sketch for Class of 1903 at Harvard," 1953, Clark Papers.

2. Clifford and Spencer, *First Peacetime Draft,* 21–22.

3. Hefner, "Legacy of a Great American," 168.

4. "Nine Old Men" was a phrase FDR, and many others, borrowed from a 1936 book criticizing the court by the journalists Drew Pearson and Robert S. Allen. Also see Latham, *FDR and the Supreme Court Fight;* Alsop, *FDR: A Centenary Remembrance;* Baker, *Back to Back,* and others.

5. Leuchtenburg, *Supreme Court Reborn*, 105. The case is *Adkins v. Children's Hospital*, 261 U.S. 525 (1923).

6. Cloyd Laporte, "G. C.," in Dimond, Cousins, and Clifford, *Memoirs of a Man*, 84.

7. Knox, *Forgotten Memoir of John Knox*, 51.

8. The professor and FDR biographer Jean Edward Smith describes the early political wrangling culminating in today's nine-justice court: "The original Judiciary Act of 1789 set the number of Justices at six. When the Federalists were defeated in 1800, the lame-duck Congress reduced the size of the court to five—hoping to deprive President Jefferson of an appointment. The incoming Democratic Congress repealed the Federalist measure (leaving the number at six), and then in 1807 increased the size of the court to seven, giving Jefferson an additional appointment. In 1837, the number was increased to nine, affording the Democrat Andrew Jackson two additional appointments. During the Civil War, to insure an anti-slavery, pro-Union majority on the bench, the court was increased to ten. When a Democrat, Andrew Jackson, became President upon Lincoln's death, a Republican Congress voted to reduce the size to seven to guarantee Johnson would have no appointments. After Ulysses S. Grant was elected in 1868, Congress restored the court to nine, [giving] Grant two new appointments." Smith, "Stacking the Court," op-ed, *New York Times*, July 26, 2007. The court has remained at nine ever since.

9. Frank E. Gannett to Grenville Clark, April 17, 1937; Clark to Gannett, June 14, 1937; Gannett to Clark, June 22, 1937, Clark Papers.

10. *Tipaldo v. Morehead*, 298 U.S. 587 (1936). Roberts maintained throughout his lifetime that his "switch in time" was not politically motivated, that legal nuances made the apparently similar cases actually quite different, and that he had declared his *Tipaldo* vote orally in closed session before the court-packing scheme was made public. Felix Frankfurter came to believe and support Roberts, although Frankfurter was initially a strong and vocal critic of the switch. See Feldman, *Scorpions*, 117–19.

11. Arthur Vandenberg to Cloyd Laporte, March 29, 1937, Clark Papers.

12. Sidney L. Samuels to Cloyd Laporte, May 4, 1937, Clark Papers.

13. Martin, *CCB*, 380.

14. Laporte, "G. C.," 85.

15. Committee for Independent Courts, organizational documents, Clark Papers.

16. E. Grey Dimond, interview by author, August 2, 2008, Diastole, Kansas City, MO. Longtime friend Sam Spencer noted how appropriate it was that as "Dublin's first citizen," Clark had the now-quaint phone number " Dublin-1," which was "taken with disbelief" by long-distance telephone operators around the world. Spencer, "Grenville Clark," 57.

17. Dunne, *Grenville Clark: Public Citizen*, 83.

18. Laporte, "G. C.," 86.

19. Baker, *Back to Back*, 200–202. For the video see "Democrats Enjoy a Picnic," June 25, 1937, *Critical Past*, http://www.criticalpast.com/video/65675058986_Franklin-Roosevelt_playing-baseball_picnic_Democrats-with-President.

20. Freedman, *Roosevelt and Frankfurter*, 400.

21. *New York Times*, July 2, 1937.

22. Dunne, *Grenville Clark: Public Citizen*, 94.

23. Harry W. Fowler and Lawrence S. Huntington, "Fiduciary Trust Company of New York: Investment Management Specialists . . . for Individuals, Corporations, Institutions," report prepared for a New York meeting of the Newcomen

Society in North America, November 13, 1974. See also Fiduciary Trust Company correspondence, March 6, 1931–December 21, 1954, Clark Papers. A tragic epilogue: Fiduciary Trust Company's home office in New York City was located on the ninety-third through ninety-seventh floors of the World Trade Center's South Tower, exactly where the second plane struck on the morning of September 11, 2001. The company was virtually wiped out in an instant; eighty-six Fiduciary employees and several business partners who were visiting the offices were killed. The company's financial records were stored off site, and Fiduciary Trust ultimately survived the loss. It now operates under its original name as a subsidiary of Franklin Resources, also known as Franklin Templeton Investments, headquartered in New York's Rockefeller Center. Julie Norwell, "Post 9-11, Companies Still Unprepared for Disasters: Ticking Time Bomb?" *Weekly Toyo Keizai*, undated article available online from the searchable Lee H. Hamilton 9/11 Commission Papers in Indiana University's Modern Political Papers Collection, http://webapp1.dlib.indiana.edu/findingaids.

24. Dunne, *Grenville Clark: Public Citizen*, 96.

25. Leonard Baker, *Back to Back*, 252–53.

26. Laporte, "G. C.," 86.

27. Leuchtenburg, *Supreme Court Reborn*, 153; Laporte to Grenville Clark, telegram, July 22, 1937, Clark Papers.

28. FDR's appointees were Hugo Black, Stanley F. Reed, Felix Frankfurter, William O. Douglas, Frank Murphy, Harlan F. Stone (chief justice), James F. Byrnes, Robert H. Jackson, and Wiley B. Rutledge. Between the appointment of Jackson in 1941 and Roosevelt's death in 1945, eight of the nine justices were FDR appointees; the only exception was the Hoover appointee, Owen Roberts, whose replacement was named by Harry Truman in 1948. Thus Roosevelt almost became the second president, after George Washington, to appoint the entire Supreme Court.

29. Leuchtenburg, *Supreme Court Reborn*, 157–60.

30. Baker, *Back to Back*, 278–80.

31. Grenville Clark, "Notes on Activities of G. Clark," October 25, 1960, Dublin, New Hampshire, Clark Papers; Spencer, "Grenville Clark," 53–54.

32. Grenville Clark to Felix Frankfurter, March 4, 1937, Clark Papers.

33. Joseph P. Baratta, note to author, June 3, 2013.

34. Felix Frankfurter to Grenville Clark, March 6, 1937, Clark Papers.

35. Freedman, *Roosevelt and Frankfurter*, 372. See entire book for the fascinating round robin of letters passed among Frankfurter, Roosevelt, Clark, and Burlingham. Also see Blum, *From the Morgenthau Diaries*, a behind-the-scenes look at the tax matter.

36. Laporte, "G. C.," 87.

9. Defending Rabble-Rousers

1. Grenville Clark, "Court Help or Self Help?" *Annals of the American Academy of Political and Social Science* 195 (January 1938): 1–11, Clark Papers.

2. Walter Lippmann to Grenville Clark, April 28, 1938; Theodore Roosevelt Jr. to Grenville Clark, July 18, 1938, both in Clark Papers.

3. Dunne, *Grenville Clark: Public Citizen*, 102–3. In October 1937, a few months before Clark's speech, the Nassau County Bar Association refused to admit five female lawyers: "It is our opinion that there are many more fine, gentlemanly lawyers living in this county who should be members of the Association." Nassau County Bar Association, "NCBA History Timeline," n.d., http://www.nassaubar.org/About Us/History.aspx.

4. Dunne, *Grenville Clark: Public Citizen*, 5; Grenville Clark to Charles C. Burlingham, September 1, 1938, Clark Papers.

5. Grenville Clark to Irving Dilliard, September 24, 1962, Clark Papers.

6. Stone, "Grenville Clark, A Tribute," Clark Papers.

7. Grenville Clark, "Notes on Activities of G. Clark," October 25, 1960, Dublin, New Hampshire, Clark Papers.

8. Roger N. Baldwin, "A Memo on Grenville Clark," Dimond, Cousins, and Clifford, *Memoirs of a Man*, 120.

9. *Hague v. CIO*, 307 U.S. 496, 504 (1939).

10. Clark to Dilliard, October 8, 1962, Clark Papers. The legal scholar was Richard Primus, in testimony during a 1952 U.S. Senate subcommittee hearing.

11. Feldman, *Scorpions*, 181–82.

12. Clark to Dilliard, October 8, 1962. The case in which the Supreme Court reversed its ruling in *Minersville v. Gobitis* was *West Virginia Board of Education v. Barnette*, 319 U.S. 624 (1943).

13. Laporte, "G. C.," in Dimond, Cousins, and Clifford, *Memoirs of a Man*, 83; Clark to Dilliard, November 12, 1962, Clark Papers.

14. Grenville Clark, "The Preservation of Civil Liberties," *New York Law Journal*, June 6, 1941, Clark Papers.

15. Grenville Clark to Henry Friendly, September 30, 1955, Clark Papers.

16. Clark to Dilliard, November 12, 1962.

17. Charles Wyzanski Jr., "Grenville Clark and the Harry Bridges Episode," in Dimond, Cousins, and Clifford, *Memoirs of a Man*, 125.

18. Ibid., 124–26.

19. Grenville Clark to Mary Clark Dimond, 1931, Mary Clark Dimond Papers. This handwritten treasure is one of dozens that Mary D. kept with her private papers throughout her life.

10. Preparedness Redux

1. Grenville Clark, "Five Years of Crisis, 1939–1941," September 19, 1944, Clark Papers.

2. J. Garry Clifford, "Grenville Clark and the Origins of Selective Service," *Review of Politics* 35, no. 1 (January 1973): 40.

3. George Roberts, article about Clark in *Cleargolaw News*, October 20, 1967. Roberts was a senior partner in Winthrop, Stimson, Putman, and Roberts, and a friend of GC's, and wrote the essay about GC for the *Memorial Book of the Association of the Bar of the City of New York*, October 1967, Clark Papers. Roberts's essay includes this long passage from a letter by Clark dated summer 1940 to Edward S. Greenbaum, one of his associates in the Plattsburg program.

Clifford and Spencer list three, not four, conditions given by Stimson: Stimson would be free to express his own views on such issues as conscription and aid to the allies; he would be excused from any partisan activities; and he could choose Patterson as his assistant secretary. Clifford and Spencer, *First Peacetime Draft*, 89.

4. Olson, *Those Angry Days*, xvii–xviii.

5. Eiler, *Mobilizing America*, 1.

6. The Clark Papers include literally dozens of such letters. See, for example, Clark to Augustus "Gus" Hand, May 28, 1941; Augustus Hand to Grenville "Grennie" Clark, January 18, 1948; Learned Hand to "Grennie" Clark, August 14, 1938; Clark to Learned "B" Hand, May 25, 1934. The nickname "B" apparently comes from Hand's given name, Billings, which he dropped because he found it pretentious.

7. Grenville Clark to Franklin Roosevelt, May 16, 1940, Clark Papers.

8. Dunne, *Grenville Clark: Public Citizen*, 123.

9. Eiler, *Mobilizing America*, 34.

10. Dunne, *Grenville Clark: Public Citizen*, 126.

11. Felix Frankfurter to Grenville Clark, May 16, 1957, Clark Papers.

12. Clifford and Spencer, *First Peacetime Draft*, 87, 93.

13. Pogue, *George C. Marshall*, 57.

14. Ibid., 58.

15. Clifford and Spencer, *First Peacetime Draft*, 87–88.

16. Clifford, "Grenville Clark and the Origins of Selective Service," 33.

17. Olson, *Those Angry Days*, 173.

18. Clifford and Spencer, *First Peacetime Draft*, 193, 192–95.

19. Ibid., 208–10, 232.

20. Averell Harriman, "Tribute to Grenville Clark," in Dimond, Cousins, and Clifford, *Memoirs of a Man*, 60; Louis W. Douglas, "Grenny in the 1930s and 1940s," in Dimond, Cousins, and Clifford, *Memoirs of a Man*, 198.

21. Clifford and Spencer, *First Peacetime Draft*, 224.

22. Hefner, "Legacy of a Great American," 64.

23. Stimson to Clark, August 22, September 2, 1941; and Clark to Stimson, September 8, 1941, all in Clark Papers.

24. Samuel Spencer Jr., "Autumn 1941—Key Papers," a summary of Clark's Selective Service campaign that quotes the Stimson diaries (which are at Yale), Clark Papers.

25. Clifford and Spencer, *First Peacetime Draft*, 224; Grenville Clark, "Notes on the Activities of G. Clark," October 25, 1960, Dublin, New Hampshire, Clark Papers. Judge Henry Friendly remembered the Clarks' temporary quarters at the Carlton: "He had an apartment [there]; the room would be in a delightful state of litter, and he would be writing out on those yellow pads those messages to Senator this and Congressman that. . . . One thing would be sure, he would have a program. One can almost see him with his coattails flying, going down to Washington and saying, 'Get out, get out, all of you. We've really had enough.'" Dunne, *Grenville Clark: Public Citizen*, 133.

26. Isaacson and Thomas, *Wise Men*, 19; Joseph P. Baratta to author, June 3, 2013; Olson, *Those Angry Days*, 450.

27. Eiler, *Mobilizing America*, 6, 7.

28. Bird, *Chairman*, 19; Isaacson and Thomas, *Wise Men*, 192.

29. Stimson and Bundy, *On Active Service in Peace and War*, 344.

30. Ibid., 340.

31. Marshall, *George C. Marshall: Interviews and Reminiscences*, 202.

32. Eiler, *Mobilizing America*, 99, 109.

33. Pogue, *George C. Marshall*, 102; Marshall, *George C. Marshall: Interviews and Reminiscences*, 203, 300.

34. Pogue, *George C. Marshall*, 103; Eiler, *Mobilizing America*, 100.

35. Dunne, *Grenville Clark: Public Citizen*, 135; Olson, *Those Angry Days*, 60–62.

36. Dunne, *Grenville Clark: Public Citizen*, 135.

37. The same reasoning undoubtedly was a factor in Clark's silence about the 1942 internment of 120,000 Japanese, mostly American citizens, in the panicked wake of Pearl Harbor. Clark did not speak publicly on the internments at the time, nor when their legality was upheld by the Supreme Court in the fall of 1944.

38. Bird, *Chairman*, 19.

39. Ibid., 141. One man even more relieved than Stimson was the beleaguered

Winston Churchill. Desperate for U.S. intervention for many months, the British prime minister "slept the sleep of the saved and thankful" on the night that he learned the news, understanding that Pearl Harbor meant, as FDR confirmed, "We are all in the same boat now." Olson, *Those Angry Days*, 429.

40. Eiler, *Mobilizing America*, 43; Chester R. Hope, "This Man Tells Uncle Sam How to Put the Finger on You in the Compulsory Work-Service Bill," undated clipping in Clark Papers that does not identify the newspaper in which it appeared.

41. Eiler, *Mobilizing America*, 377.

42. Ibid., 376.

43. Grenville Clark to Felix Frankfurter, September 29, 1944, Clark Papers.

44. Grenville Clark, "Family Policy," February 26, 1942, Clark Papers.

45. Spencer, "Autumn 1941—Key Papers."

46. Hefner, "Legacy of a Great American," 64; Grenville Clark, Grenville Clark, "Notes about Myself from Grenville Clark for Messrs. Ogilvy & Mahony," December 28, 1948, Clark Papers. John J. McCloy later speculated that Clark left Washington a year too soon and may have been able to help McCloy persuade Harry Truman to make one final attempt to force a surrender from Japan before dropping the bomb. McCloy favored giving the Japanese emperor an ultimatum, disclosing the fearsome new technology, perhaps with an offshore demonstration. But the brand-new president, facing one of history's most momentous decisions with an essentially vertical learning curve, was persuaded by the otherwise unanimous consensus of the small team of cabinet, military, and scientific advisers privy to the new technology. McCloy reportedly later mused: "The result might have been very different if I had had Grennie Clark alongside me to persuade the decision-makers." Dunne, *Grenville Clark: Public Citizen*, 141–42.

The top-secret eight-member nuclear advisory team, known as the Interim Committee, included Henry Stimson, secretary of war; George L. Harrison, Stimson's close adviser on the nuclear project; James F. Byrnes, former U.S. senator from South Carolina and former Supreme Court justice; William L. Clayton, undersecretary of the navy; Dr. Vannevar Bush, director of the Office of Scientific Research and Development, which was in charge of the top-secret Manhattan Project; Dr. Karl T. Compton, president of MIT; and Clark's good friend James B. Conant, president of Harvard and chair of the National Defense Research Committee. Also closely involved in the bomb discussions were generals Leslie R. Groves and George C. Marshall; Harvey Bundy, Stimson's former assistant secretary of state (in 1931) and now close adviser; another Stimson assistant, Arthur W. Page; and the four members of the Scientific Advisory Panel, Ernest O. Lawrence, Enrico Fermi, Arthur Compton, and Robert Oppenheimer. Bird, *Chairman*, 243.

11. Retreat to Dublin

1. Grenville Clark to Franklin Roosevelt, December 31, 1944, Clark Papers.

2. Arthur Krock, obituary for Franklin D. Roosevelt, *New York Times*, April 12, 1945; Isaacson and Thomas, *Wise Men*, 254.

3. Feldman, *Scorpions*, 257.

4. Krock, FDR obituary.

5. Ibid.; Hefner, "Legacy of a Great American," 168.

6. Grenville Clark to Henry Stimson, September 21, 1945, Clark Papers.

7. "World War II by the Numbers: World-wide Deaths," National World War II Museum, New Orleans, http://www.nationalww2museum.org/learn/

education/for-students/ww2-history/ww2-by-the-numbers/world-wide-deaths
.html; Wittner, *One World or None*, 35.

8. Dunne, *Grenville Clark: Public Citizen*, 160; Hefner, "Legacy of a Great American," 168.

9. Samuel Spencer Jr., interview by author, December 5, 2008. Spencer's 600-page doctoral dissertation about the creation and passing of the Selective Service Act is on file at Harvard's Widener Library. More than thirty years later, with new scholarship and collections available, J. Garry Clifford turned the dissertation into a superb 1986 book, *The First Peacetime Draft*, bearing the names of both Spencer and Clifford.

10. Almost ten years later the result of Conant's suggestion was Grenville Clark, "Notes about Myself from Grenville Clark for Messrs. Ogilvy & Mahony," December 28, 1948, Clark Papers.

11. James G. Hershberg, *James B. Conant: Harvard to Hiroshima and the Making of the Nuclear Age* (New York: Alfred A. Knopf, 1993).

12. Grenville Clark, "A New World Order—The American Lawyer's Role," *Indiana Law Journal* 19, no. 4 (1944): 289–300.

13. Baratta, *Politics of World Federation*, 1:112, 96.

14. Ibid., 104. See also R. W. Apple Jr., obituary for James A. Reston, *New York Times*, December 7, 1995.

15. Clark, "Notes about Myself."

16. Annan and Mousavizadeh, *Interventions*, 141–42.

17. Baratta, *Politics of World Federation*, 1:98.

18. Ibid., 115.

19. Johnstone, "Americans Disunited," 1; Baratta, *Politics of World Federation*, 1:115.

20. Clark, "Notes about Myself." The Dumbarton Oaks delegates were actually building on work that had begun back in 1942, at the height of World War II. An advisory committee comprised of high-ranking State Department officials, legal advisers, educators, historians, military leaders, the editor of *Foreign Affairs*, and even FDR's special representative to the Vatican "formed a grand alliance under a name suggested by Roosevelt, the 'United Nations.' They pledged to fight until victory, not to make a separate peace, and to adhere to the principles of the new Atlantic charter. One of which set the goal of establishing 'a wider and permanent system of general security.'" As with America's Constitutional Convention in 1787, the proceedings were held in secret so participants could speak frankly of their concerns and political constraints "at a time when democracy was fighting for its life." Baratta, *Politics of World Federation*, 1:96.

21. Bantell, "Origins of the World Government Movement," 29; Feldman, *Scorpions*, 273–74.

22. Bantell, "Origins of the World Government Movement," 24.

23. Wittner, *One World or None*, 66. Cousins later turned his essay into a book that went through fourteen editions, was translated into seven languages, and had an estimated U.S. circulation of 7 million (66–67).

24. Meyer, *Facing Reality*, 44.

25. Baratta, *Politics of World Federation*, 1:121–22.

26. *New York Times*, October 15, 1944.

27. Bantell, "Origins of the World Government Movement," 26.

28. Stringfellow Barr, "The Governed Temper," in Dimond, Cousins, and Clifford, *Memoirs of a Man*, 247–48.

29. Bantell, "Origins of the World Government Movement," 27; Alan Cran-

ston, "Memoir of a Man," in Dimond, Cousins, and Clifford, *Memoirs of a Man*, 254.

30. Bantell, "Origins of the World Government Movement," 27.

31. *Korematsu v. United States*, 323 U.S. 214 (1944); Baratta, *Politics of World Federation*, 1:149–50.

32. Report by Dublin Conference Committee, October 1945, Clark Papers.

33. Baratta, *Politics of World Federation*, 1:152.

34. Bantell, "Origins of the World Government Movement," 30–31.

35. Cranston, "Memoir of a Man," 259.

36. "Princeton's History," Princeton University, n.d., http://www.princeton.edu/main/about/history/.

37. Wittner, *One World or None*, 6, 10.

38. I. A. Richards, "The Princeton Conference of 1946," in Dimond, Cousins, and Clifford, *Memoirs of a Man*, 243; Cranston, "Memoir of a Man," 256; Dunne, *Grenville Clark: Public Citizen*, 161.

39. Wittner, *One World or None*, 59.

40. DeBenedetti, *Peace Reform in American History*, 152.

41. Wittner, *One World or None*, 6–10.

42. Baratta, *Politics of World Federation*, 1:125, 2:312; Wittner, *One World or None*, 59.

43. DeBenedetti, *Peace Reform in American History*, 149.

44. Baratta, *Politics of World Federation*, 1:109; Meyer, *Facing Reality*, 44.

45. Meyer, *Facing Reality*, 44.

46. Baratta, *Politics of World Federation*, 1:225, 216.

12. Resisting Cold Warriors

1. Grenville Clark to Paul Dudley White, February 18, 1947, Clark Papers.

2. Samuel Spencer Jr., "Grenville Clark," in Dimond, Cousins, and Clifford, *Memoirs of a Man*, 57.

3. Grenville Clark to Charles C. Burlingham, September 13, 1947, Clark Papers.

4. Samuel Spencer Jr.'s mentor at Harvard was Arthur M. Schlesinger Sr., head of Harvard's History Department and father of Arthur M. Schlesinger Jr., who also taught at Harvard but is more famous for serving as a close adviser to John F. Kennedy. Samuel Spencer Jr., telephone interview by author, December 5, 2008.

5. Henry Stimson to Grenville Clark, September 20, 1947, Clark Papers; Harold Dodds, "My Friend Grenville Clark," in Dimond, Cousins, and Clifford, *Memoirs of a Man*, 139.

6. Spencer, interview.

7. Grenville Clark to Louisa Spencer, June 1948, Clark Papers.

8. Baratta, *Politics of World Federation*, 1:216.

9. Ibid., 1:243.

10. Ibid., 1:201, 216, 199; Wittner, *One World or None*, 308.

11. Baratta, *Politics of World Federation*, 2:365–66.

12. Dunne, *Grenville Clark: Statesman Incognito*, 195.

13. Baratta, *Politics of World Federation*, 2:367; Clifford, "President Truman and Peter the Great's Will," 384.

14. Dwight D. Eisenhower, remarks at the Department of State 1954 Honor Awards Ceremony, October 19, 1954; remarks at the Republican Women's National Conference, May 10, 1955; "Radio and Television Report to the American People on the Developments in Eastern Europe and the Middle East," Octo-

ber 31, 1956, Dwight D. Eisenhower Presidential Library and Archives, http://
www.eisenhower.archives.gov/all_about_ike/quotes.html.

15. Dunne, *Grenville Clark: Public Citizen*, 192.

16. Hefner, "Legacy of a Great American," 168.

17. Dodds, "My Friend Grenville Clark," 139.

18. James B. Conant, "Grenville Clark: Stalwart Defender of Academic Freedom," in Dimond, Cousins, and Clifford, *Memoirs of a Man*, 162.

19. Grenville Clark, "Sketch for Class of 1903 at Harvard," 1953, Clark Papers.

20. Grenville Clark to Frank Ober, May 27, 1949, Clark Papers, reprinted in
Dimond, Cousins, and Clifford, *Memoirs of a Man*, 279–91. A note on the Ober
event of particular interest to my campus, the University of Missouri—Kansas
City: Outside the entrance to UMKC's Swinney Recreation Center, carved in
stone beneath the building's name, are the lines: "Exercise Renews the Body
/ Supports the Spirit / And Keeps the Mind in Vigor / Run Hard / Leap High
/ Throw Strongly and Endure." The author is John Ciardi, borrowing from
Cicero in the first four lines. Ciardi was a professor in the English Department of UMKC in 1941 when the building was dedicated. He was a prolific
and widely acclaimed poet, and one of the two Harvard professors named by
Clark in his response to the incensed alumnus Frank Ober. The story is told
in Smith and Bender, *American Higher Education Transformed*, which includes
Grenville Clark's famous "Ober correspondence" and discusses Ciardi's background, including his Kansas City ties. Cifelli also addresses the Ober incident
in his 1997 biography of Ciardi.

13. Uneasy Peace

1. Ambrose, *Cold War*, 85.

2. York, *Race to Oblivion*. York was the first director of the Lawrence Liver-
more Labs and was among the small group of scientists who created the atomic
bomb in the 1940s.

3. Baratta, *Politics of World Federation*, 2:487.

4. Clark, *A Plan for Peace*, ix–x.

5. Hefner, "Legacy of a Great American," 64.

6. Ibid.

7. Ibid.; Baratta, *Politics of World Federation*, 2:498. In 1959 Hutchins founded
(with Ford Foundation money) the Center for the Study of Democratic Institutions, an influential think tank high on a hill in beautiful Santa Barbara, California. The center sponsored the work of many prominent leaders and thinkers
until it closed in 1987, a decade after Hutchins's death. Perhaps it could be considered a ripple effect of Clark's early vision?

8. Joseph Baratta to author, June 12, 2013; Grenville Clark, distribution lists
for *World Peace through World Law*, Clark Papers.

9. Louis Sohn, "Grenville Clark: As Seen from a Co-author's Perspective," in
Dimond, Cousins, and Clifford, *Memoirs of a Man*, 50.

10. Simon Adebbo, "Grenville Clark: The Great Internationalist," in Dimond,
Cousins, and Clifford, *Memoirs of a Man*, 229.

11. DeBenedetti, *Peace Reform in American History*, 156.

12. Wittner, *One World or None*, 70–71.

13. Ibid., 44; Baratta, *Politics of World Federation*, 1:179.

14. Sohn, "Grenville Clark . . . from a Co-author's Perspective," 52.

15. Carlos Romulo, "Grenville Clark," in Dimond, Cousins, and Clifford,
Memoirs of a Man, 251–52.

16. Grenville Clark to Henry Friendly, July 28, 1951, Clark Papers.

17. Mary Clark Dimond, "A Daughter's Viewpoint: Lighter Moments and Many Exposures," in Dimond, Cousins, and Clifford, *Memoirs of a Man.*

18. Grenville Clark, "Sketch for Class of 1903 at Harvard," 1953, Clark Papers.

19. Spencer, "Clarks of Clark Botanic Garden."

20. J. Garry Clifford, e-mail to author, April 14, 2009.

21. James B. Conant, "Grenville Clark: Stalwart Defender," Dimond, Cousins, and Clifford, *Memoirs of a Man,* 162.

22. Spencer, "Clarks of Clark Botanic Garden."

23. Leo Gottlieb, "Excerpts from proposed History of the firm of Cleary, Gottlieb, Steen & Hamilton for information of Professor Gerald Dunne," n.d. (ca. 1978), Mary Clark Dimond Papers.

24. Ibid.

25. Dunne, *Grenville Clark: Public Citizen,* 196–97.

26. Ibid., 196–98.

27. The case was *Uphaus v. Wyman,* 360 U.S. 72 (1959). Clark attributed Frankfurter's ruling in the *Uphaus* case to increasingly bitter infighting among the sitting Supreme Court justices. Clark wrote to the journalist and Supreme Court watcher Irving Dilliard: "The real question [with the Supreme Court's rejection of the *Uphaus* appeal] is why F.F. [Felix Frankfurter] is on the wrong side. The answer of course is because [Justices] Black and Douglas are on the right side, and [Black, Douglas] and Murphy reversed F.F. in Gobitis, the first flag salute case. F.F. would not agree to this of course but he is human and [former Chief Justice Oliver Wendell] Holmes said we are motivated by forces and influences we don't recognize. It is tragic that because of it Willard Uphaus . . . and others should go to jail but there it is! I say F.F. on the S.C. [Supreme Court] is both a personal and national tragedy." Grenville Clark to Irving Dillard, n.d., Clark Papers.

28. Robert Reno, "Grenville Clark and the Uphaus Case," in Dimond, Cousins, and Clifford, *Memoirs of a Man,* 127.

29. Ibid., 129.

30. Ibid.

31. Dissenting opinions are not ordinarily attached to denials of appeal, although all dissents are attached to the majority decisions of the court, thereby becoming part of the permanent legal record. Dissenting opinions are often said to "appeal to the wisdom of a future day." They are not infrequently used to help reverse previous decisions; settled cases are regularly revisited as circumstances change, new laws are written, and/or new applications of existing law emerge.

32. Justice Black's dissent in *Uphaus v. Wyman,* 364 U.S. 388, 392 (1960).

33. Grenville Clark to Justice Hugo Black, February 27, 1961; Black to Clark, March 1, 1961, both in Clark Papers.

34. Reno, "Grenville Clark and the Uphaus Case," 131. An epilogue to the *Uphaus* case: fearing Uphaus would be rearrested, friends helped him leave New Hampshire; he later returned to his World Fellowship for five years, then founded a similar center in Florida, where he remained active until his death in the early 1980s. Uphaus's zealous prosecutor, New Hampshire Attorney General Wyman, was elected to Congress, where he served for twelve years.

35. Felix Frankfurter to Grenville Clark, August 31, 1959, Clark Papers.

36. Grenville Clark to Irving Dilliard, January 24, 1951, Clark Papers.

37. W. Averell Harriman, "Tribute to Grenville Clark," in Dimond, Cousins, and Clifford, *Memoirs of a Man,* 62.

38. Lyman V. Rutledge, "Reminiscences of Grenville Clark," in Dimond, Cousins, and Clifford, *Memoirs of a Man,* 200–3.

14. Sprint to the Finish

1. Maurer, "Grenville Clark: Statesman Incognito," 192.

2. Norman Cousins, "A Man for All Seasons," in Dimond, Cousins, and Clifford, *Memoirs of a Man*, 5–6. Norman Cousins had been president of the United World Federalists since 1952, but the Dartmouth event was privately organized by Clark.

3. Elizabeth Hollins, "My Father's Friend," in Dimond, Cousins, and Clifford, *Memoirs of a Man*, 184.

4. Ibid., 222, 223, 224.

5. Grenville Clark Jr. to Mary Clark Dimond, March 6, 1978; Mary Clark Dimond to Grenville Clark Jr., March 7, 1974, both in Mary Clark Dimond Papers. Note: The first phase of the World Law Fund's inaugural project, the World Order Models Project, nicknamed WOMPS, was completed in 1972, with teams of scholars and public figures submitting manuscripts about alternative models for world systems to resolve disputes without violence. The organization is now a global policy think tank in New York called the World Policy Institute, "identifying critical emerging global issues in an interdependent world and gives voice to compelling new global perspectives and innovative policy solutions." See its website at http://www.worldpolicy.org.

6. Daniel, "Grenville Clark and His Plan for Peace," 139, 140, 144; Clifford, "Grenville Clark and His Friends," in Dimond, Cousins, and Clifford, *Memoirs of a Man*, 21.

7. Baratta, *Politics of World Federation*, 1:121.

8. Daniel, "Grenville Clark and His Plan for Peace," 144.

9. Clifford, "Grenville Clark and His Friends," 22. Clark's phone bills during the missile crisis attest to his close contact with McCloy.

10. McCloy and Clark both would be pleased to learn that a half-century after their strenuous efforts, in April 2013 the UN General Assembly adopted the landmark Arms Trade Treaty, regulating the international trade in conventional arms, from small arms to battle tanks, combat aircraft, and warships. Reflecting post–Cold War realities, the treaty focuses more on conventional weapons than nuclear stockpiles, but the overarching goal of a safer, saner planet is the same.

11. Grenville Clark to Irving Dilliard, October 30, 1963, Clark Papers.

12. Grenville Clark, ABA medal acceptance speech, Clark Papers.

13. An organized mob wielding lead pipes and chains met one bus at the bus station in Birmingham, Alabama. The authorities apparently had given the mob a fifteen-minute head start in which to attack the Freedom Riders before police finally arrived. Riders suffered gruesome injuries and eventually were flown to New Orleans. A mob in Aniston, Alabama, stopped and attacked another bus. One attacker tossed a firebomb through a bus window while others barricaded the bus doors to trap the passengers inside. The men barring the doors were frightened away when something inside the bus exploded, and the passengers narrowly escaped. Dittmer, *Local People*, 91.

14. Dittmer, *Local People*, 95; Michael Dalzell, "Grenville Clark: Someone to Know on Martin Luther King Day," *Unitarian Examiner*, January 17, 2011, http://www.examiner.com/article/grenville-clark-someone-to-know-on-martin-luther-king-day.

15. The historian Mary Dudziak has written extensively about how Cold War tensions inadvertently fostered progress on civil rights in the United States. See Mary Dudziak, "Desegregation as a Cold War Imperative," *Stanford Law Review* 41, no. 1 (November 1988): 61–120.

16. Grenville Clark to Paul Dudley White, July 24, 1961, Clark Papers.

17. Ibid., July 21, 1961.

18. Jack Greenberg, "Grenville Clark," in Dimond, Cousins, and Clifford, *Memoirs of a Man*, 122–23.

19. Spencer, "Clarks of Clark Botanic Garden"; Jack Greenberg to E. Grey Dimond, July 9, 1983, Mary Clark Dimond Papers.

20. Grenville Clark to Nicholas Katzenbach, July 28, 1966, The King Center, http://www.thekingcenter.org/archive/document/support-lawyer-grenville-clark-attorney-general-nicholas-katzenbach.

21. Grenville Clark to Martin Luther King, The King Center, July 28, 1966, http://www.thekingcenter.org/archive/document/letter-grenville-clark-dr-king-regarding-naacp-legal-defense-fund.

22. John Dickey, "Conservation Through Conversation," in Dimond, Cousins, and Clifford, *Memoirs of a Man*, 153.

23. Ibid.

24. Francis E. Rivers, "One Man's Conception of Grenville Clark," in Dimond, Cousins, and Clifford, *Memoirs of a Man*, 114–18.

25. Grenville Clark to Paul Dudley White, July 6, 1961, Clark Papers.

26. William Worthy, "Grenville Clark: A Vignette," in Dimond, Cousins, and Clifford, *Memoirs of a Man*, 132.

27. Ibid.

28. Ibid., 133.

29. Grenville Clark to Fanny Clark, August 15, 1937, Clark Papers.

30. Grenville Clark to Felix Frankfurter, May 1965, Clark Papers.

31. Grenville Clark to Ina (Mrs. Paul) White, April 14, 1964, Clark Papers.

32. Einar Rørstad, "Grenville Clark as I Met Him," in Dimond, Cousins, and Clifford, *Memoirs of a Man*, 234–36.

33. Joseph Clark, "Memories of Grenville Clark," in Dimond, Cousins, and Clifford, *Memoirs of a Man*, 41.

34. E. Dimond, *Take Wing*, 305–6.

35. Ibid.

36. E. Dimond, interview by author, September 4, 2009, Kansas City, MO.

37. E. Dimond, *Take Wing*, 306–9.

38. Shewmaker, "Grenville Clark–Edgar Snow Correspondence," 598.

39. Ibid., 599.

40. Ibid., 600.

41. E. Dimond, interview; Baratta, *Politics of World Federation*, 1:87; Shewmaker, "Grenville Clark–Edgar Snow Correspondence," 601.

42. Snow arranged the Dimonds' 1971 China visit so that E. Grey Dimond, a cardiologist, could verify three articles Snow had written for the *Saturday Review of Literature* about the surprisingly advanced state of Chinese medicine. One was about limb transplantation, one described the wide-scale practice of birth control, and another explored acupuncture anesthesia during major surgery. The articles were greeted with great skepticism in the United States. Dimond spent two weeks in China and independently verified that all three articles were accurate. He published his findings in the *Saturday Review of Literature*, as well as in the *Journal of the American Medical Association*. He later expanded the experience into a book, *More Than Herbs and Acupuncture*. At Dimond's urging Snow was able to extend the invitation to include the Whites. E. Dimond, interview; E. Dimond, *Take Wing*.

43. Mary Kersey Harvey, "No Nobel Peace Prize Was Awarded in 1967," in Dimond, Cousins, and Clifford, *Memoirs of a Man*, 214–18.

44. Ibid.

45. Ibid.

46. Ibid.

47. Paul Dudley White, "Memories of Grenville Clark as Patient and Friend," in Dimond, Cousins, and Clifford, *Memoirs of a Man,* 192.

48. *New York Times,* January 15, 1967.

49. Edgar Snow to Mary Clark Dimond, January 13, 1967, Mary Clark Dimond Papers.

15. Lessons, Legacy, Relevance

1. Grenville Clark, undated handwritten note listing several possible biography titles, Clark Papers.

2. Lawrence Lessig speech to One Planet, One Net Symposium sponsored by Computer Professionals for Social Responsibility, October 10, 1998, Boston.

3. Sir Muhammad Zafarullah Khan, "Grenville Clark," in Dimond, Cousins, and Clifford, *Memoirs of a Man,* 242.

4. For more information about the Charles Taylor trial, appeal, and sentence, see the website of the Special Court for Sierra Leone, http://www.sc-sl.org.

5. "About the Court," and "Situations and Cases," n.d., International Criminal Court, http://www.icc-cpi.int/Pages/default.aspx.

6. Lyman M. Tondale Jr., "Grenville Clark: Some Stories and Personal Recollections," in Dimond, Cousins, and Clifford, *Memoirs of a Man,* 97.

7. Maurer, "Grenville Clark: Statesman Incognito," 190.

8. Harold W. Dodds, "My Friend Grenville Clark," in Dimond, Cousins, and Clifford, *Memoirs of a Man,* 145.

9. John S. Dickey, "Conservation by Conversation," in Dimond, Cousins, and Clifford, *Memoirs of a Man,* 149.

10. John J. McCloy, "A Tribute to Grenville Clark," in Dimond, Cousins, and Clifford, *Memoirs of a Man,* 63.

11. Lloyd K. Garrison, "Grenville Clark," in Dimond, Cousins, and Clifford, *Memoirs of a Man,* 98–99.

12. Kingman Brewster Jr., "Grenville Clark: Operator Extraordinary," in Dimond, Cousins, and Clifford, *Memoirs of a Man,* 159.

13. Stanley K. Platt, "Grenville Clark," in Dimond, Cousins, and Clifford, *Memoirs of a Man,* 238.

14. Hefner, "Legacy of a Great American," 164.

15. Maurer, "Grenville Clark: Statesman Incognito," 192.

16. Jack Greenberg, "Grenville Clark," in Dimond, Cousins, and Clifford, *Memoirs of a Man,* 123. Dr. E. Grey Dimond added, "Clark worked in capital letters, not fine print." E. Dimond, interview by author, September 4, 2009, Kansas City, MO.

17. Alan Cranston, "Memoir of a Man," in Dimond, Cousins, and Clifford, *Memoirs of a Man,* 257.

18. Grenville Clark, ABA medal acceptance speech, Clark Papers.

19. "W. K. Vanderbilt Dies in France in His 71st Year," *New York Times,* July 22, 1920, http://query.nytimes.com/mem/archive-free/pdf?res=F50F13FD3B 5910738DDDAA0A94DF405B808EF1D3

20. Edward P. Stuhr, "The Clark Family Financial Conferences," in Dimond, Cousins, and Clifford, *Memoirs of a Man,* 211–13. These annual conferences were intense. According to financial adviser Stuhr: "Preparation for these conferences meant considerable work. The format showing the family holdings was unique for those days. It consisted of long sheets of analysis paper listing total holding of each security, holdings of individual family groups, cost, market value, income, and columns for estimated capital gains tax as well as net market value of each

security after deducting taxes. . . . Changes in market value were stacked against the rise or fall in the Dow Jones Industrial Average for the period, a forerunner of the performance emphasis which developed in later years" (212).

21. Tondale, "Grenville Clark: Some Stories and Personal Recollections," 96.

22. U.S. Senate, "Tribute to Grenville Clark," *Congressional Record,* January 19, 1967, S611.

23. Dunne, *Grenville Clark: Public Citizen,* 225.

Postscript: Final Words from the Source

1. Grenville Clark, "Notes on My Life for My Children," January–February 1956, handwritten and transcribed versions in Clark Papers.

Select Bibliography

Ackerman, Bruce A. "In Memoriam: Henry J. Friendly." *Harvard Law Review* 99 (June 1986): 1709–27.

Alsop, Joseph. *FDR: A Centenary Remembrance.* London: Thames and Hudson, 1982.

Alsop, Joseph, and Turner Catledge. *The 168 Days.* New York: Doubleday, Doran, 1938.

Ambrose, Stephen. *The Cold War: A Military History.* New York: Random House, 2006.

Annan, Kofi, with Nader Mousavizadeh. *Interventions: A Life in War and Peace.* New York: Penguin, 2012.

Bacevich, Andrew J. "What Happened at Bud Dajo: A Forgotten Massacre and Its Lessons." *Boston Globe,* March 12, 2006. http://www.boston.com/news/globe/ideas/articles/2006/03/12/what_happened_at_bud_dajo.

Bailey, Beth. *America's Army: Making the All-Volunteer Force.* Cambridge, MA: Belknap Press of Harvard University Press, 2009.

Baker, Leonard. *Back to Back: The Duel between FDR and the Supreme Court.* New York: Macmillan, 1967.

Bantell, John. "The Origins of the World Government Movement: The Dublin Conference and After." *Research Studies* 42 (March 1974): 20–35.

Baratta, Joseph Preston. *The Politics of World Federation.* 2 vols. Westport, CT: Praeger, 2004.

Berkin, Carol. *A Brilliant Solution: Inventing the American Constitution.* New York: Harcourt, 2002.

Bird, Kai. *The Chairman: John J. McCloy, the Making of the American Establishment.* New York: Simon and Schuster, 1992.

Blanchard, John. *H Book of Harvard Athletics, 1852–1922.* Boston: Harvard Varsity Club, 1923.

Blum, John Morton. *From the Morgenthau Diaries: Years of Crisis, 1928–1938.* Boston: Houghton Mifflin, 1959.

Caro, Robert A. *The Power Broker: Robert Moses and the Fall of New York.* New York: Vintage, 1975.

Chambers, John Whiteclay II. *To Raise an Army: The Draft Comes to Modern America.* New York: Free Press, 1987.

Cifelli, Edward M. *John Ciardi: A Biography.* Fayetteville: University of Arkansas Press, 1979.

Cirillo, Vincent J. *Bullets and Bacilli: The Spanish-American War and Military Medicine.* New Brunswick, NJ: Rutgers University Press, 2004.

Clark, Grenville. "The American Bill of Rights and Its English Background." Address to the New York branch of the English-Speaking Union, April 27, 1939.

———. "Civil Liberties: Court Help or Self Help." *Annals of the American Academy of Political and Social Science* 195 (January 1938): 1–11.

———. "Federal Finances and the New Deal." *Atlantic Monthly,* December 1934, 755–62.

———. "The Limits of Free Expression." Lecture to the Association of the Bar of the City of New York, May 23, 1939.

———. "Municipal Regulation of Outdoor Public Assembly." Address to the meeting of the municipal law section, American Bar Association, July 11, 1939, San Francisco.

———. The Papers of Grenville Clark. Rauner Special Collections Library, Dartmouth College Library, Hanover, NH.

———. *A Plan for Peace.* New York: Harper and Brothers, 1950.

———. "Report of the Special Committee on the Bill of Rights." Presented to House of Delegates, American Bar Association, September 9–13, 1940, Philadelphia.

Clark, Grenville, and Louis B. Sohn. *World Disarmament and World Development Organization.* Dublin, NH: Authors, May 1962.

———. *World Peace Through World Law.* Cambridge, MA: Harvard University Press, 1958.

Clifford, J. Garry. *The Citizen Soldiers: The Plattsburg Training Camp Movement, 1913–1920.* Lexington: University Press of Kentucky, 1972.

———. "Grenville Clark: World Peace through World Law, 1882–1967." *Notable American Unitarians,* n.d., http://www.harvardsquarelibrary.org/unitarians/clark_grenville.html.

———. "Grenville Clark and the Origins of Selective Service." *Review of Politics* 35, no 1 (January 1973): 17–40.

———. "President Truman and Peter the Great's Will." *Diplomatic History* 4, no. 4 (1980): 371–86.

Clifford, J. Garry, and Samuel Spencer Jr. *The First Peacetime Draft.* Lawrence: University Press of Kansas, 1986.

Cunliffe, Marcus, and Kenneth W. Leish. *The American Heritage Pictorial History of the Presidents of the United States.* Rockville, MD: American Heritage, 1968.

Cushman, Barry. *Rethinking the New Deal Court: The Structure of a Constitutional Revolution.* Oxford: Oxford University Press, 1998.

Dalfiume, Richard. *Desegregation of the Armed Forces.* Columbia: University of Missouri Press, 1969.

Daniel, James. "Grenville Clark and His Plan for Peace." *Readers Digest,* May 1962, 139–44.

DeBenedetti, Charles. *The Peace Reform in American History.* Bloomington: Indiana University Press, 1980.

Deresiewicz, William. "The Disadvantages of an Elite Education." *American Scholar,* Summer 2008. http://theamericanscholar.org/the-disadvantages-of-an-elite-education.

Dimond, E. Grey. *Take Wing! Interesting Things That Happened on My Way to School.* Rev. ed. Decorah, IA: Anundsen, 2005.

Dimond, Mary Clark. The Mary Clark Dimond Papers. University Archives, Newcomb Hall, University of Missouri—Kansas City.

Dimond, Mary Clark, coll., Norman Cousins and J. Garry Clifford, eds. *Memoirs of a Man.* New York: W. W. Norton, 1975.

Dittmer, John. *Local People: The Struggle for Civil Rights in Mississippi.* Urbana: University of Illinois Press, 1995.

Dorey, Halstead. "The Plattsburgh Contribution to Military Training," 229–33. In William L. Ransom, ed., *Academy of Political Science.* New York: Columbia University, July 1916.

Downey, Kirstin. *The Woman Behind the New Deal: The Life of Frances Perkins, FDR's Secretary of Labor and His Moral Conscience.* New York: Doubleday, 2009.

Dudziak, Mary. "Desegregation as a Cold War Imperative." *Stanford Law Review* 41, no. 1 (November 1988): 61–120.

Dunne, Gerald T. *Grenville Clark: Public Citizen.* New York: Farrar, Straus, Giroux, 1986.

Eiler, Keith. *Mobilizing America: Robert P. Patterson and the War Effort, 1940–1945.* Ithaca, NY: Cornell University Press, 1997.

Feldman, Noah. *Scorpions: The Battles and Triumphs of FDR's Great Supreme Court Justices.* New York: Twelve, 2010.

Frankfurter, Felix. "The Case of Sacco and Vanzetti." *Atlantic Monthly,* March 1927. http://www.theatlantic.com/magazine/archive/1927/03/the-case-of-sacco-and-vanzetti/306625/?single_page=true.

Freedman, Max. *Roosevelt and Frankfurter: Their Correspondence, 1928–1945.* Boston: Little, Brown, 1967.

Fromkin, David. *A Peace to End All Peace: The Fall of the Ottoman Empire and the Creation of the Modern Middle East.* New York: Henry Holt, 1989.

Garbarine, Rachelle. "Westbury Hotel." *New York Times,* February 19, 1999.

Gordon, Robert. "Friendly Fire: How John Roberts Differs from His Hero and Mentor." *Slate,* August 11, 2005. http://www.slate.com/id/2124353.

Gottlieb, Leo. *Cleary, Gottlieb, Steen & Hamilton: The First Thirty Years.* New York: R. R. Donnelley, 1983.

Hart, Jeffrey, "What Is American?" *National Review,* April 22, 1996, 4.

Hefner, Richard. "The Legacy of a Great American: An Interview with Grenville Clark." *McCall's,* April 1967, 64, 164–65, 168.

Hershberg, James G. *James B. Conant: Harvard to Hiroshima and the Making of the Nuclear Age.* New York: Alfred A. Knopf, 1993.

Hobbs, William. *Leonard Wood, Administrator, Soldier, and Citizen.* New York: G. P. Putnam, 1920.

Hoffman, Paul. *Lions in the Street: The Inside Story of the Great Wall Street Law Firms.* New York: Saturday Review Press, 1973.

Isaacson, Walter, and Evan Thomas. *The Wise Men: Six Friends and the World They Made.* New York: Simon and Schuster, 1986.

Holmes, Oliver Wendell Sr. "My Hunt After 'the Captain.'" In *The Autocrat of the Breakfast Table.* Pleasantville, NY: Akadine Press, 1858.

Johnstone, Andrew. "Americans Disunited: Americans United for World Organization and the Triumph of Internationalism." *Journal of American Studies* 44 (2010): 1–18.

Kahn, Herman. *On Escalation: Metaphors and Scenarios.* New York: Praeger, 1965.

Keller, Frances Richardson. *Fictions of U.S. History: A Theory and Four Illustrations.* Bloomington: Indiana University Press, 2002.

Kenny, Herbert. "An Interview with Grenville Clark." *Boston Sunday Globe,* June 10, 1962.

Knox, John. *The Forgotten Memoir of John Knox: A Year in the Life of a Supreme Court Clerk in FDR's Washington.* Edited by Dennis J. Hutchinson and David J. Garrow. Chicago: University of Chicago Press, 2002.

Latham, Frank B. *FDR and the Supreme Court Fight: 1937.* New York: Franklin Watts, 1972.

Lawrence, David. *Supreme Court or Political Puppets?* New York: D. Appleton-Century, 1937.

Leuchtenburg, William E. *The Supreme Court Reborn: The Constitutional Revolution in the Age of Roosevelt.* New York: Oxford University Press, 1995.

Lewis, Anthony. *The Supreme Court and How It Works.* New York: Random House, 1966.

Lusky, Louis. *By What Right: A Commentary of the Supreme Court's Power to Revise the Constitution.* New York: Michie, 1975.

Marshall, George C. *George C. Marshall: Interviews and Reminiscences for Forrest C. Pogue.* Lexington, VA: George C. Marshall Foundation Press, 1986.

Martin, George. *CCB: The Life and Century of Charles C. Burlingham.* New York: Hill and Wang, 2005.

Maurer, Herrymon. "Grenville Clark: Statesman Incognito." *Fortune,* February 1946, 110–15, 186–92.

MacMillan, Margaret. *Paris 1919: Six Months That Changed the World.* New York: Random House, 2001.

Mayer, Martin. *Emory Buckner.* New York: Harper and Row, 1968.

Meisler, Stanley. *Kofi Annan: A Man of Peace in a World of War.* Hoboken, NJ: John Wiley, 2007.

Meyer, Cord. *Facing Reality: From World Federalism to the CIA.* Lanham, MD: University Press of America, 1980.

Morrison, Elting E. *Turmoil and Tradition: A Study of the Life and Times of Henry L. Stimson.* Boston: Houghton Mifflin, 1960.

Olson, Lynne. *Those Angry Days: Roosevelt, Lindbergh and America's Fight over World War II, 1939–1941.* New York: Random House, 2013.

Oritz, Stephen R. *Beyond the Bonus March and GI Bill: How Veteran Politics Shaped the New Deal Era.* New York: New York University Press, 2010.

Paine, Albert Bigelow. *The Boys' Life of Mark Twain: The Story of a Man Who Made the World Laugh and Love Him.* 1916. http://authorama.com/boys-life-of-mark-twain-1.html.

Patterson, Robert Porter. *The World War I Memoirs of Robert P. Patterson: A Captain in the Great War.* Edited by J. Garry Clifford. Knoxville: University of Tennessee Press, 2012.

Pearlman, Michael. *To Make Democracy Safe for America: Patricians and Preparedness in the Progressive Era.* Urbana: University of Illinois Press, 1984.

Pogue, Forrest C. *George C. Marshall: Ordeal and Hope, 1939–1942.* New York: Viking, 1966.

Postal, Bernard, Jesse Silver, and Roy Silver. "Lucius Nathan Littauer." In *Encyclopedia of Jews in Sports.* New York: Bloch, 1965. http://www.jewsinsports.org.

Rehnquist, William H. *The Supreme Court: How It Was, How It Is.* New York: William Morrow, 1987.

Rojo, Heather Wilkinson. "Mark Twain in New Hampshire" (blog). *Nutfield Genealogy,* November 12, 2010. http://nutfieldgenealogy.blogspot.com/2010/11/mark-twain-in-new-hampshire.html.

Shesol, Jeff. *Supreme Power: Franklin Roosevelt vs. the Supreme Court.* New York: W. W. Norton, 2010.

Shewmaker, Kenneth E. "The Grenville Clark–Edgar Snow Correspondence." *Pacific Historical Review* 45, no. 4 (November 1976): 597–601.

Slotkin, Richard. *Lost Battalions: The Great War and the Crisis of American Nationality.* New York: Henry Holt, 2005.

Smith, Wilson, and Thomas Bender. *American Education Transformed,*

1940–2005: Documenting the National Discourse. Baltimore: Johns Hopkins University Press, 2008.

Snow, Edgar. *Red Star over China.* Rev. ed. New York: Grove, 1973.

Spencer, Louisa Clark. "The Clarks of Clark Botanic Garden." *Nassau County Historical Society Journal* 58 (2003).

Steele, Ronald. *Walter Lippmann and the American Century.* New York: Atlantic Monthly Press, 1980.

Stevenson, David. *Cataclysm: The First World War as Political Tragedy.* New York: Basic Books, 2004.

Stimson, Henry L., and McGeorge Bundy. *On Active Service in Peace and War.* New York: Harper, 1947.

Stone, I. F. 1967. "Grenville Clark, A Tribute." *I. F. Stone's Weekly,* January 23, 1967.

Toobin, Jeffrey. *The Nine: Inside the Secret World of the Supreme Court.* New York: Doubleday, 2007.

Twain, Mark. *Weapons of Satire: Writings on Anti-imperialist Writings on the Philippine-American War.* Edited by Jim Zwick. Syracuse, NY: Syracuse University Press, 1992.

Weidman, Bette, and Linda Martin. *Nassau County Long Island: In Early Photographs, 1869–1940.* New York: Dover, 1981.

Wittner, Lawrence S. *One World or None.* Vol. 1, *The Struggle Against the Bomb.* Stanford, CA: Stanford University Press, 1993.

York, Herbert F. *Race to Oblivion: A Participant's View of the Arms Race.* New York: Simon and Schuster, 1970.

Index

ABA Medal, from American Bar Association, 2, 34, 195, 222
academic freedom, Clark defending, 3, 85–86, 179–82
Acheson, Dean, 155, 230n18
Adebo, Simeon, 186, 188
Adler, Julius Ochs, 139
African Americans: civil rights for, 3, 33, 202–4; Clark outraged by discrimination against, 203, 206–8; Clark trying to improve access to education for, 206–7; Clark's longtime interest in equality for, 11, 207–8; discrimination against, 111, 218; military training camps and, 63, 65
Air Plattsburg, 63–64
Aldrich, Winthrop, 31
American Bar Association: Clark chairing Judiciary Committee of, 79; Clark urging to defend civil liberties, 126–27, 131; Clark's ABA Medal from, 2, 34, 195, 222; loyalty oaths proposed for, 192; working for judicial independence, 115–16. *See also* Bill of Rights Committee
American Civil Liberties Union, 128
American Federation of Labor (AFL), 61
Americans United for World Organization (AUWO), 161–62
anarchy, as root cause of war, 201
Annan, Kofi, 161
anti-Semitism, 26, 121–22
appearance, Clark's, 30, 55, *85–108*, 211–12
Arabic, Germany sinking, 53–54
Arant, Douglas, 127
arms race. *See* nuclear arms race
Arnold Arboretum, 189–90
Asia, WWII in, 148–49, 151, 155–56
Atlee, Clement, 4, 77, 187
atomic bombs, 163; Clark's involvement with, 157–58, 243n46; danger of, 165, 170, 186; dropped on Japan, 157,

243n46; Dublin Conference and, 162, 165; effects of existence of, 153, 164, 170; guilt over, 157–58, 169; peace movement after, 168. *See also* nuclear weapons
atomic scientists, in peace movement, 157–58, 169
Austin, Warren K., 150
autobiography, Clark's unwritten, 217
Avery, George, 190–91

Bacon, Robert, 59, 71
Bailey, Josiah, 116
Baker, Leonard, 120
Baker, Newton, 70, 138
Baldwin, Roger, 128
bankruptcies, in Clark's law specialties, 24, 29
Baratta, Joseph, 161, 187
Barr, Stringfellow, 164
Bass, Robert P., 162
Bell, Ulric, 161
Bigelow, Albert, 74–75
Bill of Rights Committee, of American Bar Association, 33, 192, 217; Clark chairing, 126–27; goal of, 127–28; not surviving Clark's departure, 128, 131; publishing *Bill of Rights Review*, 130; using amicus curiae briefs on civil rights cases, 128–29
Bird, Charles Sumner, 22
Bird, Francis W., 21–22, 24
Black, Hugo, 194, 240n28, 247n27
Blagden, Crawford (cousin), 14
Bohlen, Charles, 230n18
Bolling, Raynal C., 51, 64, 71
Bonus March, 88
Boone, Perley, 142
Brandeis, Louis D., 27–28, 77, 111–12
Brewster, Kingman, Jr., 163, 221
Bridges, Harry, 132
Brooklyn Botanic Garden, Clarks' home donated to, 74, 191, 210, 223

259